100 Best Plants
for the Coastal Garden

100 Best Plants
for the Coastal Garden

The Botanical Bones of Great Gardening

STEVE WHYSALL

WHITECAP BOOKS
VANCOUVER/TORONTO

Edited by Daphne Gray-Grant
Copy edited by Elizabeth McLean
Cover and interior design by Warren Clark
Photographs by Paddy Wales: *Acer palmatum, Betula utilis jacquemontii,*
Cotinus coggygria 'Royal Purple', *Enkianthus campanulatus, Geranium psilostemon,*
Rhododendron augustinii, Robinia pseudoacacia 'Frisia', *Rosa* 'Ballerina', *Viburnum plicatum.*
Photo courtesy of All-American Selection: *Lavandula angustifolia*

Printed and bound in Canada

Canadian Cataloguing in Publication Data

Whysall, Steve, 1950–
    100 best plants for the coastal garden

    Includes bibliographical references and index.
    ISBN 1-55110-704-X

    1. Gardening—British Columbia. 2. Gardening—Northwest, Pacific.
I. Title. II. Title: One hundred best plants for the coastal garden.
SB453.3.C2W59 1998   635.9'09711'1   C98-910013-8

For more information on this and other Whitecap titles, please visit our website
at www.whitecap.ca

Contents

Acknowledgments

This book is dedicated to my wife, Loraine, without whose loving support this work would not have been possible. My children, Joel, Aimee and Peter, were also immensely encouraging as well as admirably tolerant of all the disruption the project brought to their lives. I am extremely grateful to Alleyne and Barbara Cook of North Vancouver for their advice and unflagging affirmation. They are two of the kindest and most knowledgeable gardeners I know.

I would like to thank the following for providing information and photographs: Max Brown, of Jacques Amand: The Bulb Specialists, England; The Netherlands Bulb Information Centre, Toronto; and John Schroeder, of Valleybrook Gardens, B.C. The following garden centers and nurseries were also very helpful in supplying details about the availability of specific plants: Adera Nursery, Sidney, B.C.; Clearview Horticulture, Aldergrove, B.C.; Ferncliffe Gardens, Mission, B.C.; GardenWorks, Burnaby, B.C.; Mandeville Garden Centre, Burnaby, B.C.; Monrovia Nursery, Oregon; and Rainforest Gardens, Maple Ridge, B.C.

Many gardeners—too many to mention here by name—have played a major role over the years in introducing me to all the exciting and beautiful plants listed in this book. I know their love for gardening and passion for plants has found its way into the following pages. Every success.

Before We Begin

What is gardening?

If you're a new gardener, you will undoubtedly feel overwhelmed by the mind-boggling array of gardening information being thrust at you. There are now more magazines, books, radio and television shows on gardening than ever before competing for your attention. It is perfectly natural if you feel bombarded and pressured by it all. But gardening is not supposed to be a tense race to acquire knowledge or a difficult project to undertake or a perpetual goal to achieve. It is not something we do with the calculated precision of a mathematician. It is a life-long adventure with nature—creative, playful, intuitive—that often involves a degree of trial and error.

Gardening is all about observation, about looking closely and learning from the physical world around you, noting where the sunlight falls, where shadows are cast, where frost lingers, where rain puddles, where the wind blows. In gardening, we learn from nature and we find out how to co-operate with nature to grow healthy, beautiful plants. From doing all this, we end up creating lovely gardens that are not only esthetically pleasing but heavenly places in which we can find a deep refreshment for the soul.

Why do we do it?

The question I always love to ask gardeners is: "Why do you do it, what do you get out of gardening?" Some tell me it gives them peace of mind and a deep sense of tranquility to be surrounded by the color and fragrance of beautiful plants.

For them, the garden is a special retreat, an oasis for quiet contemplation in a world frantic with activity. These gardeners enjoy the hard work and physical exercise involved in digging and planting and weeding and doing general garden chores, but their main motivation is to have a beautiful place in which they can rest and relax at the end of the day.

For others, gardening is a creative outlet for their artistic talents. They see the space in their yard as a blank canvas on which they like to "paint" with plants to create beautiful 3-dimensional pictures. They get pleasure out of making lovely landscape scenes that don't just hang on a wall and look pretty, but are beautiful, real-life pictures—tangible, living masterpieces you can actually step into and walk around, where you can touch the trees and smell the flowers. These gardeners like to see what happens when they mix colors and blend the textures of different plants. Most important to them is the artistic satisfaction they derive from creating a picturesque landscape.

Most gardeners are a mixture of these two types—the person looking for a quiet, restful retreat, and the artistic person looking for creative challenge and artistic fulfilment. What about the gardeners who are only interested in growing fruit and vegetables? I tend to regard them more as farmers than gardeners, which is not to say that their enthusiasm, skill and intelligence are less valid or valuable. Their passion for chemical-free, organically grown food is always impressive and their skill at growing fruit and vegetables to perfection is laudable. They have the attitude and vitality we all hope for in large-scale farmers. But I don't think these gardeners are touched by the same spirit as the ones who look to the garden as a place for spiritual and emotional renewal and as a vehicle for artistic expression. Food gardeners are often quite disparaging about ornamental gardeners. "If you can't eat it why grow it?" is the kind of thing they say.

This book is not for them. It is really for gardeners interested in ornamental horticulture, particularly in the beauty of plants and how they can be used to create places for soothing the soul and stimulating the senses.

For me, gardening is a satisfying union of the artistic and the spiritual. It is about working hard to create a place of extraordinary visual and sensory loveliness into which you can also step and find spiritual nourishment through a direct and intimate encounter with the special kind of beauty that is timeless and transcendent.

Stages of a gardener

Most gardeners go through a series of stages. We start out buying a few annuals to grow in a pot or a window box. Then we hear about perennials—plants that come back every year. This is often when we really get bitten by the gardening bug. Suddenly, the world looks different. There are all these fabulous plants we've never noticed before at the garden center. Then comes plant lust. Lusting after plants is all part of a gardener's natural maturing process. Falling in love with every plant at the local nursery is a stage every new gardener seems to go through. It stems in part from reading and listening to the likes of world class garden-makers like Beth Chatto, Rosemary Verey, John Brookes, Christopher

Lloyd and Penelope Hobhouse. These popular English garden gurus talk with such passion about the beauty of different plants—the color and variation of hosta leaves, the open-faced beauty of a Christmas rose, the enchanting fragrance of old garden roses—it is hard not to come away from having read one of their books or having attended one of their lectures and not want to own every plant mentioned.

The truth is that most of the world's great gardens don't have every plant going. They don't need to. What they have is a wonderful collection of outstanding plants, arranged in intelligent, practical combinations. The fact is, less can indeed be more in the garden when it means restricting your choices to the best of the best. A restrained planting of 3 or 4 identical high-quality performance plants looks infinitely more attractive than a more complicated scheme involving a jumble of different plants of dubious caliber.

Less is more

There are millions of fantastic plants in the world. How is it possible to reduce that vast and magnificent plant world down to a mere 100? Is it not extraordinary arrogance to say there are only 100 great plants? Yes, of course, it is, but that is not what this book is saying. I am saying that you don't need every plant in the botanical encyclopedia to make a great garden. There is a common error many of us make. We are somehow persuaded when we first get into gardening that we have to find room for hundreds of different plants in order for our garden to be any good. Unfortunately, this kind of thinking is a major stumbling block to success. It is the reason so many of our gardens end up a jumbled, disjointed, unsatisfying mess. They are often simply packed with far too many mundane plants.

We need to reduce the number of plants and variety of plant material in our borders and flower beds to a more reliable, effective, streamlined selection. We can do this by learning to use the plant world's top performers—those specimens that not only grow best in our climate, but also look terrific most of the time.

100 best plants

What this book does is identify 100 of the best performance plants for creating a great garden in the Pacific Northwest. It tells you why they are first-rate plants, where to plant them, how to take care of them and what other plants to grow with them. Once you have established the basic botanical bones of your garden, using all or a selection of the plants listed here in confident combinations, you can relax and take your time to add finishing touches like hanging baskets, window boxes, specialty bulbs, container plantings and garden decorations. Our main goal is to provide you with a list of the most reliable plants that will allow you to construct a wonderful garden from scratch.

All the plants listed in this book have been specifically chosen for their reputation as no-nonsense, workhorse plants that will do their job without fuss or bother. They all have at least one outstanding characteristic. It could be that they have impressive flowers, great foliage, eye-catching form or exquisite perfume, or all of these attributes. You can bring home from your local garden center any of the plants listed in this book and know that they will not disappoint and can be used to create a garden of exceptional charm and beauty.

Plant hunting

You won't find all the plants you're looking for at your local garden center. Even the best ones have limited inventory and you will sometimes find they don't have the plant you want. You sometimes have to become a plant hunter. This means visiting specialty, home-based nurseries and more than one garden center.

Plant shopping is a lot like shopping for clothes—you need to look around to find what you want. Then, you may find the plant you are looking for, but it may not be healthy. Or perhaps, in the case of a tree or shrub, it may not have the shape you like. So you need to keep looking. However, you will find garden centers today are very keen to keep customers happy and they will do the plant hunting for you provided you can give them the precise name of the plant you want.

What's in a name?

You will find all the plants in this book have been given both their common name(s) and correct botanical name. This is not to impress you with clever botanical nomenclature. No, it is simply to make sure that you get the right plant. For instance, if you were to wander into your local garden center and ask for a viburnum, the first thing you will be asked is, "What kind of viburnum?" The problem is there are over 200 species of viburnum. Unless you can say specifically which one you want, you are more than likely to come away with one you don't want.

You will find the same problem if you use only common names. For instance, if you ask for a pink geranium, the person at the garden center will want to know whether you really want a geranium or do you mean a pelargonium (which is the correct name for what most people call geraniums) or are you looking for a hardy geranium (which is a true geranium) and if so, which kind? Now, there is no reason to be alarmed. Staff at most garden centers are very helpful in these matters, but it makes a world of difference if you can walk confidently into your garden center and ask for the plant you want by its specific botanical name. This eliminates 90 per cent of the risk of coming away with the wrong plant. (There is also the possibility of mislabelling but that is happening less and less.)

Botanical names can be a pain. They are often difficult to say and even more challenging to remember. You will be surprised, however, how quickly you pick up the habit of saying them and how beautiful some of them sound as they roll off the tongue. The secret is to say the name three times in a row. By the third time, you will have it down pat and it will be safely stored in your memory.

When it comes to botanical names, there are things you need to know, and certain things that are really not worth worrying about. You need to know that each plant belongs to a specific group or genus. This is indicated by the plant's first name. Maples, for instance, have the word *Acer* as their genus name. So you know whenever you are looking at an *Acer*, you are looking at some kind of maple. Think of it as a kind of surname. Now within that group of maples, there are many kinds or species. To narrow things down to the precise species we are talking about, each plant has been given a special second (species) name—for instance, *Acer griseum*, *Acer davidii* and *Acer palmatum*. But if you went to the garden center and asked for an *Acer palmatum*, they would then ask you, "What cultivar?" This is why plants have a third name—a cultivar name. This appears in single quotation marks—*Acer palmatum* 'Bloodgood', for example. With this information, you can ask for precisely the plant you want and get it. You need all three names to be sure.

Botanical names get more complicated after this. Sometimes a plant has an extra latinized name after the species name that indicates something about the plant's growth habit (*fastigiate*—erect; *pendulous*—weeping), or color (*alba*—white; *glauca*—blue-green), or flowers (*campanulata*—bell-shaped; *stellata*—star-shaped), or geographical origins (*japonica*—of Japan; *sinensis*—of China). This does not change things very much—all you really need for shopping is a plant's first name (genus), second name (species) and third name (cultivar).

When a plant is a hybrid between two or more species, taxonomists use a multiplication sign to let you know. *Epimedium × rubrum*, for example, is a hybrid produced by crossing *Epimedium alpinum* with *Epimedium grandiflorum*. Do you care? Probably not. Most home gardeners don't. If you go to your garden center and ask for *Epimedium rubrum* and neglect to include the multiplication sign, you will still come away with the right plant. For botanical accuracy, you will find plants in this book have been given their correct full botanical name and, in some cases, this includes an × sign.

Coastal gardens

There are few better places in the world to be a gardener than right here in the Pacific Northwest. This is not mere regional pride, it's a scientific fact. Those of us lucky enough to live on the west coast can grow thousands of plants that gardeners in other parts of North America can only dream of having in their garden. We tend to take all this for granted. We see such marvelous plants as Mexican orange, Japanese maples, lacecap hydrangeas, passion vines and pink dogwoods growing in coastal gardens and we think nothing of it. Yet none of these plants would survive in gardens outside the protection of the coast's mild climate. Left to endure a punishing winter in Toronto or Winnipeg, Chicago or Detroit, they would quickly curl up and die.

A quick look at hardiness zones tells some of the story. North America is mapped out into 10 climate zones, based on average minimum winter temperatures. The lower the zone number, the colder it gets; the higher the zone number, the warmer it gets and the more plants you can grow. Most of the Pacific Northwest falls into either Zone 7 (0° to 10°F/–18° to –12°C) or Zone 8 (10° to 20°F/–12° to –7°C). There are, however, colder inland areas where winter temperatures dip to –10° to –30°F (–23° to –35°C), and there are hot spots where temperatures rarely fall below freezing. Zone numbers are a useful guide when buying plants. If the label on a plant indicates that it is only hardy in Zone 9–10, you can assume the plant is too tender to survive outdoors in most coastal gardens over winter.

This doesn't tell the whole story. There are other climatic factors such as rainfall and winds and freeze-thaw cycles to take into account. They also play an important role in the life of plants. This is often the reason why identical plants perform differently in neighboring gardens: one is basking in the warmth of a microclimate with a higher zone rating, while the other plant is fighting for survival in subzero temperatures in poorly drained ground that keeps freezing and thawing. Zone numbers are useful, but should not stop you from experimenting with plants. Many plants brought to Europe from China were initially thought to be tender and were overwintered in heated greenhouses until someone had the nerve to try growing them outside . . . and discovered that they were actually as hardy as nails. So keep pushing the envelope.

Six steps to success

1. Remember, plants are living things: In so many ways they are no different from people. If you neglect them, don't feed them, don't care for them, if you force them to live in the dark when they need light, or in the hot sun

when they need shade, they will experience stress. They will either live out their life weak and failing, unhappy and frustrated, or they will just give up and get sick and die. The first rule of good gardening is to make sure plants get every chance to live healthy lives. Often what makes a plant beautiful is not the color of its flowers or the shape of its leaves, but the healthiness and vigor it projects. You can have a garden full of the most wonderful plants, but if they are sick and stressed, your garden has immediately lost its intrinsic beauty. It can take years to bring a garden to maturity, but there is no reason you can't get off on the right foot by deciding at the outset to observe the following simple rules.

2. Know your garden: All the plants mentioned in this book are so dependable, you could beat them with a stick and they would not give up on you. But you need to do a little homework to get everything to work out. Take time to figure out where the hot spots are in your garden and where the frost pockets are. You don't need a detailed scale plan of your garden. Just make some mental notes about such things as where the shady areas are and where the damp, boggy spots are. You learn all this by walking the garden in all weather and at all hours of the day. Don't weary yourself with this, but do take time to walk around your garden and get to know the different microclimates, the places where the sun shines most, where the rain falls hardest, where the ground drains rapidly, where the shadows linger longest, and where the ice and frost cling on to the bitter end. All this knowledge will make a lot of difference to your success as a gardener.

3. Get the right plant in the right place: The key to successful gardening is to get a great plant in a good location . . . next to other right plants in right places. The most common garden error is to put shade-loving plants in sunny spots and sun-loving plants in cool damp places. You would be amazed how often it happens and it is almost always because the gardener has not taken the time to get in touch with the garden at the soil level. Promise that you won't just push a plant in the ground without first doing all the necessary soil preparation.

    It is such a shame to take all the time to pick out beautiful plants and then to go and stick them in ground that has barely 6 inches (15 cm) of decent soil. Most plants need at least 18 inches (45 cm) of decent, fertile, well-drained soil. Some like moist soil, others like it dry, but the majority like their roots in nutrient-rich, well-drained earth. If you can't promise a plant that, it shouldn't go in the ground. It might just as well stay in the pot and live out its life at the garden center. Before planting, dig out all the bad soil—the hard, lifeless, dead-looking earth—and replace it with fertile, loamy, humus-rich soil. If you can't go 18 inches (45 cm) deep, settle for

12 inches (30 cm), but make it the best foot of soil in the garden. This is the way to get plants off to a healthy start. And healthy gardens are beautiful gardens.

4. Think about the borrowed landscape: This basically means being conscious of the bigger world around your garden and thinking about what you get from it and what you can contribute to it. For instance, is your garden made prettier by all the lovely trees growing in the neighbor's yard? Do you enjoy impressive views of the mountains or ocean, distant lake, sunny hilltop or spinney? Is there a beautiful flowering shrub or a scrambling vine that tumbles into your yard and gives you a wonderful show or fills the air with an intoxicating fragrance?

   The borrowed landscape is a term garden designers use to describe landscaping you get for free. You didn't plan it, you didn't plant it, you did nothing to deserve it, you just inherited it. It was there before you came along and you got to draw on it and work it into your garden scene to enrich the total picture.

   It is important to make the most of whatever borrowed landscaping you have. This means looking up and around and thinking about how to incorporate whatever beautiful trees or shrubs or views are available on the outskirts of your garden. Is there a lovely flowering tree in the neighbor's yard that would provide a complementary background contrast to your rhododendrons? Does the trellis on the neighbor's wall fill out with purple clematis in summer? When the trees in the back lane lose their leaves in winter, do you get a clear view of the mountains or ocean? Framing views or calculating how to pick up color from blooms in neighboring yards is all part of borrowed landscaping.

   You also need to think about how what you do in your garden affects your neighbors and the neighborhood. You certainly have the right to take down a tree on your property, but is it a tree that is loved by the entire neighborhood and how will its loss affect the landscape of the area? True gardeners think about these things. If you garden with a sensitivity to your neighbor, you will make better decisions and end up with a better garden. You will think twice about planting a tree that will grow too big or a vine that is too vigorous or a color that is too jarring. Thinking about the borrowed landscape will make you a better gardener.

5. Share what you grow: All expert gardeners know the best way to ensure that you have a plant forever is to give some of it away to a friend. That way, if your plant should suddenly die, you always have a friend who can give you back a replacement. The Victoria Horticulture Society has a marvelous motto: "Show what you grow, share what you know." Gardeners should be willing to open their gardens and let others see what they are doing. This is a great way to encourage and inspire others. It is also an opportunity to

exchange ideas and share what you know. Gardening is all about sharing—sharing plants, sharing knowledge, sharing stories of successes and failures.

6. Don't let the fun go down: The saddest thing that happens to new gardeners is that they get serious and forget gardening is supposed to be fun. It is playing with plants. What tends to happen is that they get pushed and prodded by fanatical gardeners to become just as fanatical and . . . unhappy. Make a decision that if ever gardening stops being fun, you will stop what you are doing and do something else. Don't let gardening become a pain in the neck. If a plant dies, you can always get another one. If you make a mistake, don't be hard on yourself—that's how most people learn what works and what doesn't. Sometimes mistakes will turn out to be huge successes. You will always be making changes, taking plants out, even if they look fine, to try something new. The important thing is to have fun gardening.

100

Best

Plants

Acer palmatum dissectum 'Crimson Queen'

Common name: Laceleaf Japanese maple

Chief characteristics

There are many fine maples suitable for growing in small- and medium-sized gardens, but you won't go wrong if you pick a cultivar of *Acer palmatum*.

Location: Part shade
Type: Deciduous tree
Size: 5 feet (1.5 m)
Conditions: Moist, acidic soil, protected from winds

One of the best forms for use in the home garden is *Acer palmatum dissectum* 'Crimson Queen', which is acclaimed for its deep red foliage that holds on to its color throughout the year. It is also extremely heat tolerant and has good fall color as the leaves turn orange-red and then bright scarlet. Other popular cultivars to look for include 'Garnet', 'Red Dragon' and 'Ever Red'.

'Crimson Queen' is totally reliable. It grows slowly to form a small, mushroom-shaped tree. It has soft, finely cut leaves that create a relaxed, cascading look in the landscape. It is a very useful tree for growing over low retaining walls or as a special feature in a planter box or container. You will often find it combined, in both casual and formal gardens, with its green-leaf lookalike, *A.p. dissectum* 'Viridis'. Together they provide balance, harmony and visual relief. Red-leafed forms of *A.p. dissectum* are by far the most popular, outselling the green-leafed cultivars by at least 4 to 1.

Dissectum maples are mostly rounded shrubs with cascading branches, whereas *Acer palmatum* are mostly upright trees. However, the cultivar 'Seiryu' is unusual in that it is a dissectum that grows upright. There are many outstanding cultivars of *Acer palmatum*. Few exceed 30 feet (9 m); most grow to little more than 20 feet (6 m). The coral bark maple (*A.p.* 'Sengo kaku', also known as 'Senkaki') has coral-pink bark and branches. The leaves turn a pleasant golden color in fall. Other top cultivars to consider include 'Bloodgood', 'Oshû-beni', 'Shishigashira', 'Red Dragon', 'Sherwood Flame', 'Osakazuki', 'Koto no ito' and 'Butterfly'.

Part of the beauty of these graceful upright maples is their ability to cast gentle, dappled shade that is not only pleasant to sit under, but provides the perfect light for growing a wide variety of plants that thrive in lightly shaded areas.

Where to plant it

The low-growing dissectum forms of *Acer palmatum* as a rule do not do well in open, exposed sites. They prefer a semi-shaded location where they will be well protected from the morning sun of early spring and the hot afternoon sun in summer. They thrive in rich, acidic soil that stays reasonably cool and moist without being excessively wet or boggy.

How to care for it

Prune away dead, damaged and diseased branches in spring. Make sure the tree gets well watered and the ground never becomes parched. Scorching of the delicate foliage can be a problem if the tree gets no protection from afternoon sun. This is something to avoid by thinking carefully about the appropriate location at time of planting.

Good companions

There is usually not much room to plant under the cascading foliage of dissectums. The branches tend to keep tumbling downward until they reach the ground. Some people try, without a great deal of success, to weave clematis or annual vines through the lacy, deeply divided leaves. The best companions for the green and red cultivars of *Acer palmatum dissectum* are each other. For a dramatic contrast you could combine a red laceleaf with the lime-green foliage of *Spiraea japonica* 'Lime Mound', which also has pink flowers. Most common partners for *A. p. dissectum* are well-behaved neighboring shrubs such as rhododendrons, evergreen azaleas, pieris, photinia and cotinus.

For your collection

Here are a few other quality maples you might like to try.

- Paperbark maple (*Acer griseum*): When the soft dying light of the setting sun strikes the peeling, cinnamon-colored bark of this special tree, the sight can be quite mesmerizing. The fall foliage is also very attractive. It grows 24 to 36 feet (7 to 11 m) at maturity.
- Golden fullmoon maple (*Acer japonicum aureum*): This has beautiful, tightly clustered yellow-green leaves that can light up the corner of the garden. It grows to about 20 feet (6 m).
- *Acer palmatum* 'Aka Shigitatsusawa': This has light, darkly veined green leaves that turn reddish in spring for a striking display. It grows into a tall, bushy shrub about 10 feet high (3 m).
- *Acer palmatum* 'Red Pygmy': A relatively new, slow-growing variety, this tree becomes more beautiful as it ages. It grows only 5 feet tall by 4 feet wide (1.5 by 1.2 m).

$\mathcal{A}$cer pseudoplatanus 'Brilliantissimum'

Common name: *Sycamore maple*

Chief characteristics

Why don't more people grow this lovely, slow-growing tree? It has outstanding shrimp-pink new foliage in spring that easily compares to the cherry blossom for elegance and charm. It has an extremely graceful form, slowly rounding at the top as it matures into a full, lollipop shape. Once the shrimp-pink leaves have unfolded, they turn a pale green. New leaves continue to appear through the summer and they decorate the tree with bright patches of pinkish-green. The effect is very subtle and attractive.

Location: Full sun to semi-shade
Type: Deciduous tree
Size: 15 feet (4.5 m)
Conditions: Ordinary soil
Flowering time: Excellent foliage color from March to April

'Brilliantissimum' was awarded the Award of Merit by the Royal Horticultural Society in 1925 and won the Award of Garden Merit from the same illustrious society in 1973. Yet the tree is still quite a rarity in coastal gardens. If you do go looking for it, don't be palmed off with the plain old sycamore, *Acer pseudoplatanus*. This is not the same thing at all. It is a fast-growing street tree that can shoot up 50 or 60 feet (15 to 18 m) in no time at all.

'Brilliantissimum' is very slow growing. Nor should you be told that the cultivar 'Leopoldii' is much the same thing. It again is a much larger tree. Make sure you see the name 'Brilliantissimum' on the label before you part with your money.

Try to pick a specimen that is already showing the tree's attractive mophead look and avoid ones that have been pruned like a regular maple tree.

Where to plant it

'Brilliantissimum' has one drawback. In the hot afternoon sun of summer the delicate pale green leaves can scorch and end up looking a little tatty. For this reason, it is best if the tree is planted where it will get afternoon shade from taller trees or hedging. The tree's natural color stands out best against a dark background. Gardeners in England and Ireland use 'Brilliantissimum' in their mixed borders as well as a stand-alone specimen. Its slow-growing habit allows it to blend very comfortably with evergreen or deciduous shrubs. The tree's short stubby trunk leaves plenty of room for underplanting.

How to care for it

Grow 'Brilliantissimum' in ordinary, well-drained soil. It can be pruned while dormant in late winter or early spring before the sap rises. Remove dead, damaged or crossing branches. The pink foliage may attract aphids and ants but these can be dissuaded by applying a collar of sticky Tanglefoot around the trunk at the end of winter. (Tanglefoot is a "tree paste" that is used around the trunk of a tree to make a sticky barrier against insects.)

Good companions

The pink-flowering bleeding heart (*Dicentra spectabilis)* is an excellent choice to grow beneath 'Brilliantissimum'. The bright red, heart-shaped flowers harmonize beautifully with the tree's pale pink foliage during March and April. Maidenhair fern, hardy geraniums and hellebores are also good partners. In the mixed border, 'Brilliantissimum' will rub shoulders happily with viburnums, rhododendrons, cotinus, pieris, photinia and magnolias. You can create a first-class underplanting using blue- and yellow-leafed hostas. For the blues, use 'Halcyon', 'Blue Cadet', 'Hadspen Blue'. For the yellows, mix 'September Sun', 'Piedmont Gold' and 'Gold Scepter'.

For your collection

Here are a few other great small- and medium-sized trees worth considering.

- Fullmoon maple (*Acer japonicum* 'Aconitifolium'): An excellent shade tree, this grows to about 25 feet (7.5 m). It has distinctive, deeply cut leaves with good fall color.
- Paperbark maple (*Acer griseum*): This has peeling, cinnamon-colored bark which is spectacular when the late-afternoon sun strikes it. It can reach 30 feet (9 m) at maturity.
- Sourwood or sorrel tree (*Oxydendrum arboreum*): This has white, scented flowers and spectacular fall color. It likes acid soil and grows at a moderate rate, reaching about 35 to 40 feet (11 to 12 m) at maturity.
- The weeping pussy willow (*Salix caprea* 'Pendula'): This has attractive grey catkins with yellow flowers in late spring. It grows 10 feet (3 m) and thrives in moist soil.
- Hakuro Nishiki willow (*Salix integra* 'Albamaculata'): With its bright variegated green leaves, this attractive willow grows about 12 to 15 feet (3.6 to 4.5 m) in a sheltered spot.
- Persian ironwood (*Parrotia persica*): A lovely deciduous tree, this is spectacular in the fall when its leaves turn various shades of red and yellow. Grows slowly to about 40 feet (12 m) at maturity.

🪶 Staghorn sumac (*Rhus typhina*): This small tree or large shrub grows to 20 feet (6 m) and has brown velvety branches like a stag's antlers. Its leaves turn bright red in fall.

🪶 Japanese stewartia (*Stewartia pseudocamellia*): This superb deciduous tree grows 35 to 40 feet (11 to 12 m). It has white flowers in mid-summer and good fall foliage.

*A*ctinidia kolomikta

Common name: Kolomikta vine, Arctic beauty vine, super-hardy kiwi vine

Chief characteristics

Location: Full sun
Type: Deciduous vine
Size: 10 to 14 feet (3 to 4 m)
Conditions: Ordinary soil
Flowering time: June to August

The heart-shaped leaves of *Actinidia kolomikta* are what make it so magical. In full sun the tips turn a strawberry pink or creamy white. Once the vine is well established, the decorative effect of the variegated color can be striking. Not everyone likes this. Critics have described the vine as "a horror of horrors" and "temperamental." I find such comments needlessly exaggerated and unfairly harsh. The vine is a popular, useful, handsome climber with a remarkable foliage color that knowledgeable gardeners have described as "magnificent." It is obviously all in the eye of the beholder!

Actinidia kolomikta is certainly a lot more graceful and easier to accommodate in the average-sized home garden than its rampant cousin, *A. chinensis*, the Chinese gooseberry. That species is so vigorous it will clamber 30 feet (9 m) into a large tree or smother the wall of a house. Don't bring home the wrong plant.

As well as the interesting leaf coloring, the Kolomikta vine produces mildly fragrant, cup-shaped white flowers in June. The vine gets its intriguing nickname, Arctic beauty vine, because it is capable of enduring intense cold. Although it is rarely grown on the prairies, gardeners there should consider it since it can survive even when temperatures plummet to as low as –40°F (–40°C).

Where to plant it

Actinidia kolomikta looks best against a south- or west-facing wall of a house or over a fence. It can grow more than 12 feet (3.6 m) and cover a sizable area but it must have plenty of sunshine if the leaves are going to perform their unique conjuring trick and change color at the tips.

This, however, doesn't always happen until the plant has been established for a few years. Being deciduous, it loses its leaves in winter, so it would not be the right choice if you want an area perpetually covered or screened. (Ivy would be a more suitable pick for that task.)

When not planted in the right place, A. *kolomikta* will struggle along and look rather unhappy and bedraggled. This is how many people have seen it and dismissed it. Pity. Seen at its best, it's a plant for everyone's garden.

How to care for it

While it can tolerate extreme cold, *Actinidia kolomikta* can be killed by excessively wet winters, especially if planted in poor-draining soil. It also suffers during freeze-thaw cycles when moisture in the ground around the plant turns alternately from water to ice.

The answer is to ensure it is planted in a well-draining spot in a sunny, sheltered area. Prune in late winter or early spring. The way to get it to spread and increase its coverage is to cut it back to about 2 feet (60 cm) off the ground when it is still quite young. This treatment gets it to bush out. From then on it is simply a matter of pruning to size and shape.

Good companions

Climbing roses, especially pink and red ones like 'High Hopes', 'Altissimo', 'Dublin Bay', 'Francois Juranville' and 'New Dawn', and purple clematis like *Clematis × jackmanii* or 'Polish Spirit' make lively companions, although *Actinidia kolomikta* is mostly seen working alone.

For your collection

Actinidia kolomikta has been used successfully to cover the side of garden sheds in summer. Other shed-covering vines worth considering include those below.

- The golden hops vine (*Humulus lupulus* 'Aureus'): This deciduous vine has yellow foliage and produces dangling hops in late summer. It thrives in full sun.
- The chocolate vine (*Akebia quinata*): With soft green leaves arranged in clusters of 5, this deciduous vine produces fragrant dark plum-purple flowers. It grows 15 to 20 feet (4.5 to 6 m).
- Russian vine (*Polygonum baldschuanicum*): This immensely vigorous deciduous vine may cover more than the shed by the time it is done. It can stretch 30 feet (9 m) and produces panicles of pink-tinged flowers.

- Winter jasmine (*Jasminum nudiflorum*): Looking for winter flowers? This deciduous vine, which likes sun or partial shade, will climb 10 to 15 feet (3 to 4.5 m) and produces yellow flowers from January to March.
- Common white jasmine (*Jasminum officinale*): This has fragrant white flowers in summer and is especially useful for covering arbors and walls. Semi-evergreen, it will grow 30 feet (9 m) or more. There is a golden-leafed form, *J. officinale* 'Fiona Sunrise'.
- English ivy (*Hedera helix*): Not the most creative choice of vines but certainly one of the most reliable evergreen climbers for covering walls, sheds or fences. The sturdy, solid green leaves will quickly form a lush cover. The variegated Persian ivy (*H. colchica* 'Dentata Variegata') may have more appeal, but it is also more tender than English ivy. Evergreen, both will easily grow 15 to 25 feet (4.5 to 7.5 m).

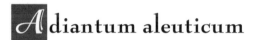diantum aleuticum

Common name: Western or five-fingered maidenhair fern

Chief characteristics

You may have thought a fern is a fern is a fern. Not so. It can come as a bit of a shock to discover just how many kinds of ferns there are being commercially cultivated today. Take a deep breath and give this short list a whirl: arching wood fern, crested royal fern, ostrich fern, parsley fern, shield fern, Japanese lady fern, hard fern, fragile fern, oak fern, log fern (pause for breath), soft tree fern, scaly tree fern, Korean rock fern, licorice fern, crisped golden-scaled male fern, champion's wood fern. And on and on. The list seems endless. Actually, there are no fewer than 132 kinds in commercial cultivation.

Location: Shade to light shade
Type: Perennial
Size: 12 to 24 inches (30 to 60 cm)
Conditions: Moist soil

Ferns are magnificent foliage plants for the shade. Along with hostas, they are the royalty of shade plants. Their main role in the garden is to provide architectural form and foliage texture and contrast. We don't expect them to have colorful flowers, although some have patterned fronds. We mainly appreciate them for their reliable, long-lasting greenness and dependable structure.

Where to begin? A great fern for any garden is *Adiantum aleuticum*, the graceful maidenhair fern. It has delicate fan-shaped fronds and thin back-ribbed stems. This is a supremely elegant plant, indispensable for adding a light, airy, romantic touch to the shade under trees. I have a large clump growing next to a birdbath beside a maple tree in my garden. *A. aleuticum* grows about 2 feet tall (60 cm) and will hold its form all summer, slowly giving way to frost and dying down in fall, only to return the following spring. It is truly one of the best ornamental plants available to the gardener's palette.

Where to plant it

The majority of ferns perform best in loose, fertile, well-drained soil that is regularly amended with compost or manure. Grow them under trees in dappled shade along with hostas and astilbes. You can use ferns to get a lush, jungle-like look or a soft, romantic textured look. It is interesting to mix species to achieve even more dramatic contrast, but think carefully about their size at maturity or you may end up losing smaller plants beneath the billowy fronds of stouter giant ferns.

How to care for it

Don't let your ferns struggle in poor, arid soil in summer. Water them with the same care you show other plants in the garden. Old, faded fronds can be cut away in spring to allow new, fresh green fronds to emerge unhindered. Add organic material every year. Mulch in spring as a moisture-retaining measure. This is also an effective way of enriching the soil.

Good companions

There is no shortage of chums for ferns: hostas, hardy geraniums, astilbes, cimicifuga, polygonatum, astrantia, pulmonaria, hydrangeas, rhododendrons, light shade–loving bulbs such as scilla, trilliums and erythronium, and lovely lush green ornamental grasses such as lazula.

For your collection

Other top ferns, some bigger and more architectural than others, include those named below.

- The western sword fern (*Polystichum munitum*) is the vigorous, clump-forming, native species with marvelously long, strong fronds that unfurl in the most delightfully entertaining way.
- The Japanese painted fern (*Athyrium niponicum* 'Pictum') has deep green fronds with a decorative gray-pink marking.
- The royal fern (*Osmunda regalis*) will ultimately reach 4 feet high (1.2 m) and makes a very bold feature plant that provides structure for your garden.

🌿 The ostrich fern (*Matteuccia struthiopteris*) grows 3 to 4 feet (90 to 120 cm) and gets its common name because the fronds look rather like the plumes of an ostrich.

🌿 Any of the durable workhorse *Dryopteris* ferns tend to define what the word "fern" means for most people. Notable ones include the autumn fern, *D. erythrosora*, which has striking copper-pink fronds, and the lacy crested broad buckler fern, *D. dilatata* 'Lepidota cristata'.

🌿 If you have room, how about a Tasmanian tree fern (*Dicksonia antarctica*), which has huge fronds that make it look rather like a palm tree? Slow-growing, it can eventually reach 15 feet high (4.5 m) and have a thick tree-like trunk 3 feet (90 cm) around. It is designated a Zone 8 specimen, which means it needs protection from heavy frost in most of the Pacific Northwest.

 *A*juga reptans 'Bronze Beauty'

Common name: Common bugleweed

Chief characteristics

One of the basic rules of gardening is that all soil should be covered, especially in summer when the sun can suck all the life-giving moisture from the ground and put your plants under stress. Grass is what most of us use to cover large, exposed expanses of

Location: Shade to part sun
Type: Groundcover
Size: 6 inches (15 cm)
Conditions: Moist, well-drained soil
Flowering time: May to June

ground. Mulch is more routinely used to protect soil around perennials in borders. If you have large areas of exposed soil under trees or shrubs, you will want to plant a suitable groundcover, preferably a thick plant cover that not only holds and protects the soil, suppresses weeds and reduces moisture-loss, but also has attractive flowers or foliage. A groundcover should provide a low-growing, closely structured, carpeting plant cover.

Ajuga reptans is one of the best and most versatile groundcovers. A sturdy creeping plant with small, shiny, rounded leaves, this is dense enough to smother most weeds. Watch for its 4- to 6-inch (10- to 15-cm) spikes of blue flowers from May to June. There are many cultivars on the market. The best is 'Bronze Beauty', which has brilliant blue flowers in spring and reliable, ground-hugging bronze foliage the rest of the year. There are a few others that offer slight variations in foliage color that are also worth checking out. 'Purple Torch' has glossy green foliage while 'Burgundy Glow' has striking variegated leaves that are a mixture of white, pink and silvery green. Other popular cultivars include 'Braunherz', 'Silver Carpet' and 'Catlin's Giant'.

Ajuga pyramidalis 'Metallica Crispa' is a little more unusual than the common bugleweed. The crinkled leaves are compact and attractive and not bothered by a little sun.

Where to plant it

Ajuga is a fast-growing groundcover that forms mats of crinkly foliage in full sun to part shade. You should plant it where you will be able to see and enjoy the bright blue flowers in spring and the lush carpeting foliage the rest of the year.

Use 'Bronze Beauty' under trees and shrubs or to form a low edging for paths. It can be combined with other groundcovers but is fairly competitive, gaining ground by invasive runners, and will squeeze out all rivals but those that can hold their own.

Hostas have sufficiently sturdy root systems to contend with it, but daintier specimens like lamium or creeping jenny will lose out most of the time. Most groundcovers thrive in light or full shade. The best test is to grow a few different groundcovers in the same area and let them fight it out. It is surprising sometimes which one wins.

How to care for it

The best rule of maintenance for ajuga is not to let it become too invasive. It will want to creep and cover as much ground as possible. It can, however, be very easily contained by chopping it back into bounds. Ajuga's blue flowers are wonderful, but you should not plant it for the flowers alone.

Your main decision to plant it should be to cover ground under trees and shrubs. When the flowers come, you should regard them as a bonus. When they are finished blooming, you can shear them off or allow them to disappear in their own time. Ajuga is rarely troubled by pests and diseases and can be very easily transplanted. Simply separate one of the offshoots and relocate it. Provided this is not done in the heat of summer, the offshoot will easily root and should be well watered.

Good companions

Mix ajugas with other ajugas. Blue-leafed hostas make nice companions, as do lungwort (*Pulmonaria*) and maidenhair ferns. Astilbes and hardy geraniums can also be mixed in to create foliage contrasts.

For your collection

There are many other notable groundcovers. Here are some of the best.

- Wild ginger (*Asarum*): Not widely used, nevertheless this is an excellent groundcover plant with dark green, glossy, evergreen heart- or kidney-shaped leaves on thin stems. It gets its name from its gingerlike fragrance. Look for A. *canadense* or A. *europaeum*. Wild ginger performs best in moist, acidic, deep shade under rhododendrons or hydrangeas.

- Giant rockfoil or large-leafed saxifrage (*Bergenia cordifolia*): This has large, leathery bright green leaves that turn coppery red in fall. It thrives in sun or shade and sends up a striking pink, red, white or purple flowerhead in spring. Look for 'Baby Doll', 'Bressingham Ruby', 'Bressingham Salmon', 'Bressingham White'.

- Bunchberry (*Cornus canadensis*): A member of the dogwood family, native to North America, it takes a little longer than other groundcovers to get established and is not your best pick if you want to quash weeds. It does have attractive, broad foliage and white flowers in late spring followed by red berries in late summer. Grow C. *canadensis* in light shade with lily-of-the-valley or epimedium or sweet woodruff.

- Lily-of-the-valley (*Convallaria majalis*): This may not be the most original groundcover, but it is one of the most dependable and hardy. In spring, it puts out sweetly scented white, bell-like flowers.

- Bishop's hat or barrenwort (*Epimedium*): Mainly grown for its leaves, which are heart-shaped and held up on delicate, wiry stems, *Epimedium* also flowers, producing tiny pink or white blooms in spring. In mild areas, the leaves will change color and hang on all winter, needing only to be cut back just before spring. *Epimedium* gets its folk name, barrenwort, from the belief that it was supposed to be able to prevent conception.

- Sweet woodruff (*Galium odoratum*): This has delightful white flowers and lacy foliage. It is the perfect choice for underscoring boxwood hedges or shrubs in the shady woodland border. It is a notorious colonizer. If planted in an unrestricted area, it will self-sow freely and spread rapidly. But this is perhaps precisely what you want. If you don't, then plant it under low hedges next to concrete driveways or paths, or next to lawns that get mown regularly.

- St. John's wort (*Hypericum*): A bit too common for the taste of some gardeners, it is always reliable, producing attractive leaves on low arching stems, and distinct yellow flowers for great summer color. Look for H. *calycinum*, which is not bothered about the quality of soil in which it is planted and flourishes in both sun or part shade.

🐾 English ivy (*Hedera helix*): This plant provides the easy answer to many coverup problems. It will clamber into trees, over walls and fences and cover large areas under shrubs. Evergreen, it quickly forms a thick, leafy carpet, and it is indifferent to whether it is grown in sun or shade. While acknowledging its tremendous value as a woodland plant, critics tend to see ivy as a boring, monotonous choice for the home garden. But it does have its uses.

🐾 Spotted dead nettle (*Lamium maculatum*): Not to be confused with stinging nettles, this has the look but not the stinging hairs of its pain-inflicting cousin. The soft, green leaves have a greenish-white stripe, or midrib, and purple flowers. It will quickly form a mat of foliage in sun or light shade. 'Beacon Silver' has silvery leaves and purple flowers. Also look for 'Pink Pewter', 'White Nancy', 'Chequers' and 'Aureum'.

🐾 Creeping jenny (*Lysimachia nummularia*): One of the prettier groundcovers, this has soft yellow-green leaves and tiny, bright yellow flowers. It is ideal for brightening up a dampish, semi-shady corner in summer. The trailing stems should be snipped to make the plant thicken up. It also goes by a variety of other names including moneywort, twopenny grass, meadow runagates, string of sovereigns and wandering tailor.

🐾 Japanese spurge (*Pachysandra terminalis*): This will do as thorough a job as ivy at covering ground with a thick carpet of handsome, evergreen foliage, only it will take longer to do it. Hardy and drought tolerant, Japanese spurge has creamy white flowers in late spring. It is especially useful in areas where nothing else will grow.

🐾 Periwinkle (*Vinca minor*): Next to grass, this is probably the most widely grown groundcover in coastal gardens and for good reason: It does such a steady, dependable job and requires minimal attention. Flourishing in shade or part sun, its spreads rapidly, rooting its trailing stems as it goes. The dainty, 5-petal, lilac-blue flowers are not unattractive either.

🐾 *Lamium galeobdolon* 'Hermann's Pride': A fine plant with decorative variegated leaves, this is a noninvasive groundcover for edging or for providing foliage contrast in semi-shaded areas.

🐾 *Houttuynia cordata* 'Chameleon': This has small, showy heart-shaped leaves with yellow, green, bronze and pink coloring. It is a vigorous grower, especially in moist soil, and produces white flowers in summer. It grows 2 to 3 inches (5 to 8 cm) high.

$\mathcal{A}$kebia quinata

Common name: Chocolate vine

Chief characteristics

The chocolate vine has two endearing qualities: it has superbly graceful 5-lobed leaves, which are a delicate shade of green, and it has mildly vanilla-scented chocolate-colored flowers in spring.

Location: Full sun
Type: Semi-evergreen vine
Size: 20 to 26 feet (6 to 8 m)
Conditions: Well-drained, average soil
Flowering time: June

The worst thing anyone is going to tell you about this vine is that it is too vigorous. How vigorous? In ideal conditions, it can travel 30 feet (9 m), although it may take its time to get started on that journey.

The pluses far outweigh the minuses. Its ambitious ways can be controlled and the plum-purple flowers, which some have compared to the fragrance of expensive French soap, more than compensate for any overenthusiasm.

Where to plant it

The chocolate vine is ideal for covering fences or growing into trees and shrubs. Its vigor can also be harnessed to bring the garden up to isolated decks and balconies. Pergolas and arbors also provide ideal homes. Akebia likes moist soil and plenty of sunshine. It grows by twining skinny tendrils around whatever it can get a grip on, so you want to provide a little support at the beginning. Train the vine where you want it to go and, once it is established, you can simply concentrate on pruning it to shape. The roots don't like to be disturbed once they are settled.

How to care for it

How do you keep the chocolate vine from taking over? You prune it late in the spring the second it has finished flowering. The new growth that occurs will be less invasive.

Good companions

The chocolate vine combines well with clematis and roses. Consider planting such roses as 'Albertine' or 'Francois Juranville' or a wine-red clematis like 'Madame Julia Correvon'.

For your collection

- 🌿 Chocolate-scented flowers are an interesting talking point in the garden. To go with your chocolate vine, you could grow a chocolate cosmos (*Cosmos atrosanguineus*).
- 🌿 If you're interested in unusual climbers, how about a flame creeper (*Tropaeolum speciosum*), which has leaves quite similar to those of the chocolate vine? It has bright, red flowers in July and is a tender perennial climber.
- 🌿 Also, consider the trumpet vine (*Campsis radicans*), also known as the trumpet creeper or trumpet honeysuckle. This does well in a sunny, sheltered, moist, but well-drained location. The red, trumpet-shaped flowers are especially popular with hummingbirds. Cultivars to look for are *C. r.* 'Flava' or *C. × tagliabuana* 'Madame Galen'.

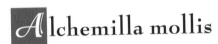lchemilla mollis

Common name: Lady's mantle

Chief characteristics

Location: Full sun to light shade
Type: Low mounding perennial
Size: 12 to 14 inches (30 to 36 cm)
Conditions: Ordinary garden soil
Flowering time: May to June

All the great cottage gardens of England have this old-fashioned favorite. It is loved for its seemingly magical ability to display raindrops like diamonds on its rough, hairy leaves. It is also valued for the light lime-green color and frothy texture of its effervescent sprays of flowers that first appear in June and last for several weeks.

The name *Alchemilla* is rooted in the word alchemy. When the plant was used as a herb it was thought to possess magical healing properties. The word *mollis* refers to the soft hairs of the leaves, which lock together in a way that looks rather like a lady's cloak or mantle.

While its performance is always predictable, lady's mantle can be used in a variety of ways—as a groundcover or container plant or for foliage contrast. Its most popular use is as a mounding foliage plant for filling out the front of a perennial border or as a plant for overgrowing and softening the straight edges of a path or walkway.

Originating in meadows and woodlands of eastern Europe and western Asia, *Alchemilla mollis* copes comfortably with cold winters. Hardy to −20°F (−29°C), it reaches about 14 inches (36 cm) high when in full bloom and is one of the first perennials to bounce back to life in the garden in spring. A time-bomb of a plant, lady's mantle is certainly a specimen to pass over the fence if you want your neighbor's empty yard to turn into a garden. It will quietly tick over the first year, then seed itself so rampantly that by the second year the whole yard will be covered.

Where to plant it

Lady's mantle will grow almost anywhere, but it looks best planted where it gets at least 3 hours of sun a day and protection from the afternoon sun. Grow it in well-drained soil in light shade in a place open to the sky, but shaded on the west side. In a container, it will do well provided it is not forgotten and left to wilt. Some gardeners have used the frothy lime-green flowers of lady's mantle very artistically along the banks of a stream or creek to mimic the rush and spray of water. Others have used it to create the effect of a lush oasis in a dry gravel area or alongside a stone path.

How to care for it

Lady's mantle requires minimal maintenance. It grows happily for several years without needing to be divided and flourishes even in poor soil. When clumps do become dense, they should be lifted and divided. Do this in early April when the soil is most workable.

Lady's mantle is a prolific self-seeder. If you are not careful it will propagate itself with almost promiscuous abandon in a free-spirited bid to take over your entire garden. The simple solution is to remove the browning flowerheads before they have a chance to shake down their seeds. The plant can also become somewhat untidy in late summer. The solution again is to take your pruners and clip off the unsightly leaves; this will encourage fresh new foliage to form. Shear back old foliage at the end of fall as part of your routine garden cleanup.

Good companions

The tiny lime-green flowers and the thick green leaves work well with almost any other garden plant, but lady's mantle combines exceptionally well with such shade-lovers as astilbe, bleeding heart, hostas, aquilegia, solomon's seal and sunnier performers like yellow achillea and white *Lychnis coronaria*. The sprays of lady's mantle's tiny chartreuse flowers can be used in floral arrangements.

For your collection

🌢 The compact rockery plant, alpine lady's mantle (*Alchemilla alpina*), grows to only 5 or 6 inches (13 or 15 cm) high and also produces tiny yellow-green flowers in summer. It is not as versatile as its cousin *Alchemilla mollis*, so show it more care and grow it in slightly moist, well-drained, fertile soil.

*A*llium aflatunense

Common name: Ornamental onion, flowering garlic, cricketball allium

Chief characteristics

Close your eyes and picture this: dozens of perfectly spherical purple flowerheads reaching up beneath a canopy of yellow blooms, cascading from rows of laburnum trees. Purple *Allium aflatunense* looks equally sensational popping up to complement the pink bottlebrush spikes of *Polygonum bistorta* (knotweed). Both these images are testament to the talent of gardeners who had the wit and wisdom to plant allium bulbs in the fall with a vision of what a spectacular picture they would create for spring.

> **Location:** Full sun or light shade
> **Type:** Bulb
> **Size:** 3 feet (90 cm)
> **Conditions:** Well-drained soil
> **Flowering time:** May to June

Allium aflatunense, sometimes called the cricketball allium, is the most companionable and versatile of the flowering garlics to use in the garden landscape. It has a more stately presence than its diminutive relative, *A. schoenoprasum* (chives). But, at 3 feet (90 cm) high, *A. aflatunense* is less towering than its robust relative, *A. giganteum*, which stands 4 feet (120 cm) and has flowerheads the size of a grapefruit.

Both add charm, character and regal color to the early summer garden. Bulbs are not expensive and they come back year after year to give the same magnificent display. An extra bonus: squirrels hate the smell of them and won't disturb them unless there are tulips planted nearby.

Rosemary Verey, the grand dame of English horticulture, was one of the first to see how well they fit under laburnum trees. Others have copied her celebrated planting in her garden at Barnsley House in Gloucestershire. *Allium aflatunense* also performs very well interplanted with roses.

Where to plant it

Plant the bulbs in late September or early October, at 3 or 4 times their own depth in fertile, well-drained soil in a sunny or lightly shaded spot. They will have no trouble pushing up through hardy geraniums or daylilies or rising up through the soft leaves of *Polygonum bistorta*.

How to care for it

Once they are in the ground there is very little that can go wrong with alliums. Slugs will sometimes nibble young foliage and bulbs have been known to rot in excessively boggy ground. One of the most common mistakes is to buy the wrong bulb. It can be disappointing if you plant *Allium karataviense* instead of *Allium aflatunense* and then discover in spring that the lovely flowerhead is lost in a jungle of taller foliage.

The decision to leave the faded flowerheads is purely an esthetic one: some gardeners love the look, others don't. English gardener, author and photographer Nigel Lawson once saved the dried flowerheads and re-introduced them to his garden in the winter to add architectural interest and intrigue.

Good companions

Without doubt, the best partner for *Allium aflatunense* is the knotweed (*Polygonum bistorta* 'Superbum'), which has pink, bottlebrush flowers that harmonize perfectly with the graceful purple flowerheads of the cricketball allium for about a month starting around the middle of May. Together these two plants make an extremely striking partnership. *Allium aflatunense* also appears at its best when mass planted under a row of yellow-flowering *Laburnum* × *watereri* 'Vossii' trees. Other excellent partners for the outstanding ornamental onion include yellow-leafed hostas, blue-flowering *Centaurea montana*, and the delicate magenta-red flowers of *Geranium macrorrhizum*.

With *Allium christophii*, contrast its magnificent starry flowerhead against the dark foliage of *Cimicifuga simplex* 'Brunette' or against the soft foliage of bleeding hearts. *Allium christophii* flowers around the same time as *Aubrieta*, *Phlox subulata*, foxgloves (*Digitalis purpurea*), perennial cornflower (*Centaurea montana*) and coral bells (*Heuchera sanguinea*).

For your collection

Allium aflatunense is not the only star performer in the allium family. It has a few relatives that also deserve a place in the home garden. All the alliums make excellent cut flowers, especially the Star of Persia. If you have the nerve take them out of the garden when they are at their most glorious. When they finish flowering, the large globular heads slowly fade to brown and produce tiny charcoal-black seeds that add an unexpected beauty to the spheres.

- Star of Persia (*Allium christophii*) resembles a space station when it is fully formed from a cluster of countless 5-point stars, each one a shiny, metallic purple-silver color.

- *Allium karataviense* produces a light purple-pink globe only 8 inches (20 cm) off the ground.
- *Allium caeruleum* brings the sky to the ground with its gorgeous light blue flowers in mid-summer.
- The most common of all alliums, chives (*Allium schoenoprasum*) also can be incorporated into the perennial border, or used as a decoration in a pot on the patio close to the kitchen.
- *Allium sphaerocephalum* (drumstick allium, roundheaded leek) has a spherical, reddish-purple flowerhead at the top of a 2-foot (60-cm) stem. It makes an excellent cut flower in a sunny perennial border in late July and August.

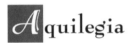 quilegia

Common name: Columbine

Chief characteristics

Columbines are exquisite woodland plants. Their bell-shaped flowers nod expressively and look rather like a committee-decision to cross a daylily with a daffodil and toss in the wings of a dragonfly for good measure. They are a perfect plant for mild, coastal gardens, flourishing in the moist, dappled shade of overhanging trees and popping up serendipitously between perennials and shrubs to form lovely pictures.

Location: Sun to light shade
Type: Perennial
Size: 2 to 3 feet (60 to 90 cm)
Conditions: Ordinary soil
Flowering time: April to May

The columbine's foliage is graceful and distinctive, but it is the modest, lantern-shaped flowers most gardeners fall in love with. Colors range from rich blues to muted pinks to soft pastel shades of purple and yellow. The plain columbine, *Aquilegia vulgaris*, is the old-fashioned "granny's bonnet" flower, which can be found in most English cottage gardens. It is the parent of many of the new cultivars, including the blue 'Hensol Harebell', the green-red 'Nora Barlow', and the maroon-white 'Biedermeier'.

Other modern favorites include the McKana Giants hybrids, which produce big flowers in pastel and two-tone hues and grow to just over 2 feet (60 cm), and the Mrs. Scott Elliott's hybrids, which are slightly more purple and darker than the others.

Although relatively short lived, especially in heavy and wet soils, columbines are easily raised from seed, so there is no reason to lose them once you have them established in the garden. Other well-known ones to watch out for include the dragonfly hybrids, which have long spurs and bright colors. They are very similar to the McKana hybrids but do not grow quite as tall.

Where to plant it

Grow columbines in well-drained leafy soil in a sunny or partly shady location. They flourish naturally under trees or in among the lush foliage of hostas and bleeding hearts. They have been known to attract hummingbirds but their main role is to provide a romantic cottage-garden atmosphere to the garden. They make fine cut flowers.

How to care for it

Columbines are short lived but come easily from seed, which should be collected and germinated in trays or pots and then re-introduced to the garden each year.

Watch out for aphids. Red spider mites can sometimes be a problem but columbines are mostly trouble-free.

Good companions

Purple alliums and late-blooming tulips mix well with columbines, which tend to blend most naturally with other cottage garden favorites such as bleeding hearts, lady's mantle, ferns, hostas, campanulas, cornflowers, foxgloves and shade lovers such as masterwort and ligularia.

Columbines also thrive happily among shrub roses and they always find their own place in the cheerful chaos of a spring perennial border with hardy geraniums, peonies and blue salvia.

For your collection

In the rock garden, try growing any or all of these.

- *Aquilegia caerulea* is a pale blue and white flower from Colorado's mountains.
- *Aquilegia bertolonii*, the dwarf species from Italy, grows only 6 inches (15 cm) high.
- The Swiss columbine (*Aquilegia alpina*) grows only 12 inches (30 cm) high and has gray-green leaves.

$\mathcal{A}$rtemisia 'Powis Castle'

Common name: Wormwood

Chief characteristics

Gray foliage is essential for creating
wonderful, classy color and textured
contrasts in the perennial border. There
are quite a few plants that will give you
the look you want, but few are as
reliable as the artemisias, which not
only have outstanding gray-silvery foliage but a respectable tolerance for
spells of drought. One of the best cultivars is 'Powis Castle'. It has
delightful, feathery, almost bushy, silver foliage. It is noninvasive and
blends superbly with other plants in the perennial border.

Location: Full sun to part sun
Type: Perennial
Size: 2 to 3 feet (60 to 90 cm)
Conditions: average, well-drained
   soil

When it first appeared a few decades ago, it caused quite a stir in
English garden circles. It was immediately recognized as one of the new
aristocratic plants, was welcomed wholeheartedly into the garden, and
has never left. It is actually the offspring of two older, well-known forms
of artemisia—the common wormwood, *Artemisia absinthium*, and
A. arborescens, considered by some to be the most attractive of all silver
foliage plants. With such parents it was perhaps predictable that the
child would be special. Although now grown in countless gardens,
'Powis Castle' is still regarded as a connoisseur's plant, a true botanical
treasure. The common name, wormwood, refers to the plant's history—
herbalists used it for a medicine to kill parasitic worms.

Where to plant it

Grow 'Powis Castle' in well-drained soil in full sun. It will tolerate some
shade. It is best planted toward the middle or back of the border since it
can grow taller than 3 feet (90 cm). It looks good when allowed to
intermingle freely with other perennials.

How to care for it

Cut back 'Powis Castle' to a few inches off the ground in April or early
spring to encourage new growth. Buds will break easily from the old
wood. It needs to be grown in almost perfectly free-draining soil or it
will be lost in a wet winter.

Good companions

Shrub roses combine very well with artemisia. The silvery foliage is a
perfect foil for the soft, pink, fragrant blooms of shrub roses such as

'Mary Rose' and 'Ballerina'. 'Powis Castle' also works well with bronze fennel. Other possible partners include lilies, baby's breath, rock rose, *Helianthemum*, the striking red dahlia 'Bishop of Llandaff', red potentilla, and the red-flowering *Lobelia cardinalis*.

For your collection

- *Artemisia ludoviciana* 'Valerie Finnis' has lovely, soft, willowlike silver-white leaves on erect stems.
- *Artemisia schmidtiana* 'Silver Mound' is a smaller, compact plant with soft, feathery silver foliage, wonderful to touch, that mounds to only 12 to 15 inches (30 to 38 cm). 'Silver Mound' can be used in the rockery or in containers or as a front-of-the-border plant.
- *Artemisia stelleriana* 'Silver Brocade' is a low-growing, compact plant with similar soft gray foliage to dusty miller. It is useful for rockery edging, groundcover or hanging baskets.
- White mugwort (*Artemisia lactiflora* 'Guizhou') has very different foliage—dark maroon-colored stems with purple, near black leaves and sprays of creamy white flowers from late summer to early fall. It grows about 4 feet (120 cm) high, making it a good choice for growing at the back of the perennial border.

ster × frikartii 'Monch'

Common name: Michaelmas daisy

Chief characteristics

Location: Full sun	
Type: Perennial	
Size: 28 inches (70 cm)	
Conditions: Moist, well-drained soil	
Flowering time: July to October	

You know the end of summer is just around the corner when you start to see asters coming into bloom along with rudbeckia and Japanese anemones. Asters, better known as Michaelmas daisies, are available in a wide range of colors from red to pink, light blue to purple-blue. They also range in size from tall, gangly 5-foot (1.5-m) giants to short compact dwarf specimens that can be grown in a rockery. Asters are valued for their long blooming period, the cheerfulness of their daisylike flowers, and their late season appearance when it seems as though the festive fun of summer is finished. They are a welcome late arrival to the party.

The best Michaelmas daisy for the average garden is *Aster × frikartii* 'Monch', which has bright lavender-blue flowers with yellow centers. It grows 3 feet (90 cm) tall and about 18 inches (45 cm) wide and flowers from the end of July to October. It is sturdy enough not to require staking, provides excellent cut flowers, and is a useful addition to any perennial border.

Where to plant it

Grow *Aster* × *frikartii* 'Monch' in full sun in rich soil that stays moist in summer but does not become water-logged in winter. Taller forms of aster often need staking, although they can be pinch-pruned to make them bushier. They are best placed at the back of the border where they can provide a wall of color.

The best place to grow 'Monch' is mixed in with other perennials and shrubs in a location where it can come into its own in August, bringing reinforcements of color to flagging flower beds, but not where it has too prominent a profile from spring to mid-summer. The shorter asters can be grown at the front of the border, tucked in between such early flowering fare as echinacea, daylilies, liatris and phlox.

How to care for it

The key to growing asters successfully is to make sure they get plenty of sun and are planted in fertile soil that does not dry out completely in the drought days of summer. Staking needs to be done early in July or even in late June to make sure the taller forms don't flop all over or start to twist.

Good companions

Gray-leafed plants such as *Artemisia ludoviciana* 'Valerie Finnis' and *Stachys byzantina* 'Primrose Heron' make effective partners, as do canna lilies, the peanut butter plant (*Melianthus major*), the steel-blue flowers of the globe thistle (*Echinops*) and sea holly (*Eryngium*), and the gold-yellow blooms of black-eyed susan (*Rudbeckia fulgida*). The exquisite flowers of Japanese anemones such as 'Honorine Jobert' (white), 'Queen Charlotte' (pink) and 'September Charm' (silvery pink) are also good partners. You can also select your asters so they flower when such ornamental grasses as *Miscanthus* and *Pennisetum* are at their peak in late summer and early fall.

For your collection

🌺 The bushy dwarf hybrids (*Aster dumosus*): These grow only about 12 to 15 inches (30 to 38 cm) tall and are ideal for the front of the border. Best bet: 'Lady in Blue', which has violet-blue flowers with a yellow center. This is easy to place in the border and it keeps its color long into fall. Other names to look for include 'Audrey' (mauve-blue), 'Diana' (rose-pink), 'Lady-in-Blue' (blue), 'Little Pink Beauty' (bright pink), 'Violet Carpet' (violet-blue), 'Nesthaskchen' (clear pink), 'White Opal' (white) and 'Jenny' (red).

- The New England asters (*Aster novae-angliae*): This is a taller species growing 5 feet (150 cm) high. These can become gangly and benefit from being pinch-pruned at the tips in early July to make them bushier. Good names to look for include: 'Andenken an Alma Potschke', 'Hella Lacy', 'Pink Winner', 'Purple Dome', 'September Ruby', 'Mrs. S. T. Wright' and 'Harrington's Pink'.
- The New York asters (*Aster novi-belgii*): These grow 3 to 4 feet (90 to 120 cm) tall and are the hybrids of a species that is native to New York State. Top cultivars include: 'Alert' (crimson), 'Coombe Rosemary' (violet-purple), 'Royal Ruby' (deep red), 'Coombe Margaret' (reddish-pink), 'Ada Ballard' (mauve-blue) and 'Chequers' (purple-violet).
- The heath aster (*Aster ericoides*) will mound into a bush about 3 feet (90 cm) tall with clouds of lilac-blue or pale pink flowers. Look for 'Blue Cloud' or 'Pink Cloud'.
- The white wood aster (*Aster divaricatus*) will grow in light, dry shade and produce a bright spray of white flowers that can add interest to the dappled woodland area of the garden.

$\mathcal{A}$stilbe × arendsii 'Elizabeth Bloom'

Common name: False spiraea

Chief characteristics

It is impossible to imagine a garden without astilbes. It was once rumored that the English had given up on them completely and had banned them from their borders. If ever that were true, it would have been a most foolish choice.

Location: Part sun to full shade
Type: Perennial
Size: 2 to 3 feet (60 to 90 cm)
Conditions: Good, moist soil
Flowering time: June to July

Astilbes are such thoroughly dependable plants. They send up lovely white, pink or red feather duster–like plumes from spring to late summer and their foliage forms great healthy mounds of leaves, which give the shade border its necessary bulk and full-bodied appearance. An old country garden plant, astilbe has had hybridizers playing with its genes for years with the result that now we have literally dozens of names with outstanding flower color and performance.

'Elizabeth Bloom' is one of the best of the newer cultivars, producing delightful, blowsy, pink plumes in late June. It will grow to a very respectable 2 feet (60 cm) high. What makes this plant so special is its utter reliability, its cheerful coloring allowing it to blend effortlessly with other perennials, and its good timing, producing abundant plumes from June to July, which is precisely when the garden needs to start exhibiting a sense of vitality and fullness.

Astilbe chinensis taquetii 'Superba' is another first-rate performer. It flowers later in the summer and has tall, deep purple-pink plumes reaching over 3 feet (90 cm). It is usually the last of the astilbe family to flower. Other astilbe cultivars include 'Fanal' and 'Etna' (red); 'Intermezzo', 'Bressingham Beauty', 'Sprite', 'Finale' and 'Koln' (pink); 'White Gloria', 'Queen of Holland', 'Brautschleier' and 'Snowdrift' (white). There are so many kinds of astilbe now on the market, you might prefer to shop for them the way you do for rhododendrons—wait until they are in bloom and then pick the color you like best.

Summer is a good time to make a note of plants and flowers you like. Be sure to find out not only the first name but the specific species and cultivar names so you can buy exactly what you want with confidence in spring. Keep in mind flowering times when choosing astilbes. You will want to get a few late-blooming types such as 'Superba', 'Purple Lance' or 'Intermezzo'. You also might have a spot for a shorter astilbe. One that can be used almost as a low-growing groundcover in drier soil or in the shady rock garden because of its dwarf habit is *A. × crispa* 'Perkeo', which has reddish-pink spikes and grows to less than 12 inches (30 cm) tall.

Where to plant it

Astilbe is outstanding when grown in bold drifts, especially by small streams that keep the surrounding soil perpetually moist. It doesn't take a lot to create a drift. Put in 3 or 5 plants to start and within a few years you will have twice that number. Grow astilbe in light shade in rich soil that does not dry out completely. It will flourish in a sunnier spot provided the soil is constantly moist. It can also be grown in full shade, although it blooms more impressively when it gets a few hours of warm sunlight.

How to care for it

If clumps of astilbe are not divided every 3 or 4 years, they start to flower poorly and the whole plant begins to look unhappy. Division invigorates the plant and gets it to bloom enthusiastically again. The magnificent plumes can be cut and used in flower arrangements and you may find them giving off a sweet sugary scent that cannot really be described as perfume but is not unpleasant.

Good companions

Hostas, ligularias, primulas, iris, lady's mantle, Jacob's ladder and a whole range of other light shade–loving plants work well with astilbes. The blues of the late summer–blooming monkshood (*Aconitum carmichaelii* 'Arendsii') would look great planted behind a drift of late-flowering *Astilbe chinensis taquetti* 'Superba'. The delicate, muted white or soft pink flowers of *Astrantia major* are outstanding combined with astilbe blooms in a vase.

For your collection

- If you like the light airy plumes of astilbe, you will probably love the giant plumes of goatsbeard (*Aruncus sylvester*). It looks like a giant astilbe with large attractive white plumes and it grows 5 feet (1.5 m) tall.
- Also check out *Rodgersia pinnata* 'Superba', which has impressive astilbe-like white or pink flower spikes held up above large, distinct leaves, rather like those of the horse chestnut.

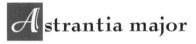# strantia major

Common name: Masterwort

Chief characteristics

Astrantia major is loved by gardeners for the delicacy and sophistication of its flowers. They are a gentle, greenish-white with light pink centers. Very charming, very elegant. Astrantia grows happily in the shade or light shade of trees or protective shrubs. It is an old-

Location: Part sun to part shade
Type: Perennial
Size: 30 inches (75 cm)
Conditions: Moist, but well-drained soil
Flowering time: June to July

fashioned perennial, one with a long history of being used in English cottage gardens. And yet it is invariably overlooked at garden centers because it has a difficult time drawing attention away from more showy annuals and perennials with vivid blooms. In the garden, however, astrantia brings a natural refinement to the shade border because of its low-key, non-pushy presence. The flowers are excellent for cutting. Indoors they can be appreciated close up for the true beauties they are.

Where to plant it

Astrantia thrives in ordinary, well-drained soil in semi-shade. It will grow in deep shade, but you tend to forfeit some of its remarkable flower power. The clumps of leaves smother out weeds and associate well with the foliage of other shade plants like bleeding hearts and solomon's seal.

How to care for it

Astrantia is a most reliable, clump-forming perennial. It needs very little care. It may topple onto its neighbors, especially after a heavy rain storm, but while some see it as untidy, others recognize the relaxed look as rather charming and natural. If you do want your astrantia to behave more formally, install link stakes as the new growth emerges in early spring and establish some parameters.

It should be watered well in the dog days of summer. Dry shade can kill it. Cut back the foliage after flowering to promote healthy new growth. Divide clumps every few years.

Good companions

Astrantia combines well in the shade border with astilbe, hostas, rodgersia, ligularias and ferns. It can also be worked in with shrub roses in light shade areas. One excellent combination puts *Astrantia major* 'Rubra' against the young burgundy leaves of the dwarf shrub *Berberis thunbergii* 'Atropurpurea Nana'. Also try marrying it with the blue cranesbill (*Geranium pratense*).

For your collection

- *Astrantia major* is the most dependable, although *A. major* 'Rubra' is now also very popular because of its wine-red flowers.
- *Astrantia maxima* has slightly larger, more pronounced shell-pink flowers with densely clustered pincushion centers, somewhat similar to scabiosa.
- There is also a variegated form, *Astrantia major* 'Sunningdale Variegated', which does not look as sickly as so many plants with green-white variegated foliage. In spring, this cultivar produces a bright mound of yellow-cream leaves.
- There is a dwarf red masterwort, *Astrantia carniolica* 'Rubra'. It grows less than 18 inches (45 cm) tall, has crimson-red flowers, and is slightly more compact, making it a useful plant for the front of the border.
- *Astrantia major* 'Shaggy' or 'Margery Fish' has larger, frillier white bracts and forms bold clumps of deeply cut leaves.

*A*ubrieta deltoidea 'Dr. Mules'

Common name: Rock cress

Chief characteristics

At its best, aubrieta will form a soft
cushion of tightly knitted evergreen
foliage and a cascade of pink, purple or
lilac-blue flowers in rockeries or over
low retaining walls. At its worst,
planted in fast-draining soil that dries
out and overheats at the height of summer, aubrieta can turn
disastrously brown and strawlike and end up looking very messy indeed.
Fortunately, with a little care at planting time, this can be avoided.

Location: Full sun to part shade
Type: Evergreen perennial
Size: 6 inches (15 cm)
Conditions: Well-drained soil
Flowering time: April to May

Aubrieta is certainly one of the most useful wall-tumblers. 'Dr.
Mules' is an old favorite with tiny red-purple flowers in early May that
last 2 or 3 weeks. It grows 4 to 6 inches high (10 to 15 cm) and spreads
12 to 15 inches (30 to 38 cm). Most other aubrieta do much the same.
Top performers include: 'Red Carpet', 'Purple Heart', 'Novalis Blue',
'Whitewell Gem' and 'Blue Carpet'. Buy aubrieta when it is in bloom to
make sure you get the color you want. Labels get switched around by
accident in garden centers and it is very easy to end up with red instead
of blue.

Where to plant it

Right at home in a well-drained location, aubrieta gives a magnificent
show of color in the spring. It is tolerant of drought to a degree, but
don't grow aubrieta in blistering hot spots. It performs best if it is rooted
in moderately cool, moist soil with its foliage and flowers in full sun. It
will die if its roots are forced to constantly alternate between being very
dry and very wet—so be careful with your watering. It is said that
watering the plant from the front will encourage it to grow over a wall as
it reaches for the water. I have not found this to be true but it is certainly
capable of filling crevices in sunny rockeries or dry-stone walls. It is
exceptional when left to tumble in a well-behaved manner and form a
soft matlike carpet over low retaining walls.

How to care for it

Take your shears and trim back aubrieta once it has finished flowering.
This will tidy it up and encourage it to bloom sporadically throughout
summer. Maintain an even watering pattern, so that the soil is not
pushed to extremes. You can try to divide aubrieta but you may find the

tangled clumps difficult to sort out. It is often a lot more trouble than it is worth. Either buy inexpensive small pots of new plants or grow a new crop from seed, which germinates very easily when sown directly into the garden.

Good companions

Purple or red aubrieta go well with white and pink evergreen *Phlox subulata* and white sandwort (*Arenaria montana*) and the frothy pink flowering soapwort (*Saponaria* 'Bressingham'). For a striking contrast, try using aubrieta to underscore the yellow-green flowers of *Euphorbia polychroma*. Mixing different types of aubrieta will not only give you happy combinations but also a slight variation in flowering time.

For your collection

- *Aubrieta* 'Silver Queen' has lavender flowers and green and white variegated foliage while 'Gurgedyke' has deep purple flowers.
- Other top wall-tumblers include *Alyssum montanum* 'Mountain Gold', *Iberis sempervirens* 'Little Gem', 'Snowflake' or 'Purity', and snow in summer (*Cerastium tomentosum*).

*B*etula pendula 'Youngii'

Common name: Young's weeping birch

Chief characteristics

Location: Full sun or light shade
Type: Deciduous tree
Size: 10 feet (3 m)
Conditions: Good, well-drained soil

In his superb poem, "Birches," Robert Frost imagines himself escaping the troubles of the world for a while by climbing a birch tree's "snow-white trunk toward heaven". Perhaps he was thinking of a grove of magnificent European weeping white birches (*Betula pendula*), one of the most widely planted deciduous trees. The white-barked birch is certainly a heavenly tree with graceful, drooping branches and attractive fall foliage. But if you are wondering which birch to plant in your garden, you will likely want either Young's weeping birch (*Betula pendula* 'Youngii') or the pure snow-white–barked Himalayan birch (*B. utilis jacquemontii*), depending on how much space you have.

Young's birch is ideal for the courtyard or small garden because it is short and compact. It is usually sold as a weeping standard, grafted onto a trunk about 6 to 8 feet (2 to 2.4 m) off the ground. It soon forms an attractive umbrella shape that can look particularly handsome next to a small pond or as the centerpiece of a flower bed. The leaves often drape to the ground, hiding the silvery white trunk, which goes unnoticed until the bare days of winter.

The Himalayan birch, on the other hand, grows much taller—to an ultimate height of 40 feet (12 m) in 20 years. Its most attractive attribute is its brilliant white bark—the brightest white of any tree—which is exceptional in the barren winter landscape.

Where to plant it

Birches are relatively short-lived trees. After 25 years they tend to lose their vigor and start to go downhill. More optimistic estimates give them 50 years, still not a long life in tree terms. Often decay starts with attacks from insects like the bronze birch borer and leafminers, but birch trees also suffer from inadequate watering after being wrongly planted in an excessively sunny, fast-draining location. All birches are happiest in rich, acidic soil where the roots can get down into moist, cool soil while the top of the tree can enjoy full sunshine. They suffer miserably if exposed to too much hot sun in summer while being denied plenty of water.

Plant your birch in early fall or mid-March. Where space permits, a clump of upright white-barked birches such as the Himalayan can be dramatic, especially if contrasted against a dark background of conifers or distant hedging. One technique for growing birches in clumps is to plant a few saplings 10 to 15 inches (25 to 38 cm) apart in the same large hole with each trunk pointing in a different direction. In winter, there is nothing quite so beautiful as the brilliant white bark of *Betula utilis jacquemontii*.

How to care for it

Birches will "bleed" sap heavily if pruned at the wrong time of year. Don't prune when the sap is running in spring. Wait until fall or mid-winter. Deadwood should always be taken out. In birch, it can become more of a problem because it may signal the start of fungal rot, which can quickly spread. If you plant your birch in a lawn, remember to give it an extra drink in the summer because the grass will rob it of water.

Good companions

Both Young's weeping birch and the Himalayan birch can be underplanted with spring-flowering bulbs such as glory of the snow, grape hyacinth, scilla, snowflakes, iris, scented narcissus and exotic tulips. Or consider underplanting with low ground perennials like heuchera, ajuga, wild ginger, lamium and bergenia. Black mondo grass provides a striking contrast against the white bark in winter. You might consider making use of the shorter ornamental grasses and more sun-tolerant hardy geraniums.

For your collection

- Less common but also worth getting to know are the paperbark birch (*Betula papyrifera*), which has peeling chalky white bark, and the Chinese white birch (*B. albosinensis*), which has orangy coffee-colored flaking bark and lovely yellow foliage in fall.
- The birch that is said to be the most disease and insect resistant is the Whitespires Japanese white birch (*B. platyphylla japonica* 'Whitespire'), which has a pyramidal form and grows to 30 feet (9 m).
- For a more unusual birch, you could plant the river birch (*B. nigra* 'Heritage'), which has pinkish-brown peeling bark, or the purple-leafed weeping birch (*B. pendula* 'Purple Splendor' or 'Purple Rain').
- Where space is limited, another small weeping tree worth considering is *Prunus cerasifera* 'Kiku-shidare-sakura', which forms a low dome shape and has bright pink flowers in April.
- Weeping spring cherry (*Prunus subhirtella* 'Pendula Rosea') is a heavy blooming, slow-growing mushroom-shaped tree that grows about 15 feet (4.5 m) and produces pale pink blossoms in March to April.
- Another good choice for a small garden, the Kilmarnock willow or weeping pussy willow (*Salix caprea* 'Pendula') has weeping catkins that turn yellow. It thrives in moist soil.

Brugmansia (Datura) × candida

Common name: Angel's trumpet

Chief characteristics

You can grow all kinds of plants in pots on your balcony or deck in summer. Few of them will match the dramatic impact of angel's trumpet in full flower. At its peak in July and August, *Brugmansia × candida* can reach 6 feet (1.8 m) high and cover itself with gigantic, drooping, trumpet-shaped blooms with a very strong perfume. The golden-yellow flowers can measure up to 15 inches (38 cm) long.

Location: Full sun
Type: Annual
Size: 5 to 6 feet (1.5 to 1.8 m)
Conditions: Rich soil
Flowering time: July to September

Other varieties offer a range of flower colors from soft white to orange-red to pale green to peachy pink. The plant's genus name used to be *Datura*. It was changed by botanists to *Brugmansia*, but it is still sold at many garden centers under its old name. Fortunately, only the name has changed; the plant is still the same outstanding exotic-flowered specimen it always was.

You will most likely find the species *Datura meteloides* being sold at garden centers under the name angel's trumpet. These are short, bushy plants that grow 2 to 3 feet (60 to 90 cm) tall. They are also grown as an annual, producing white or rose-purple flowers in July. While they are fine plants, they do not have the same dramatic impact as shrubby, treelike *Brugmansia* × *candida*.

Where to plant it

Grow angel's trumpet in a pot or planter in full sun or part shade in rich soil in a location that protects it from gusts of wind. Its role in the garden is as an accent or feature plant, so it needs to be placed in a prime location to achieve the most dramatic, visual impact. The plant's exceptionally sweet fragrance is often more noticeable in the warm evening air at twilight.

How to care for it

Grow *Brugmansia* in a container that gives it room for root growth but not a lot. It performs better when it is somewhat potbound. Feed with 20-20-20 every week. It is a heavy feeder and the fertilizer will encourage a profusion of blooms.

The plant should come with a label saying "handle with care" since the leaves and flowers contain toxic chemicals. Touching the leaves and rubbing your eyes can cause your pupils to dilate.

You can overwinter these plants or take cuttings, but this could be a lot more trouble than it is worth. It is perhaps easier and best to start afresh with a new plant the next season.

Good companions

You don't need to plant anything in the pot with your angel's trumpet and there are few plants that will be able to compete with its formidable fragrance. You could surround it with smaller pots filled with different colored ornamental grasses to create the illusion of the angel's trumpet rising out of a sea of blue or yellow or burgundy. For striking contrast, fill a pot with the red-purple foxtails of *Pennisetum setaceum* 'Rubrum' and place it next to a pot of golden yellow *Hakonechloa macra* 'Aureola' or with a couple of containers of bright blue lyme grass *(Elymus racemosus*) and blue oat grass (*Helictotrichon sempervirens*). The colors will create a sensational contrast to the super-scented angel's trumpets.

For your collection

🌢 The flowering tobacco plant (*Nicotiana*) is another annual that can be grown in pots and has extremely fragrant, trumpet-shaped flowers.

🌢 Other highly scented pot plants include chocolate cosmos (*Cosmos atrosanguineus*), which has maroon-colored flowers that smell like chocolate, and the cherry-pie plant (*Heliotropium peruvianum*), which smells like fresh baked pie to some, baby powder to others.

*B*uddleia davidii

Common name: Butterfly bush, summer lilac

Chief characteristics

Walk into any garden and most of the plants you see probably come from other parts of the world. There is really no such thing as a Canadian or American garden any more than there is an English garden. Most gardens are

Location: Full sun
Type: Deciduous shrub
Size: 8 to 13 feet (2.4 to 4 m)
Conditions: Average or poor soil
Flowering time: July to October

composed of a rich assortment of plants gathered from different parts of the world over centuries of patient, and at times courageous, plant-hunting followed by years of painstaking hybridizing and propagation. Part of the fun of showing people around your garden can be to point out plants that originated in China or South Africa, Greece or Turkey, New Zealand or South America.

The butterfly bush originates from the Sichuan and Hubei areas of China. It gets its name not because its flowers or foliage look anything like a butterfly, but because it has the uncanny knack of attracting butterflies. It does this by waving around long, arching stems of sweet-scented cone-shaped flowers. The nervous butterfly apparently feels some security when it lands in the long arms of the buddleia.

Buddleia davidii comes in a rich variety of colors. Top names include the dark violet-purple 'Black Knight', rich-red 'Royal Red', bright pink 'Pink Delight', bluish-mauve 'Nanho Blue' and variegated-leafed 'Harlequin.' Excellent whites include 'White Cloud', 'Peace', 'White Bouquet' and 'White Profusion'. Buddleia has other fine qualities besides its flowers. Not particularly fussy about the ground it grows in, it will thrive in the poorest of soils in the least charming, most neglected corner of the garden, and still deliver an impressive show of colorful blooms. Even in its first year it will start to pump out fragrant clusters of flower cones that can measure up to 9 inches (23 cm) in length.

Where to plant it

Grow buddleia anywhere you like, but if you want to make it very happy, plant it in loose, loamy, ordinary garden soil that has good drainage in a spot that gets lots of sun. The only thing buddleia won't tolerate is too much lime.

How to care for it

Left unpruned, *Buddleia davidii* can get right out of hand. Within a couple of years, it can easily top 15 feet (4.5 m). After that it will start looking for new places to conquer. The key is to prune it back each year to about 2 feet (60 cm) off the ground. Do this in spring and dig in a little bonemeal at the same time. It also helps if you mulch really well around the shrub in early summer as a water-conserving measure. Even if you do this don't forget to water, especially during the first year when your buddleia is trying to establish itself.

Good companions

Ornamental grasses and flowering shrubs such as abelia, rock rose, Mexican orange and mock orange make good companions. In my garden, *Buddleia davidii* shares ground with ballotta, scabiosa, fountain grass (*Pennisetum alopecuroides*), bronze fennel, *Euphorbia characias* and assorted self-sowing annuals such as love-in-a-mist and California poppies.

For your collection

- *Buddleia alternifolia* is a very decorative form of butterfly bush. It is known as the fountain butterfly bush because it produces a cascade of arching branches of tightly knotted mauve flowers. With a little effort, it can be nicely pruned to form a very attractive small tree in the mixed border. You can also do this with wisteria, but *Buddleia alternifolia* looks particularly handsome when trained in this way.
- Another shrub worth checking out is *Buddleia fallowiana* 'Lochinch', which has silvery leaves and lavender-blue flowers that smell like vanilla.

Buxus sempervirens

Common name: English boxwood, common boxwood

Chief characteristics

Location: Sun or shade
Type: Evergreen shrub
Size: 10 feet (3 m) at maturity
Conditions: Ordinary soil

There's nothing quite like a low, well-clipped boxwood hedge to give your garden a classical elegance. It immediately conjures up images of Elizabethan knot-gardens where flowers were dressed up like candies in a chocolate box. Boxwood is still used mostly for edging rose or herb gardens or to define the edges of a flower border more purposefully. It is also used for topiary and clipped into magnificent pyramids, cones, squares and assorted creatures. You can find in some English gardens packs of hounds and flocks of birds all shaped out of box. It also has been used particularly effectively to create wonderful architectural accents such as large round "box balls."

Composed of small, glossy, dark green leaves that form an attractive, compact bush, *Buxus sempervirens* can be clipped into a wondrous variety of eye-catching shapes. In the sun, boxwood tends to give off a pungent smell that some people find mildly offensive. In most gardens, fortunately, this aroma is completely masked by the more pleasant fragrance of roses and honeysuckle.

Korean small-leafed boxwood (*Buxus microphylla koreana*) is faster growing than the common English box, but it doesn't much like our wet winters. It is best suited to drier areas where the soil is less acidic. Names to look for are 'Morris Midget' and 'Green Velvet'.

True dwarf boxwood (*Buxus sempervirens* 'Suffruticosa') is an even slower growing plant. It can take 20 years to grow 4 feet (1.2 m). This is the best type for enclosing a small formal rose or herb garden.

Where to plant it

Use box to make neatly clipped, low, rectangular-shaped hedges. Plants are not inexpensive. You will undoubtedly face the temptation of using fewer plants and leaving wider spaces between them, with the idea that they will eventually grow together and the gaps will disappear. This can happen, but you can also end up with gaps in your hedge for a very long time—or at least for longer than you really want to have gaps. So, decide at the outset to bite the bullet and buy a few extra box plants so you can close ranks. You should really not plant them more than 9 inches (23 cm) apart. If you use 'Suffruticosa', plant 6 inches (15 cm) apart.

Trimming off the top shoots will help. It will force the plants to bush out on the sides more quickly.

How to care for it

Box thrives in mild, moist climates like ours where there is a clear separation of seasons with warm summers and cool winters. Don't neglect to water your new box hedge regularly during the first year after planting. Once established, the hedge will never give you any worries, but in the beginning the new plants are vulnerable to dry periods. Box is rarely bothered by pests and diseases.

Good companions

Underplant your box hedge with sweet woodruff (*Galium odoratum*). The foliage is a perfect complement to the box's tightly knotted leaves. Sweet woodruff also has fragrant white flowers in spring, which give the hedge a lovely touch of color. This groundcover can be dreadfully invasive, so don't let it seed itself too freely.

For your collection

It is unlikely you will want to collect varieties of box, but you might like to try your hand at doing a topiary or a box ball. The ball is made by putting 3 small plants together in a triangle form and then clipping as they grow to form the desired smooth, round ball shape.

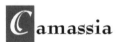 amassia

Common name: Quamash

Chief characteristics

Daffodils. Tulips. Snowdrops. Crocuses. These are flowering bulbs we all know very well. They are all useful—crucial, some would say—for providing a burst of color to lift our spirits in spring after a long dark winter. Today, you can get some

Location: Sun to light shade
Type: Bulb
Size: 2 feet (60 cm)
Conditions: Moist soil
Flowering time: May to June

superb tulips: parrot tulips, fringed tulips, lily tulips, species tulips. They are all a lot fancier than the plain old tulip of yesteryear. Even daffodils are not what they used to be. Now you can get narcissi with multiple flowerheads that are also extremely fragrant.

The best bulbs for a garden are the ones that do not need to be lifted and replanted every year but can be left to naturalize under trees and shrubs, over grassy banks and at the foot of hedgerows. Some of the best for this purpose are the grape hyacinth (*Muscari*), crocus, and scilla. But it is also fun to find room for a few more unusual, slightly exotic bulbs for a change of pace and to provide a conversation piece when you show visitors around.

Camassia is a perfect bulb for the job. It thrives in wet or moist soil and produces very elegant blue or white flowers in late spring to early summer. Prince Charles liked this bulb so much he told his head gardener to plant 3,000 of them for the prince's garden at Highgrove in Gloucestershire. After searching the nurseries of the world, the only place the gardener apparently could find enough camassias for the job was in Canada.

Look for *Camassia leichtlinii* or *C. cusickii*, both of which produce a profusion of blue flowers. *Camassia quamash* also has pale blue to deep purple-blue flowers.

Where to plant it

Grow camassias in wet or moist fertile soil in full sun. If you don't have wet or damp ground, you have to make sure to water the bulbs even when they are not in flower in summer. They will do very well even in ordinary soil and will tolerate light shade. Plant the bulbs, which are suprisingly large, in groups (the more the merrier) in September or early October.

If you have a stream running through your property, you can plant them on the sunny banks at the side. They are also very comfortable in damp, open grassy areas, which is camassia's natural habitat. In the small garden, they are a choice plant to mix in with the perennial border where they can rise and shine and then disappear without leaving untidy gaps.

How to care for it

After a few successful years of growing camassias, you will need to lift and divide clumps and space out the bulbs to avoid congestion.

If they are planted in well-drained soil, remember to water during dry periods. Once the flowers have faded, snip the flower stalks back to the ground.

Good companions

Iris sibirica, daylilies, gooseneck loosestrife, catmint, masterwort, hardy geraniums and astilbes can all thrive in moist soil in sunny or partial shade locations. For color companions, however, you could try white campanulas and fritillarias. Not everyone likes fritillarias because they stink, but there are a few worth adding to your garden. They make good supporting plants, especially when mixed in with other spring-flowering bulbs. *Fritillaria meleagris*, sometimes called snake's head fritillaria, has a colorful purple and white checkerboard flower. But one of the most eye-catching fritillarias is *F. imperialis* 'Lutea', which has giant yellow flowers.

For your collection

Here's a list of other exciting bulbous plants that can liven up your garden.

- The foxtail lily (*Eremurus*): Not technically a bulb, with its spidery, tuberous root, *Eremurus* produces majestic 6- to 8-foot (1.8- to 2.4-m) spires of yellow or pale pink flowers that resemble long, bushy foxtails. Despite being somewhat temperamental (it requires a well-drained, sunny spot), it is a spectacular flower, especially when planted in clumps. Look for *E. stenophyllus (bungei)*, *E. robustus*, *E. himalaicus*, or the two most popular hybrid strains, 'Ruitery' or 'Shelford'.

- The autumn crocus *(Colchicum)*: We've all seen crocuses in spring, but these crocuslike flowers bloom in fall. Look for *C. autumnale* (mauve), 'The Giant' (rose-lilac) and 'Princess Astrid' (deep purple-pink). The species crocus, *Crocus speciosus*, also flowers in fall, producing striking violet-blue, goblet-shaped flowers.

- Dog's tooth violets *(Erythronium)*: These are graceful woodland flowers with extremely attractive, nodding, lanternlike heads. They get their rather unflattering common name from the appearance of the corms, which look rather like dog's fangs. You won't go wrong with *E. dens-canis* 'Purple King', 'Pink Perfection', 'Frans Hals', 'Rose Queen' and 'Pagoda', which has terrific yellow flowers. 'White Beauty', sometimes listed as a trout lily, is one of the most beautiful erythroniums currently available, with delightful white flowers. You can find it under the name *Erythronium californicum*.

- Summer hyacinth (*Galtonia candicans*): This has pure white, drooping, bell-shaped flowers on 2-foot (60-cm) stems in late summer. Use it to add a boost of color to the perennial border in August.

- Pineapple lily (*Eucomis bicolor*): Yes, the flower really does look just like a pineapple. *Eucomis* grows 18 inches (45 cm) tall and flowers in July. It is best to grow it in a pot and then tuck the pot into the flower bed. This allows you to bring the pot into a frost-free place over the winter.

- Giant Himalayan lily (*Cardiocrinum giganteum*): A real showstopper in any garden, this grows 9 feet (2.7 m) tall and has pure white, 6-inch-long (15-cm) fragrant, trumpet-shaped flowers with red throats. The heart-shaped leaves also live up to their name, being a gigantic 18 inches (45 cm) long. Gardeners often leave the seed heads of the plant for decoration in the garden. Great conversation piece.
- Tiger flower (*Tigridia pavonia*): This is a true exotic beauty with yellow or red flowers and speckled throat. It flowers from August to September and grows about 18 inches (45 cm) high. The daylily-like flowers last only a day but new ones continue to appear for a time.
- Snowflake (*Leucojum*): This is certainly a spring bulb worth planting. It has small, nodding white flowers somewhat similar to snowdrops but with distinctive fine green or yellow spots on the tip of each petal. Look for *Leucojum vernum*, which flowers in February or March. *L. aestivum* 'Gravetye Giant', the later flowering summer snowflake, gets its name from the garden of 19th-century British garden guru William Robinson.
- Canna lilies: These large, bold, tropical-leaved specimens add drama and exotic color to the August garden. Start the rhizomes indoors in March and plant out in June in a hot, sunny spot. Lift and store the roots in a frost-free place over winter. They go well with dahlias.

Campanula persicifolia

Common name: Bellflower

Chief characteristics

Location: Full sun to semi-shade	
Type: Perennial	
Size: 3 to 4 feet (90 to 120 cm)	
Conditions: Well-drained soil	
Flowering time: June to September	

There are few flowers as cheery in the June garden as the light sky-blue blooms of *Campanula persicifolia*. They have immense charm and bring a natural, relaxed style to the perennial border. They also make a first-rate cut flower. The campanula family is large and serves reliably, year after year, in various parts of the garden. *C. persicifolia* is usually found in the perennial border, but you will find other campanulas tumbling over walls, filling crevices between stepping stones, adding color to the rockery or alpine garden or just giving flower beds the charming look of an old English cottage garden.

Campanula persicifolia, also known as the peach-leaved bellflower, is one of the most popular perennials partly because of the loveliness of its flowers and partly because it is so easy to grow. *C. persicifolia* 'Alba' has dazzling white flowers with the same delightful bell shape as the blue version. After flowering, the long stems can be cut down, allowing the plant to duck out of sight back to ground level where it can act as a low-mounding groundcover.

Unfortunately, my favorite campanula is not so easy to find at local garden centers. It is the giant bellflower, *Campanula latifolia* 'Alba', which grows about 4 feet (1.2 m) tall and has very attractive white flowers. The flowers are a more tubular, bonnet shape than the blooms of *C. persicifolia*. They are a highlight in my garden in late June.

Where to plant it

Grow *Campanula persicifolia* in a sunny location in ordinary well-drained soil. It will also flourish in light shade. In the middle or at the back of the border it will look terrific. You get to see the flowers without having to look at the less attractive stems on which they appear. The worst use is as a solitary clump on an exposed boulevard or alone in an empty flower bed. The peach-leaved bellflower will generally stand tall and erect, but expect some flower stems to flop over. This is often preferable to having the flowers stand perfectly at attention.

How to care for it

New clumps will form without permission or invitation. Bellflowers like to self-seed and new plants are always cropping up in unexpected places. If you don't like where they are, simply shovel them out and move them to a better spot. Clumps divide easily. You'll have plenty of plants to give away to friends.

Good companions

A truly gregarious plant, *Campanula persicifolia* gets along well with roses and lilies and is at ease sharing ground with perennial cornflower (*Centaurea montana*), foxgloves, lupins, geraniums, lady's mantle, daylilies, artemisia, asters and phlox. It invariably ends up forming its own associations, creating its own good companions.

For your collection

There are dozens of campanulas, all with slightly different growth habits, making them useful in different ways in different parts of the garden.

- The clustered bellflower (*Campanula glomerata* 'Superba') has eye-catching spherical clusters of dark violet-purple flowers from June to July.

- The milky bellflower (*C. lactiflora*) forms compact clumps and sends up tall stems of star-shaped flowers. There is a pink-flowering cultivar called 'Loddon Anna'.
- The traditional Canterbury bells (*C. medium*) produce deep purple-blue flowers with a bonnet shape.
- The delicate Carpathian harebell (*C. carpatica*) grows only 9 inches (23 cm) high.
- Fairy thimbles (*C. cochleariifolia*) is a low-growing plant for the rockery, with tiny, nodding thimble-shaped flowers colored either white or blue.
- The Serbian bellflower (*C. poscharskyana*) is a trailing rockery plant that produces masses of star-shaped blue flowers and can be used as a groundcover.
- The Korean bellflower (*C. takesimana*) has large pale-lilac flowers with strawberry spots inside. A good plant for dry shade.

Campsis radicans

Common name: Trumpet vine, trumpet creeper, trumpet honeysuckle

Chief characteristics

The trumpet vine is a beautiful hot-blooded creature. The rich, deep-throated, red flowers have an extremely sensual, pouty look to them. That's why hummingbirds can't stay away. But love will not make this vine flower. Only hot sun will do it. The vine is also a vigorous climber, capable of clambering at least 15 feet high (4.5 m) and 3 or 4 feet (90 to 120 cm) wide in the right spot.

Location: Full sun
Type: Deciduous vine
Size: 20 feet (6 m)
Conditions: Fertile, well-drained soil
Flowering time: July to August

You can grow *Campsis radicans* into trees or use it to cover sheds or old tree trunks. All it needs is a simple trellis or post for support to get started. It climbs stealthily, without a lot of wasted effort, clinging as it goes to whatever it can use to attach its tiny aerial roots. If exposed to too much frost, it will die back to the ground, but, being a born survivor, it invariably rallies the following year. The trumpet vine is a little tougher and more free-flowering than its Asian cousin, the Chinese creeper vine (*C. grandiflora*), which has scarlet-colored blooms. Neither vine is as famous as the hybrid they produced—*C. × tagliabuana* 'Madame Galen', which has salmon-red flowers and is more winter resistant than both parents.

Where to plant it

Without plenty of sun (and heat), your trumpet vine will put on lots of leafy growth and will end up looking extremely lush and healthy, but may not bloom. To get it to flower freely, the vine needs a warm, sunny spot, which is why it does so well in places with hot, arid summers. Grow it in fertile, free-draining soil.

One of the best plantings I've seen was over the roof of a carport in a very sheltered west-facing courtyard garden. In my garden, I have a trumpet vine smothering an old telegraph pole. For the last 3 years, it has leafed out very enthusiastically, but has yet to flower. This is partly because it is lightly shaded by nearby trees at the crucial time of day when it needs more heat. This is probably easily remedied by clipping back a few branches to allow in more light. Working with your plants to help them to achieve their purpose is part of the thrill of gardening.

How to care for it

Protected from cold winds and severe frosts and planted in well-drained soil, your trumpet vine will sail through a winter of heavy rain and snow. It flowers on the current season's growth and should be lightly pruned in early spring just for size and to thin out the vine's top.

Good companions

Stonecrop, daylilies and agapanthus will all fill out ground around the base of a trumpet vine. For a dramatic contrast you could grow it up a wall in the California microclimate of your garden alongside a blue-flowering ceanothus or against a yellow-flowering fremontodendron.

For your collection

- You might want to look for the yellow-flowering trumpet vine (*Campsis radicans* 'Flava').
- For something a little more daring you could try your hand at growing the Chilean glory vine (*Eccremocarpus scaber*), which will scramble up 10 feet (3 m) and has bright orange-red tubular flowers. It can be grown successfully in sheltered spots in mild areas in rich, well-drained soil.
- Another vine that is a real challenge for coastal gardeners is *Bougainvillea spectabilis*. Vigorous, growing 20 to 30 feet (6 to 9 m), and producing amazing pink or red flowers from June to August, it is an extremely tender plant that has been grown to 5 or 6 feet (1.5 to 1.8 m) in a pot just for fun. It is classified as a Zone 10 plant, which means even our summers are rather cool for it. But don't let that stop you from trying to crack gardening zone barriers!

Catalpa bignonioides 'Aurea'

Common name: *Golden Indian bean tree*

Chief characteristics

The catalpa tree has large, attractive, heart-shaped leaves and white flowers with yellow and purple markings in summer. The flowers have been compared to foxgloves and the blooms of a horse-chestnut tree. The catalpa has oodles of character and probably deserves to be planted more in the urban landscape. It is an exotic, ornamental specimen, best suited to a medium-sized garden. *Catalpa bignonioides* 'Aurea' is exceptional. It has golden-yellow leaves that bring brightness and lightness to a garden. Growing 20 to 30 feet (6 to 9 m), a catalpa can be pruned into a handsome framework for showing off the leaves at their best.

> **Location:** Full sun or semi-shade
> **Type:** Deciduous tree
> **Size:** 30 feet (9 m)
> **Conditions:** Ordinary well-drained soil
> **Flowering time:** August

The nonblooming dwarf cultivar, *Catalpa bignonioides* 'Nana' (umbrella catalpa), is a more suitable choice for smaller gardens, growing to only 15 feet (4.5 m) at maturity. It has an attractive, umbrella-shaped canopy and no flowers. Catalpas are called "bean" trees because the seed pods resemble skinny broad beans. The pods hang in bunches from the tree, appearing soon after flowering has finished.

Where to plant it

The golden catalpa thrives in virtually any kind of soil in light shade or full sun. You want to show off its fine foliage and form, so it is best to plant it where it can be seen from all angles and where people can walk up and touch the leaves (something they will want to do) without trampling through flower beds. Catalpa looks especially good planted by a pond or stream or as a dramatic focal point with dark conifers or hedging as a backdrop.

How to care for it

Left to grow to maturity, 'Aurea' will expand to fill an area 30 by 30 feet (9 by 9 m). It is best to control it by pollarding. This involves pruning the tree's canopy back to a shapely crown every year or two. The tree responds well to pruning and its shape can be enhanced. Routine cleanup of flowers and seed pods is more work than some gardeners are prepared to do, but as with so many good things that give pleasure in life, there is invariably something you have to give in return.

Good companions

Squeezed between other trees or shrubs, the golden catalpa rarely looks happy. Planted on its own in the middle of a great sweep of lawn or by the far end of a pool it is magnificent. Underplant it with spring-flowering bulbs or primulas. Once the catalpa's large leaves are fully formed, the bottom of the tree is plunged into deep shade.

For your collection

There are a few other trees with outstanding golden or handsome yellow-green leaves that are suitable for medium-sized to large gardens.

- The golden black locust (*Robinia pseudoacacia* 'Frisia'): Exceptionally graceful, it grows 30 feet (9 m) and has outstanding bright, yellow-green leaves that are particularly attractive when seen against the backdrop of dark, brooding conifers.
- The golden fullmoon maple (*Acer japonicum* 'Aureum'): Its handsome, tightly clustered yellow-green leaves bring a cheery brightness to any corner of the garden. It grows slowly, reaching 20 feet (6 m) at maturity.
- The golden hop tree (*Ptelea trifoliata* 'Aurea'): This small, deciduous tree is usually grown as a bushy shrub. It grows about 15 feet (4.5 m) and has bright yellow leaves that slowly turn pale green.

Ceanothus impressus 'Victoria'

Common name: California lilac

Chief characteristics

Ceanothus impressus is a warm-blooded plant. It comes from California and it likes hot summers and frost-free winters. It will thrive in slightly cooler zones if it is planted in a sheltered corner of the garden, possibly protected from chilly winds by a wall or up against the house,

Location: Full sun
Type: Evergreen shrub
Size: 6 to 10 feet (1.8 to 3 m)
Conditions: Ordinary, well-drained soil
Flowering time: April to May

where radiant heat will trick it into thinking it is back where winter temperatures dip to a mere few degrees below freezing at worst. When in bloom, the California lilac is a glorious sight. It can be espaliered into an elegant and cleanly defined form or left to billow into a giant cloud of spectacular blue flowers.

There are both evergreen and deciduous types. Evergreens such as

Ceanothus thyrsiflorus, *C. burkwoodii* and *C. impressus* all flower in May or June. The deciduous cultivars such as 'Gloire de Versailles' and 'Topaz', two of the most famous, bloom in mid-summer and put out a second flush in fall.

Ceanothus thrives beautifully in balmy seaside locations. The best cultivar is *C. impressus* 'Victoria', which grows to about 10 feet (3 m). What makes it superior to other cultivars is its attractive, compact growth habit, its ability to thrive even in chilly coastal gardens, and the large, bright blue flowers it produces in profusion from spring through to summer. It was discovered on Vancouver Island and quickly caught the attention of the nursery industry as it outperformed all other cultivars used in the Pacific Northwest.

Where to plant it

In the right spot, the California lilac can be used to create a privacy screen or as a colorful backdrop in a mixed shrub border. Finding the right microclimate is the key to success. This is a good opportunity to see how well you know your garden. Where are the frost pockets? What areas are well drained? Knowing such details is all part and parcel of becoming an accomplished gardener.

If frigid temperatures don't kill your ceanothus, waterlogged soil will. So it is just as important to locate ceanothus in full sun in well-drained ground. My neighbor has two California lilacs growing perfectly happily, espaliered against an east-facing wall on the north side of his house but in a fast-draining raised bed.

How to care for it

Prune evergreen varieties for shape and size after they have flowered. Prune the late summer–flowering, deciduous ones in early spring. Don't overwater, which can lead to root-rot problems.

Good companions

Climbing roses, red or white, make a striking contrast. Also try red hot pokers, white clematis and the bright yellow flowers of the Warminster broom (*Cytisus praecox* 'Allgold'), which grows about 5 feet (1.5 m) high.

For your collection

🐾 There are pink-flowering ceanothus available—'Perle Rose' and 'Marie Simone'. Both are extremely tender in cooler coastal gardens but if you always love a challenge, why not give them a try?

Acer palmatum: Outstanding tree with superb autumn color, page 13–14.

Alchemilla mollis: Raindrops are held like diamonds on the shapely leaves, page 26–27.

Allium sphaerocephalum: Distinctive drumstick alliums have reddish-purple flower-heads, page 30.

***Aquilegia* McKana Giants:**
Unique spring blooms come in
assorted pastel shades,
page 30.

***Astilbe* × *arendsii* 'Elizabeth
Bloom':** Soft pink plumes in
June, page 35–37.

Betula utilis jacquemontii:
Elegant tree with dazzling white
bark, page 40–41.

Camassia cusickii: Blue star-shaped flowers with enduring charm, page 48.

Cardiocrinum giganteum: Giant white trumpet-shaped flowers with red throats, page 50.

Clematis **'Henryi':** Divine vine with creamy white flowers, page 59.

Clematis montana **'Pink Perfection':** Ideal vine for growing into trees or over fences, page 60.

***Cotinus coggygria* 'Royal Purple':**
Purplish-red leaves add great foliage
contrast, page 67–68.

Crocus speciosus: Violet-blue, goblet-shaped flowers have classic elegance, page 49.

Enkianthus campanulatus: Bushy shrubs with delicate, bell-shaped flowers in spring, bright red foliage in fall, page 78.

Eremurus stenophyllus (bungei):
Golden yellow-orange spires appear like
giant candles from June to July, page 49.

**Erythronium dens-canis
'Pagoda':** Nodding sulfur-yellow
flowers appear in April, page 49.

Euphorbia griffithii 'Fireglow':
Eye-catching orange flowers and superb foliage, page 83.

Fritillaria imperialis 'Lutea':
Golden yellow flowers in spring, page 49.

Choisya ternata 'Aztec Pearl'

Common name: Mexican orange or Mexican orange blossom

Chief characteristics

All the experts agree, Mexican orange blossom is a top-of-the-line, 5-star shrub. It has handsome, glossy, evergreen foliage, a well-behaved, compact form, and attractive, fragrant clusters of white flowers in April and May. Being remarkably drought resistant, it also performs very respectably in a container. This makes it an ideal plant for apartment or townhouse dwellers to grow on their deck or balcony.

Location: Full sun to light shade
Type: Evergreen shrub
Size: 5 feet (1.5 m)
Conditions: Ordinary, well-drained soil
Flowering time: April to May

The flowers have an orange fragrance and the plant is native to Mexico, which is how it earns its common name. The leaves also give off a pleasant, fruity aroma when bruised or when the plant is trimmed. The only drawback to choisya is that it can be tender if planted in very open, unprotected spaces where it is exposed to hard frosts. Apart from that, it really doesn't need to be pampered. It can be easily propagated from cuttings taken in summer. This not only guarantees that you won't lose it, but allows you to try it out in other locations around the yard and fill up a few containers.

The best cultivar to get is 'Aztec Pearl', although you can also get a bright yellow-leafed cultivar called 'Sundance', which also grows between 4 and 6 feet (1.2 to 1.8 m).

Choisya can be used to add foliage texture and contrast to the mixed border. This is really its primary function in the garden since the flowers are only significant for a few weeks in spring. Choisya's habit is to grow wide rather than tall, which makes it very useful as a short hedge or as a leafy shrub to soften the look of a stone wall. If planted in too much shade, it tends to become straggly and not to flower very generously.

Where to plant it

Grow choisya in nutrient-rich, well-drained soil in full sun or part shade. The more sun you give it the better it will flower. In very hot inland areas, however, it should be planted in light shade where it won't suffer from scorching. Frost is its worst enemy and icy winds are no better. If you fear for your Mexican orange, use burlap to build a protective screen around it during the coldest part of winter but don't get carried away with extraordinary measures. Remember, you're living on the coast.

How to care for it

Prune choisya, mainly for size and shape, after it finishes blooming. Cut below the old flowerheads and you will encourage the plant to put out a second, less vigorous flush of white blooms. If you want more plants, take cuttings in summer. They root very easily.

Good companions

The variegated dogwood (*Cornus alba* 'Elegantissima'), and the evergreen shrub *Elaeagnus pungens* 'Maculata' make excellent partners. *Edgeworthia chrysantha* and *Viburnum carlesii* are also interesting companions. Pineapple broom (*Cytisus battandieri*) also likes full sun and produces distinctive yellow pineapple-scented flowers around the same time as the choisya.

For your collection

- Once you have enjoyed the plain green choisya, you might like to add the golden cultivar 'Sundance' to your garden, although some find the bright lime-yellow leaves a little too cheerful.
- If you like the smell of orange, you will probably also like mock orange (*Philadelphus*), which produces white flowers that have a fruity, orangy fragrance.

Clematis × jackmanii

Common name: Virgin's bower, old man's beard, traveler's joy

Chief characteristics

The most sociable of climbers, clematis is deservedly called the "queen of vines." No garden should be without at least one or two. Some gardeners have planted as many as half a dozen at a time to cover a single trellis or arbor.

Location: Full sun to light shade
Type: Deciduous vine
Size: 12 to 20 feet (3.6 to 6 m)
Conditions: Fertile, well-drained soil
Flowering time: June to July

Choosing the right clematis is the key to success. The selection can be overwhelming. In commercial cultivation at the moment there are at least 50 blue-flowering clematis, 34 pinks, 30 purples, 16 two-tone, 34 whites, 21 reds, and 10 yellow-blooming varieties. Once you've chosen the color you like, the next step is to decide what time of year you want it to flower. You can get clematis that bloom in early spring or summer or fall.

The most popular and dependable of them all for coastal gardens is *Clematis × jackmanii*, the most reliable performer of the summer-flowering cultivars. It grows 12 to 20 feet (3.6 to 6 m) and produces masses of 4- to 6-inch (10- to 15-cm) purple flowers from June to August. 'Jackmanii Superba' is very similar to *C. × jackmanii* but the flowers are more substantial and bloom a little longer. Other outstanding summer bloomers include the red 'Ville de Lyon', blue 'Polish Spirit', white and pink 'Nelly Moser', and white 'Henryi'.

Where to plant it

Grow clematis so the roots are in the shade and the foliage and flowers are in full sun. Plant the vines deeply, at least 18 inches (45 cm). This includes the crown, which probably means burying a little more of your new plant than seems right.

To flower properly, clematis need at least 5 hours of full sun. The ideal location is a west-facing trellis that is shaded at its base all afternoon. This allows the vine to get maximum light and warmth at the top while the roots get the cool, moist shade they need. Plant a small shrub in front or use large stones to create shade for roots if there is no other available protection.

How to care for it

"How do you prune it?" is the most commonly asked question about clematis. There is no simple answer: it really depends on what kind of clematis it is. 'Nelly Moser', for example, requires only modest pruning in early spring while *Clematis × jackmanii* should be cut back to 2 feet (60 cm) off the ground every February.

The key is to know your vine. Watch it and make note of when it flowers and how it grows. As a general rule, if it flowers in spring on last year's wood, prune after flowering. If it flowers in summer on new supple shoots, prune in early spring. If it blooms twice, on old wood in spring and new wood in fall, prune lightly for appearance and size after it has finished blooming.

Good companions

Clematis are their own best friends. You can plant several side by side. The art, however, is to plant those that will give you a natural sequence of blooms from spring to fall. This is easier said than done. Your best bet is to play with the colors and forms you like and see what happens.

Clematis is a natural partner for climbing roses, especially to complement an arch arbor. The purple smoke bush (*Cotinus coggygria*) is an excellent companion for red-flowering clematis such as 'Madame

Julia Correvon' or 'Ville de Lyon'. *Magnolia × soulangiana* is also a good partner to provide a frame for the early flowering outstanding *Clematis alpina* 'Pamela Jackman' (deep blue) or 'Jacqueline du Pre' (rosy mauve).

For your collection

There are a few other excellent clematis that are also worth accommodating.

- The evergreen clematis (*Clematis armandii*): This has shiny, dark green, slender leathery leaves and powerfully scented masses of white flowers in March or April. It has been used successfully to drape fences, cover arbors and gazebos and to dress up porches and patios. It is slightly tender in parts of the Pacific Northwest and needs to be planted in a protected spot or a cold winter can kill it. Many gardeners, however, have found the perfect place for this marvelous harbinger of spring.

- *Clematis montana*: This vigorous, deciduous species flowers in early spring, usually a little after the evergreen variety. Look for the names 'Tetrarose', 'Elizabeth', 'Pink Perfection' and *C.m. rubens*. The montana clematis originates from the Himalayas and has been used to form thick, leafy coverings over arches or arbors. It is even vigorous enough to scramble high into tall trees. This type of clematis flowers on growth produced the previous year.

- The golden clematis (*Clematis tangutica*): This is an exceptionally vigorous form that produces nodding, yellow lantern-shaped flowers in July. The flowers magically transform into soft, silvery seed heads in the fall.

- *Clematis florida* 'Sieboldii': A more unusual vine with creamy white blooms with distinctive deep purple centers, it can be grown in a pot on a patio as it grows only 8 feet (2.4 m) high and requires minimal pruning. It is more tender than other clematis, but can be overwintered if protected from frost. Two other star performers are deep violet-purple 'Mrs. N. Thompson' and white 'Guernsey Cream'.

Coreopsis verticillata 'Moonbeam'

Common name: Tickseed

Chief characteristics

Yellow is not everybody's favorite color in
the garden. It is, however, one of nature's
favorites. There are some exceptional plants
that produce first-rate yellow flowers and
Coreopsis verticillata 'Moonbeam' is one. It
flowers profusely from late spring into
summer, growing about 18 inches (45 cm)
tall and producing hundreds of small, pale
yellow flowers that are not at all jarring to the eye. Called a thread-leafed
coreopsis because of its lacy foliage, 'Moonbeam' was named Perennial
Plant of the Year in 1992 by the Perennial Plant Association of North
America.

Location: Full sun
Type: Perennial
Size: 18 inches (45 cm)
Conditions: Ordinary, well-
drained soil
Flowering time: June to
August

    Other cultivars to look for include 'Golden Showers', which has large
6-petaled open-faced flowers and 'Zagreb', a more compact dwarf form
that grows only 15 inches (38 cm) high. *Coreopsis grandiflora* 'Early
Sunrise' has much larger yellow flowers. It is a fuss-free award winner
that forms a small bushy mound about 2 feet (60 cm) high and won't
stop flowering until you force it to by cutting down the stems in early
fall. Other notable cultivars of *Coreopsis* include 'Double Sunburst',
'Sunray' and 'Baby Sun'. Coreopsis earns its nickname—tickseed—from
its seeds which look like tiny bugs.

Where to plant it

Grow coreopsis in well-drained but moist soil in full sun toward the
front of the border. 'Moonbeam' is perfect for growing either at the
front of the border or as a supporting plant in a container scheme.
'Golden Showers' and 'Zagreb' are also excellent choices for pots or
planters. The most endearing characteristic of 'Early Sunrise' is its ability
to keep on blooming throughout summer. The cheerful sunny flowers
can be cut and used to add zest to floral arrangements.

How to care for it

While it will perform in fairly dry, well-drained soil, coreopsis still needs
to be watered. It is a common mistake to treat coreopsis like an utterly
drought-tolerant plant. It is also a mistake to allow the 'Early Sunrise'
and other grandiflora varieties to flower perpetually until they get killed
by hard frosts in October. Much better to cut back the stems in early

to mid-September and give the plant a few weeks to bulk itself up in preparation for winter.

Good companions

For striking contrast to the yellow flowers of coreopsis, look to blues and purples. There are the blue spikes of *Lavandula angustifolia* 'Munstead' and 'Hidcote Blue' or the blue flowers of agapanthus or vivid blue grasses such as *Festuca glauca* or *Helictotrichon*. The blues of *Salvia × sylvestris* 'May Night' or the annual *Salvia farinacea* are also very useful. The woody shrub *Caryopteris × clandonensis* 'Dark Knight' (sometimes called blue spiraea) flowers late in August and offers an exciting contrast to the yellows of rudbeckia as well as coreopsis.

There's also the purple of blazing star (*Liatris spicata*) or *Verbena canadensis* 'Homestead Purple' or plain old chives (*Allium schoenoprasum*). For lively pastel combinations, you could try using some of the Galaxy hybrids of yarrow such as *Achillea* Summer Pastels, 'Heidi', 'Appleblossom' or, for a little more punch, how about the cherry red of *Achillea millefolium* 'Paprika' or 'Red Beauty'?

Coreopsis verticillata 'Moonbeam' will also partner very well with the silvery gray foliage of *Artemisia ludoviciana* 'Valerie Finnis' or 'Silver King', the pale pink flowers of *Penstemon digitalis* 'Husker's Red', and daylilies such as the pale pink 'Catherine Woodbury' or the richer red of 'Velveteen' and 'Summer Wine' or the plum-purple of 'Russian Rhapsody'. Also consider mixing it up with the pink-purple foxtails of *Pennisetum setaceum* 'Rubrum', the maroon flowers of *Cosmos atrosanguineus* or the orange-red flowers of *Crocosmia* 'Vulcan', a shorter, more compact montbretia.

For your collection

There are several other superb yellow-flowering perennials that deserve a spot in your garden. Here's a pick of the best.

- Yellow waxbells (*Kirengeshoma palmata*): This is an excellent plant for cool woodland gardens and considered a choice specimen by plant connoisseurs. It has yellow, waxy bell-shaped flowers from July to October that hang down from purplish stems of 4 or 5 feet (1.2 to 1.5 m). It thrives in rich, moist, but well-drained leafy soil.
- *Ligularia stenocephala* 'The Rocket': A bold background plant with large, decorative leaves, this has long rocket-tail spikes of yellow flowers. It looks wonderful in June and July and not so terrible even when the flowers have faded. Even so, you should still cut down the spikes once they are done.

- Evening primrose (*Oenothera tetragona*): This grows 2 feet (60 cm) tall and produces striking lemon-yellow flowers from June to August. It is drought resistant and can spread to fill a sizable area. It is best displayed with another low-growing plant to cover the gawkiness of its stems at the front.

- Black-eyed susan (*Rudbeckia*): The large yellow daisy flowers with dark purplish-brown centers are a mainstay of the fall border, flowering from late summer into October. *R. fulgida* 'Goldsturm' is very reliable, growing 2 feet (60 cm) high, but there are also excellent taller cultivars such as 'Double Gold' and 'Irish Eyes'.

- False sunflower (*Heliopsis*): These tall daisies make a bright backdrop, growing up to 4 feet high (1.2 m). They are also long lasting, flowering from early summer to fall. *H. helianthoides* 'Summer Sun' is the best and can be combined with blue veronica or salvia for a striking mix of colors.

- *Verbascum bombyciferum*: Not only does this have striking yellow flowers, it also has attractive, soft, silvery gray leaves. It is a plant full of impact that needs plenty of room to achieve its potential. Grows 5 to 6 feet (1.5 to 1.8 m) in full sun.

- *Argyranthemum* (formerly *Chrysanthemum*) *frutescens* 'Jamaica Primrose': This perennial has lovely yellow flowers that mix in well in the mid-summer border.

Cornus 'Eddie's White Wonder'

Common name: Dogwood

Chief characteristics

Location: Sun to light shade
Type: Deciduous tree
Size: 25 feet (7.5 m)
Conditions: Moist, acidic soil
Flowering time: May to June

Dogwoods have always occupied a prominent and popular place in coastal gardens. The hybrid *Cornus* 'Eddie's White Wonder' is one of the most outstanding. Not only does it have a handsome form and generous flowering habit, it has a fascinating history. The tree was bred in the early 1940s when Henry Eddie, a nursery owner from Vancouver, B.C., successfully managed to cross the eastern dogwood (*Cornus florida*) with the native western dogwood (*Cornus nuttalli*). The outcome was a better tree than either parent. The new dogwood, named 'Eddie's White Wonder', went on to achieve international fame because of its usefulness in home gardens as a disease-resistant tree that produces abundant clusters of simple, white, cross-shaped flowers from May to June. It also has very beautiful fall color.

Where to plant it

Dogwoods grow best in full sun or light shade in rich, acidic, moist, but well-drained soil. They need some protection from cold winds.

How to care for it

Poor air circulation can lead to dogwood anthracnose, a fungal problem that is widespread in southern B.C. and other areas of the Pacific Northwest. It appears as brown spots or blotches at the tips of leaves. The native western dogwood (*Cornus nuttalli*) is particularly prone to the disease. However, 'Eddie's White Wonder', *Cornus florida* and *Cornus kousa* are more resistant to the disease. Part of the solution is to make sure the tree is pruned to allow good air circulation through the center and to rake up and dispose of any fallen leaves during the growing season and fall.

Good companions

Rhododendrons, magnolias, witch hazels, evergreen and deciduous azaleas, and native shrubs such as salal and red-flowering currant (*Ribes sanguineum*) are all perfect partners for dogwoods. Dogwoods can be underscored with spring-flowering bulbs such as dog's tooth violets (*Erythronium*) and flowering perennials like the Lenten rose (*Helleborus orientalis*) and groundcovers like ajuga and hardy geraniums.

For your collection

There are other members of the dogwood family worth getting to know.

- The red-flowering dogwood (*Cornus florida rubra*) is a very popular small tree that produces light pink flowers. 'Cherokee Chief' has the deepest red flowers and bright red foliage in spring, while 'Cherokee Sunset' has variegated yellow-green foliage that turns red in fall.
- The variegated medium-sized shrub (*Cornus alba* 'Elegantissima') is an extremely useful plant for its light, attractive two-toned foliage. It is one of the mainstays of a mixed border, bringing a change of pace to the plain greens of rhododendrons and azaleas.
- The red- and yellow-twig dogwoods (*Cornus alba* 'Sibirica' and *Cornus stolonifera* 'Flaviramea') are both used extensively to provide winter color along with pink-flowering viburnum, white-flowering hellebores, early flowering camellias and witch hazels.

🐾 The Chinese dogwood (*Cornus kousa*) is actually a native of Japan, not China. It flowers in June, about a month after most other dogwoods, and is much loved for its creamy white flowers. It grows as wide as it does tall, reaching 15 feet (4.5 m) after about 10 years.

🐾 The Cornelian cherry (*Cornus mas*) is a large deciduous tree-shrub with yellow flowers on bare branches in March and April and bright "cherry" red fruits in fall. It grows about 10 feet (3 m).

🐾 *Cornus controversa* 'Variegata' is a much a coveted tree because of its rarity, its green-white variegated foliage and its graceful habit of growing steady, tiered branches while maintaining a pyramidal shape. It also produces masses of white blooms. It is best seen with setting sunlight behind it which brings out the magic of the two-toned foliage. A fast grower, it reaches about 25 feet (7.5 m) at maturity.

Corydalis lutea

Common name: Yellow corydalis

Chief characteristics

This is a magnificent, perpetually flowering perennial for semi-shade areas of the garden. It has tiny yellow, tubular flowers that are borne in clusters above lush mounds of frothy foliage. The first flowers appear in mid-spring and continue to the end of summer. Corydalis can be mass planted in long rows to provide very effective edging for a stone or brick path in light shade or as a groundcover under trees or shrubs. The worst thing anyone is going to tell you about *Corydalis lutea* is that it likes to seed itself everywhere. Of course, this may be exactly what you want it to do. If not, you can either resign yourself to pulling out the seedlings, which can be given away to friends, or grow the plant only where its free-seeding habit is not going to be a problem. The benefits of growing corydalis far outweigh the disadvantages.

Location: Sun or part shade
Type: Perennial
Size: 12 to 18 inches (30 to 45 cm)
Conditions: Average, well-drained soil
Flowering time: April to September

There are now three other immensely popular cultivars of corydalis, all of them blue-flowering—'Blue Panda', 'China Blue' and 'Purple Leaf'. With its sky-blue, fragrant flowers, *Corydalis flexuosa* 'Blue Panda' has proven itself to be the best performer of the three in coastal gardens. None of the blues, however, flower quite as profusely as the yellow form.

Where to plant it

Corydalis will grow in average, even inferior soil. Grow it under shrubs or combined with other perennials for its foliage contrast. Even if it falls on stony ground, corydalis seed never fails to germinate.

How to care for it

Sometimes called the "yellow bleeding heart," *Corydalis lutea* has loose, lacy foliage that's similar to dicentra—in fact, it's a close relative. Clumps can be divided every few years. The foliage tends to look a little disheveled by the end of summer and can be cut back. It will soldier on for awhile, eventually dying down with the first frost. In spring, it will bounce back good as new.

Good companions

Blue always makes yellow more striking, so combine *Corydalis lutea* with one of the great blue varieties of Jacob's ladder, either *Polemonium caeruleum* or *P. reptans* 'Blue Pearl'. The blue flowers of *Geranium* 'Johnson's Blue' would also work. Other good partners include bleeding hearts like *Dicentra spectabilis* or *Dicentra formosa* 'Luxuriant'. The frothy lime-green sprays of lady's mantle (*Alchemilla mollis*) also fit well with the corydalis's yellow blooms. Experiment at growing spring-flowering bulbs—bluebells, grape hyacinths, tulips—to achieve some eye-catching contrasts.

For your collection

Yellow flowers are not everyone's favorite. Others love the cheerfulness of yellow. Here are some other great yellow-flowering perennials to check out.

- Jerusalem sage (*Pholmis fruticosa*) has soft gray foliage.
- *Lysimachia punctata* has buttercuplike flowers on tall stems.
- The Welsh poppy (*Meconopsis cambrica*) has soft yellow flowers in late spring.
- *Ligularia stenocephala* 'The Rocket' produces tall spires of golden-yellow foxtail lily–like flowers.
- Evening primrose (*Oenothera fruticosa*) flowers from spring through to the end of summer and has bright yellow flowers at the top of 3-foot (90 cm) stems.
- Black-eyed susan (*Rudbeckia fulgida*) is the flower that signals the end of summer and the coming of the cool days of September.

Cotinus coggygria 'Royal Purple'

Common name: Smoke tree, smoke bush

Chief characteristics

This is a most attractive and useful foliage shrub for gardens of any size. The distinctive plum-purple, oval-shaped leaves are exceptional when contrasted against the dark green background of a cedar or yew hedge.

Location: Full or part sun
Type: Deciduous shrub
Size: 10 feet (3 m) or more
Conditions: Well-drained, ordinary soil
Flowering time: July to August

Native to southern Europe and eastward to China, the shrub gets its common name from its delicate feathery panicles of pinkish-purple flowers that form in summer and give the impression of puffs of smoke. At one time, it was called *Rhus cotinus*. In Europe, it is known as the Venetian sumach and it is sometimes called wig tree. Left to grow without interference, *Cotinus coggygria* 'Royal Purple' will quickly soar to more than 15 feet (4.5 m) high and can achieve almost that in width. It will, however, tolerate regular pruning and can be kept down to a manageable size. In gardens where space is limited, it is often pruned back to form a small, single-stemmed tree.

Where to plant it

Cotinus coggygria 'Royal Purple' will grow in any ordinary, well-drained soil, but prefers fertile, humus-rich, moist ground. To get the best "smoke" effect, it needs full sun. In large, spacious gardens it can be used as a giant, showy specimen shrub, which will look like a great cloud of frothy purple at the height of summer. In most gardens, however, 'Royal Purple' is more realistically grown in the mixed border as a contrast plant against other medium-sized shrubs.

It can also be grown as a patio tree. In a container, its roots will be restricted, which will keep it from getting out of hand, but the soil will need to be top-dressed every year and slow-release fertilizer added.

How to care for it

It is a trouble-free shrub with no pest or disease problems. Powdery mildew can sometimes be a problem and verticillum wilt has been known to slowly kill the shrub in some locations but these are not common occurrences. Prune for size and shape and to eliminate shoots that pop up from the roots.

Good companions

Clematis 'Ville de Lyon' or 'Madame Julia Correvon', both with reddish flowers, can be grown into a smoke bush and the red flowers will provide a striking partner for the shrub's plum foliage. Plain green leaves of a magnolia or the green and red leaves of a photinia work well. The bright leaves of the mock orange (*Philadelphus coronarius* 'Aureus') are also worth considering. You can create room under a smoke bush for silver foliage plants such as lamb's ear or artemisia. For a striking color combination try *Brachyglottis* (formerly *Senecio*) *greyi* 'Sunshine' for an understory. The bright yellow flowers and silvery foliage offer an emphatic contrast.

For your collection

Other purple-leafed plants you might like include the following.

- If you have acres of space, you might like to consider planting the mighty *Cotinus obovatus*, which grows 30 feet (9 m) high by 25 feet (7.5 m) wide and has green leaves that turn red and purple in fall.
- *Euphorbia amygdaloides* 'Rubra' has evergreen wine-colored foliage that plays nicely against the small yellow flowers that appear in spring.
- Purple-leafed sage (*Salvia officinalis* 'Purpurascens') is an excellent foliage contrast plant with soft purple, slightly aromatic leaves.
- *Sedum telephium maximum* 'Atropurpureum' is one of the more unusual varieties of stonecrop. It has dark, succulent burgundy leaves, pinkish-white flowers in August and September, and grows about 2 feet (60 cm). Also look for names such as 'Matrona', 'Morchen', 'Vera Jameson' or 'Bertram Anderson', which all have darkish burgundy-purple or mahogany-red foliage.

aphne odora

Common name: Winter daphne, fragrant daphne

Chief characteristics

Daphne is said to possess the world's most powerful fragrance. Quite a claim to fame! The most popular species is the February-flowering *Daphne mezereum* which grows 3 or 4 feet (90 to 120 cm) and produces highly scented purple-red flowers on bare, erect, twiggy branches. There is also a white type. The species I like best, however, is the

Location: Full sun to light shade
Type: Evergreen shrub
Size: 4 feet (1.2 m)
Conditions: Good, well-drained soil
Flowering time: May

D. odora, which has soft, slender evergreen leaves, and extremely fragrant purple-pink flowers that appear in January and February, continuing on sporadically into spring.

The fragrance of these exquisite blooms has been described as an ambrosia dessert laced with an orangy-coconut juice. It has the most powerful scent of all daphnes. In the summer, the shrub's foliage maintains its bright shade of green provided it is not allowed to languish in excessively dry soil. It grows to 4 feet (1.2 m) tall and wide. There is a cultivar—*D. odora* 'Aureomarginata'—which is slightly more cold resistant, less prone to viral diseases, and has equally fragrant flowers. It is, however, variegated, with green leaves with creamy edges, something not all gardeners like. The best daphne for the general shrub border is *Daphne × burkwoodii*, which flowers in late spring around May and produces handsome pale white-pink flowers. It grows to a fairly compact 5 feet (1.5 m) at maturity.

Where to plant it

Daphne odora is best grown next to a doorway or entrance or beside a path where the fragrance can be appreciated. It will thrive in a sheltered position in very well-drained soil in full sun or light shade. It will also perform very respectably in a planter box, provided it is given plenty of nourishment in the form of well-rotted manure applied as a top-dressing in spring. Plant winter daphne where it gets shade in the afternoons. The shrub is relatively slow growing and will take a few years to become a full, compact bush.

How to care for it

One of the easiest shrubs to look after, daphne needs only light pruning. Remove faded flowers to keep the plant looking tidy and shapely. Feed with 14-14-14 slow-release fertilizer in spring and be sure to water well in dry spells.

Good companions

Daphne odora can be placed next to Mexican orange (*Choisya ternata*) to form a fragrant spring walkway in a sunny, frost-free location. Add *Daphne mezereum* and *Viburnum carlesii* and you'd have a combination of fragrance and color that was fantastic. The golden-leafed form of Mexican orange (*Choisya ternata* 'Sundance') and the variegated form of *Daphne odora* could also be slotted into the mixed border for foliage contrasts and heavenly fragrances.

On its own, *Daphne odora* makes a good specimen plant in a planter box or tub on a patio or deck. The container can be moved under a window or by an open door when the plant is in full bloom and relocated to a less prominent site when it has finished.

For your collection

- *Daphne bholua* 'Gurkha' is a large-sized shrub growing to 12 feet (3.6 m) and producing purplish rose–colored blooms in January and February.
- *Daphne retusa* is a shorter, evergreen member of the family, growing 2 feet (60 cm) and producing purple-pink flowers in April.
- Other first-rate fragrant shrubs include *Sarcococca humilis, Skimmia japonica, Ribes odoratum, Rhododendron* 'Dora Amateis', *Rhododendron fragrantissimum, Hamamelis × intermedia* 'Jelena' or 'Diane', *Osmanthus × burkwoodii* and *Syringa vulgaris*, notably 'Charles Joly', 'Angel White', 'Lavender Lady'. The Chinese lilac (*Syringa × chinensis*) also has very lilac-purple blooms, and *Syringa patula* 'Miss Kim', a variety of Korean lilac, is a modest shrub, growing only 3 feet (90 cm) high, perfect for a small garden or patio.

Delphinium Pacific hybrids

Common name: Larkspur

Chief characteristics

The tall, soaring spires of blue or white delphiniums can be an awesome spectacle in the summer garden. Delphiniums have been described as "glamorous" and "romantic" and "compulsory for the perennial border." The white forms can look especially lovely at twilight when all the reds and blues have faded into the dusk. Delphiniums certainly have a long and glorious association with the cutflower garden. They were one of the mainstays of the classic Victorian-Edwardian perennial border and their popularity has never subsided. When planted with care, they rarely disappoint.

Location:	Full sun
Type:	Perennial
Size:	4 to 6 feet (1.2 to 1.8 m)
Conditions:	Moist, rich soil
Flowering time:	July to August

The secret to success is picking the right type. The best and most dramatic performers are the Pacific hybrids, which grow 4 to 6 feet (1.2 to 1.8 m) tall in perfect conditions. Many of them are named after characters in the legend of King Arthur and the Knights of the Round Table. Names to look for: 'Black Knight' (dark blue), 'Galahad' (white),

'King Arthur' (purple), 'Guinevere' (lavender-pink), 'Summer Skies' (light blue), 'Camelliard' (lavender-blue), 'Blue Bird' (blue) and 'Blue Jay' (light blue).

The other popular type of delphiniums are the Belladonna types, which are shorter than the Pacific hybrids, growing only 3 to 4 feet (90 to 120 cm). They display their flowers in loose, open clusters rather than dense, garlandlike spires. The Chinese delphinium (*D. grandiflorum* 'Blue Butterfly') has intense blue flowers in June and August and grows only 10 inches (25 cm) high.

Where to plant it

Grow delphiniums in rich, well-drained soil in sun or light shade at the back or middle of the perennial border. They should be positioned so their magnificent flowers can be easily seen above medium-sized perennials. Delphiniums can also be very effectively combined with ornamental grasses to provide the height needed at the center of an island bed.

How to care for it

Cut off the flowerheads when they are faded. This will promote a second flush in late summer. Delphiniums are heavy feeders so make sure you enrich the soil at planting time with well-rotted compost or manure. An application of slow-release 14-14-14 fertilizer in late spring will ensure the plants do not starve. Staking is almost always necessary with the super-tall Pacific hybrids, especially where the towering plants are exposed to sudden gusts of wind.

Staking is also useful in preventing them from tumbling over in the event of a heavy rain storm. Give your delphiniums the support they need, but don't tie them so tightly they're throttled to death. Unfortunately, delphiniums don't go on forever. They become less and less vigorous in subsequent seasons and end up having to be replaced. But by that time they will have given many, many hours of pleasure for very little expense.

Good companions

The red flowers of *Crocosmia* 'Lucifer' or the candyfloss-pink clouds of blooms of *Phlox paniculata* 'Eva Cullum' can give bold and dramatic support to the blues and whites of delphiniums. Taller ornamental grasses such as *Miscanthus sinensis* 'Gracillimus' or *Pennisetum alopecuroides* can also join forces with the rose-pink flowers of Mexican evening primrose (*Oenothera berlandieri* 'Siskiyou') to surround your delphiniums with interesting and unusual colors and textures. For more standard companions, look to pink and red *Monarda* 'Gardenview Scarlet', silvery *Artemisia* 'Powis Castle' and the lacy foliage and buttery yellow flowers of *Coreopsis* 'Moonbeam'. Delphiniums also look first-rate rising up behind shrub roses.

For your collection

- Blue and white are not the only colors of delphinium. You can also get yellow (*D. semibarbatum*), red (*D. cardinale*) and pink (*D.* × *ruysii*). One of the best delphiniums for connoisseurs is *D. cashmerianum*, which has especially graceful and delicate blue flowers.

- If you are looking for other tall, attractive plants to add strength to the back of the border, consider the giant plume poppy (*Macleaya cordata*) or goatsbeard (*Aruncus dioicus*) or the foxtail lily (*Eremurus himalaicus*).

Dicentra spectabilis 'Alba'

Common name: Old-fashioned bleeding heart

Chief characteristics

What is the loveliest flower in the spring garden? The tulip? Daffodil? Lenten rose? All are quite wonderful but few can compare with the transcendent, classical beauty of the old-fashioned bleeding heart. It has such a simple, elegant, graceful appearance and exquisite white or red

Location: Shade to semi-shade
Type: Perennial
Size: 3 feet (90 cm)
Conditions: Moist, well-drained soil
Flowering time: June to July

blooms. It is easy to understand why it has been a favorite of gardeners worldwide for generations.

You will find dicentra listed in many people's top 10 perennials. The lovely heart-shaped flowers are suspended individually like precious ivory lockets along gently arching stems that reach out romantically from a lush clump of soft green leaves. If the outer shell, or coat, of a single flower is carefully removed, a perfectly formed, miniature Valentine's Day heart can be found in the center. The plant derives its common name from the appearance of the red form of *Dicentra spectabilis*, which has tiny white hearts enclosed by blood-red shells.

Dicentra spectabilis 'Alba' and plain old *D. spectabilis* are the most outstanding kinds, but they do have a drawback. The bushy clumps of leaves, so vigorous and full in late May and June, start to fade by the end of June. The flowers disappear and the plant slowly dies down and usually needs to be cut down to keep the rest of the border looking neat and tidy. This can leave an unsightly gap. It is not a major problem. One of the simplest solutions is to have a mature hosta—perhaps 'Krossa Regal' or 'Francee' or 'Frances Williams'—in a pot, standing by to move into the vacated spot. The pot can be easily disguised and the hosta will fit very naturally into the scheme of the border. Or you could take the opportunity to add some color to the border and bring in a semi-shade flowering perennial such as the blue- or yellow-flowering corydalis or taller forms of impatiens or begonias to fill the space.

There are, however, other cultivars of bleeding heart (none quite as attractive in my opinion as the ones just mentioned) that do not go dormant in the heat of summer. The best is *Dicentra eximia* 'Alba', one of the fringed bleeding hearts, all of which have lacy, fernlike foliage. 'Alba' grows about 12 to 15 inches (30 to 38 cm) high and produces white pouch-shaped flowers all summer, making it a good selection for the front of the border. A good red variety is *D. formosa* 'Luxuriant', which has cherry-red flowers.

Where to plant it

A native woodland plant, bleeding heart is best grown in cool shade under trees as a companion to other perennials in the herbaceous border. In my garden, both red and white forms of *Dicentra spectabilis* have a place in a semi-shaded mixed border. The red variety is tucked beneath the slow-growing sycamore maple (*Acer pseudoplatanus* 'Brilliantissimum') where, in May, the tree's light salmon-pink leaves are beautifully underscored by the red-pink flowers of the bleeding heart. The dwarf varieties of bleeding heart can be mass planted to create drifts of frothy bluish-green foliage and white flowers in summer.

How to care for it

Dicentra spectabilis can be spotted emerging from the ground in April. It will also be immediately noticed by any passing slugs. Keep an eye on the new growth to make sure it gets off to a good start. The plant does not need staking but the stems can grow 3, even 4 feet (90 to 120 cm) high, in ideal conditions and tend to cover other plants. The arching stems of flowers are not long lasting when cut but they still make a handsome, if temporary, addition to floral arrangements.

The clumps of dicentra should be cut down and tidied up at the end of June. Clumps are best left undisturbed, but if needed they can be divided and moved in fall or before flowering in spring.

Good companions

Dicentra spectabilis combines naturally with columbines, hostas, ferns, astilbes, alliums and hardy geraniums, especially the dark-flowered cranesbill, *Geranium phaeum* (mourning widow), or *Geranium pratense* and, in sunnier spots, *Geranium* 'Johnson's Blue' and the pink-flowered *Geranium sanguineum*. Early spring–flowering bulbs such as scillas and muscari can be planted around the clump to add color while the bleeding heart is getting underway and in late spring, tulips can inject interesting color contrasts.

For your collection

- *Dicentra* 'Stuart Boothman' has bright pink flowers and pale green foliage and grows about 15 inches (38 cm) high.
- *Dicentra* 'Langtrees' (also known as 'Pearl Drops') has white flowers with pink tips.
- *Dicentra* 'Bacchanal' has deep red flowers and gray-green leaves.

*D*igitalis purpurea

Common name: Foxglove

Chief characteristics

Foxgloves are majestic, romantic plants. The story goes that a fox used the silky tube-shaped flowers as gloves so he could sneak into the hen house without awakening the farmer. Foxgloves can be found in just about any medium-sized garden with a semi-shady woodland-like corner. They are superb in large groups, gently swaying in the breeze. They also have immense character and charm as solitary specimens, rising up like sentries here and there around the garden. They spend the first year establishing themselves and then flower the following year. You will always be nursing a few foxglove plants, allowing them to occupy space in the garden even though they produce no flowers and the small clumps of coarse leaves are not at all attractive.

The most common foxglove, *Digitalis purpurea*, produces lovely pink-purple tube-shaped flowers with a speckled throat. These flowers are tightly arranged in drooping layers up the sturdy stem. The flowers open first at the bottom, giving the impression that the spires of blooms come

Location: Sun to semi-shade
Type: Perennial
Size: 5 feet (1.5 m)
Conditions: Moist, well-drained soil
Flowering time: May to July

to a sharp point. The Excelsior hybrids are the most impressive foxgloves. They produce white, purple and pink flowers and grow to 5 feet (1.5 m) tall from May to July. There is also a shorter kind, *Digitalis × mertonensis*, the Merton foxglove, which is a true perennial. It grows less than 3 feet (90 cm) and has deep copper-pink flowers. Foxy hybrids are another popular kind available in a range of colors and more compact than Excelsior hybrids. They grow about 3 feet (90 cm).

Where to plant it

Plant foxgloves in semi-shade in ordinary garden soil that stays reasonably moist all the time. Grow them in colonies or small groups in the middle or at the back of the perennial border. Once they have finished flowering, they will leave a gap that will need to be filled or covered by other perennials. Foxgloves are particularly useful for creating height and architectural interest. Some people like only white foxgloves, so they pull out any with purplish leaf stalks, supposedly a sign that the flowers will not be pure white.

How to care for it

After they have finished flowering, foxgloves produce thousands of tiny coal-black seeds which spill everywhere from fragile brown pods. You can collect the seed and sprinkle it where you would like foxgloves in the future or sow it in pots and raise plants for transplanting into specific locations later on.

Plants that have established themselves through the summer can be lifted in the fall and moved to wherever you want them to flower the following year. You don't need to leave all your foxgloves until they have gone to seed. One or two produce enough seed to ensure survival. The rest can be tugged very easily from the ground and disposed of once they have finished blooming.

Good companions

Foxgloves are great minglers. They get along very well with virtually every plant in the garden, especially daylilies, campanula, hardy geraniums, bleeding hearts, ferns and columbines. The beauty of foxgloves is that they are always forming their own spontaneous partnerships. They will pop up quite unexpectedly behind rhododendrons and assorted shrubs. They even find a place next to roses. If you don't mind a little rustic, old-world charm in your garden, you won't be too hard on foxgloves and you will give them their day. If they are quite out of place at bloom time, simply snip the flower stalk and use it in an indoor bouquet for hall or table.

For your collection

🐾 The yellow foxglove (*Digitalis grandiflora*) has pale yellow flowers and smooth green leaves and grows less than 3 feet (90 cm) tall. It blooms from June to August. It can be used to form a striking contrast with red shrub roses.

🐾 *Digitalis viridiflora* has white flowers with a yellow-gold throat and green markings.

🐾 The rusty foxglove (*Digitalis ferruginea*) has yellowish flowers with rust-red speckles.

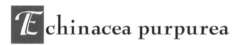

Echinacea purpurea

Common name: Purple coneflower

Chief characteristics

This native North American flower is closely related to the other very popular cottage garden perennial, black-eyed susan (*Rudbeckia fulgida*). It has a similar daisylike flower. But while rudbeckia is yellow with a black center, echinacea has bright, pink-purple petals around a large, orange-brown cone.

Location: Full sun
Type: Perennial
Size: 3 feet (90 cm)
Conditions: Ordinary, well-drained soil
Flowering time: July to August

Echinacea purpurea 'Magnus' is a dependable cultivar with cheerful rose-pink petals. There is also an attractive white cultivar, *E. purpurea* 'White Swan', which has flowers with a rather regal gold and black cone at the center. Everyone falls in love with echinacea when they first see a mature clump of it with dozens of the purple flowerheads. Yet it can take a few years of patient nurturing to get a plant to that level of lushness. The effort is worthwhile. In addition to producing spectacular, colorful, honey-scented blooms, which make excellent cut flowers, echinacea attracts butterflies to the garden. You may also come across *E. angustifolia*, which is similar to *E. purpurea* but a little taller with slender, drooping petals.

The name echinacea is derived from the Greek word for "hedge-hog"—what the prickly cone at the center of the flowers vaguely resembles. It is said to have healing properties and is still used by herbalists to stimulate and strengthen the immune system and cleanse the body of toxins.

Where to plant it

Purple coneflowers can be grown in the perennial border or for cut flowers. It thrives in average soil in a warm, sunny location. It is best planted slightly back from the front of the border where the beautiful flowerheads can be easily seen and reached for cutting while the less attractive stems are concealed by shorter flowering perennials.

How to care for it

To get the best results from echinacea, remember that it has an appetite. Work in plenty of well-rotted compost and manure at the time of planting and mulch around the plant in spring. A sprinkling of slow-release fertilizer or rose food in spring doesn't hurt either. Staking is often needed. Don't be too aggressive or you'll end up with straggled foliage and choked flowerheads—not a pretty picture. Deadhead faded flowers regularly. The whole plant can be cut down close to the ground at the end of the season. Clumps take a few years to build up, but once they have, you probably won't feel like dividing them. If you do get around to it, do it in late September.

Good companions

Ornamental grasses offer credible companionship for *Echinacea purpurea*. You can use fountain grass (*Pennisetum alopecuroides*) or giant feather grass (*Stipa gigantea*) as a light and breezy background. Shasta daisies, asters, crocosmia, rudbeckia, and other late summer–flowering perennials can create appealing combinations. One of the best ways to focus echinacea's purple blooms is to provide a backdrop of color. The orange in the flower cone will be heightened by a blue backdrop of monkshood (*Aconitum napellus*) or rich blue of *Agapanthus* 'Bressingham Blue'. Or you could try a silver background using *Artemisia ludoviciana* 'Silver King' or *Artemisia* 'Powis Castle'.

For your collection

- For something more exotic, track down *Echinacea tennesseensis*, which is native to Tennessee. It is a rarer form of the purple coneflower, growing to about 3 feet (90 cm). If you manage to get one you have something quite special.
- If you like echinacea, you will probably like the blanket flower (*Gaillardia grandiflora*) which also has large, colorful, daisy-shaped flowers with a central cone. It grows in full sun, can reach 3 feet (90 cm) high, makes an excellent cut flower, and comes in a range of colors including red with yellow tips, burgundy and yellow.

$\mathbb{E}$nkianthus campanulatus

Common name: Pagoda bush

Chief characteristics

Enkianthus is a great bush for the back of the mixed shrub border. It has abundant clusters of cream bell-shaped flowers with rosy pink veins and tips in spring. The flowers have a sophisticated delicacy to both their color, size and habit of dangling in dense clusters in late spring. In full leaf, the bush forms an attractive, structurally useful green backdrop. The small oval-shaped leaves are a soft, pleasant shade of green. In the autumn, the foliage is particularly outstanding. The leaves turn shades of crimson, yellow and orange as impressive as any maple.

Location: Semi-shade
Type: Deciduous shrub
Size: 10 feet (3 m)
Conditions: Good, well-drained soil
Flowering time: April to May

Enkianthus is really the antithesis of a blowsy hybrid rhododendron. Its flower color is quieter and refined and its form is more casual. Native to Japan, enkianthus has tended to be shunned by professional garden-makers mainly because of its low-key flowering habit, lack of color in summer and relaxed overall form. It is, however, a treasured shrub, valued by true plant lovers, who are more than willing to find a place for it if only for the beauty of the flowers, which you can often find decorating the covers of general gardening books and plant encyclopedias.

Where to plant it

Grow *Enkianthus campanulatus* in semi-shady, acidic soil in as close to a woodland setting as you have. Locate it where the spring flowers can easily be seen and appreciated and where the exceptional fall color can make a useful contribution, but not where the plant's profile becomes too high. Enkianthus will grow in full sun provided it is rooted in moisture-retentive soil. On the other hand, it can tolerate a fast-draining site if it is given plenty of cool shade in the afternoon. It looks best situated behind smaller semi-shade–loving shrubs like hydrangeas or rhododendrons.

How to care for it

Don't let the soil get sweet on you, though there is not much chance of that with the heavy rains we get on the coast. A lime-hater, enkianthus does particularly well in acidic soils. Although slow growing, it will send up tall, thin shoots to gain height at the beginning. If these are neatly pruned back, it will immediately bush out and take on a fuller, more esthetically pleasing shape. Prune away dead wood and thin the bush to size in spring after flowering. If you want more enkianthus bushes, take cuttings in early summer. They will root easily.

Good companions

The yellow, pineapple-scented flowers of *Cytisus battandieri* make a nice companion, along with soft pink-flowering rhododendrons such as 'Bow Bells' or 'Lady Bowes Lyon'. *Hydrangea aspera* would also be a good friend for enkianthus in a light woodland setting. The usual troop of high-performance spring-flowering bulbs—muscari, erythroniums, scilla and leucojums—can be put to good use to create a sequence of color until the bush flowers in May.

For your collection

Here are some other excellent enkianthus.

- *E. cernuus rubens* has red flowers and grows to just 6 to 8 feet (1.8 to 2.4 m).
- *E. perulatus* has dazzling white flowers and will reach 8 feet (2.4 m) at maturity.
- The largest member of the family is *E. chinensis*, which can grow more than 15 feet (4.5 m) and can turn into a small tree.

rica carnea 'Springwood White'

Common name: Winter heather

Chief characteristics

When is heather not heather? When it is heath. It is a curious fact, but what we often think are heathers, are actually heaths and vice versa. The most popular forms of heather are actually members of the *Erica* family (heaths), while true Scottish heather is actually part of the less well-known *Calluna* group. Who cares? Mostly passionate members of heather clubs and societies. Certainly not the average gardener.

Location: Full sun to light shade
Type: Shrub
Size: 10 to 12 inches (25 to 30 cm)
Conditions: Acidic, well-drained soil
Flowering time: January to April

What is the key difference? It basically comes down to form and flowering periods. The species and cultivars of erica (heath) cover a large

range of flowering seasons while all calluna (heather) flower from July
to October and the range of cultivars is not great. Also unlike ericas,
callunas loathe lime. Another little known fact about heather: It is not
just a spring-flowering plant. If you put together the right kinds, heather
can give you an almost seamless sequence of flower or foliage color
throughout the year. One final bit of heather trivia: Not all heathers are
low-growing, ground-hugging plants. You can also get bushy, upright
shrubby heathers, even heather trees, and they can often be put to good
use to provide height and color contrast. The big issue, however, is first
to find out whether you like or loathe heather. Gardeners either love it
or hate it. There doesn't seem to be a lot of middle ground.

Before we get to the most popular forms, let's deal with cultivars of
true Scottish heather (*Calluna vulgaris*). These lime-haters grow about
12 inches (30 cm) tall and produce pink, lilac or white flowers in
summer from July to the end of October. Some have striking foliage
such as 'Boskoop' and 'Sunset', which changes from golden to orange, or
'Bonfire Brilliance', which has bright, reddish foliage. There are no late
winter- or spring-flowering heathers in this group but there are plenty of
top performers such as 'Gold Haze' (white); 'Peter Sparkes' (deep pink);
'Devon' (pink); 'Flamingo' (lavender); and 'H.E. Beale' (pink).

Easily the most popular heather is *Erica carnea* (really a heath) that is
also known as *Erica herbacea*, but commonly called winter heather. It is a
tough, mounding shrub, growing 9 to 12 inches (23 to 30 cm) tall with
medium to dark green leaves and tiny masses of tube-shaped flowers in
shades of red, pink and white. There are countless cultivars. Some flower
from November to December, others from January to April.

One of the best and most vigorous is 'Springwood White', which has
light apple-green foliage and masses of white flowers from February to
April. There is a pink form called 'Springwood Pink'. Other top names
include: 'Vivellii', 'Ann Sparkes', 'December Red', 'Eileen Porter', 'King
George', and 'Pink Spangles'. Notable foliage heathers in this group
include 'Aurea' (golden foliage in spring/summer), and 'Foxhollow'
(yellow foliage with pink tinge in winter).

Where to plant it

Heather thrives in a sunny, open position in well-drained soil. It can be
grown as a groundcover in average soil in a rockery or in window boxes,
planters or raised beds. If you fall in love with heathers, you could
devote an entire area to them and create a heather garden, mixing
cultivars to form a tapestry of color and foliage.

How to care for it

Prune winter heather lightly in spring after the blooms have faded and new growth begins to appear. Most of the work in maintaining heathers involves tidying the plants to make them look compact and healthy. They are mostly drought tolerant, but that does not mean they don't want any water.

When old plants get too woody and messy, it is best to replace them with new stock or learn to grow new stock from cuttings and have a few plants in the wings for the day when the old stuff needs to be replaced. Remember, heathers like acidic soil so be cautious when top-dressing or mulching with mushroom manure, which often contains soil-sweetening chemicals.

Good companions

Grow heathers and heaths with slow-growing conifers and ornamental grasses. Good evergreens as companions include *Thuja orientalis* 'Aurea Nana', *Pinus pungens* 'Globosa', *Taxus baccata* 'Semperaurea' and *Chamaecyparis lawsoniana* 'Aurea Densa' or 'Minima Aureau'.

For your collection

- The bell heather (*Erica cinerea*), also known as twisted heather, is the kind found on moors or by the sea or growing in rocky places in mountain areas. It is extremely drought tolerant and flowers from July to September. Top forms are 'Ashdown Forest' (rich lavender), 'C.D. Eason' (bright magenta), 'P.S. Patrick' (purple), 'Velvet Night' (beetroot red), 'Windlebrooke' (golden foliage turning orange-red) and 'Eden Valley' (purple-white bicolored flowers).
- Other heathers worth checking out include the Cornish heath (*Erica vagans*), which grows 18 inches (45 cm) tall and flowers from August to October, and cultivars of the Darley heath (*Erica × darleyensis*), which grows 18 inches (45 cm) high to form an evergreen bush with bell-shaped white, pink or purple flowers from November to April. Top names include 'Arthur Johnson' (lilac pink), 'George Rendall' (dark pink), 'Furzey' (deep pink) and 'Kramer's Rote' (red with bronze foliage).
- The tree heath (*Erica arborea*), is an evergreen shrublike tree that can reach over 10 feet (3 m). There are shorter, more manageable forms, such as 'Albert's Gold', which grows 6 feet (1.8 m) and has fragrant, white globular flowers in early spring.

Euphorbia characacias wulfenii

Common name: Spurge

Chief characteristics

A powerful, stately member of the spurge family, this majestic evergreen sends up long sturdy flower stems with graceful, spear-shaped, blue-green leaves and produces large lime-green, multi-eyed flowerheads in spring.

Location: Full sun
Type: Evergreen perennial
Size: 4 feet (1.2 m)
Conditions: Well-drained soil
Flowering time: March to May

Certainly one of the most striking plants in the garden, it works well as a team player in the perennial border or it can be given a place of honor and grown as an accent or feature plant. It is one of my favorites.

Evergreen in most parts of the coast, *E. c. wulfenii* is a fairly large, bulky specimen, quickly growing 4 feet high by 4 feet wide (1.2 by 1.2 m) within a couple of years. It is, however, extremely well behaved. Its sturdy stems can be trimmed easily, making it far more manageable than its appearance suggests. This also makes it a perfectly suitable candidate for even smaller town gardens since it can be contained without fuss against the wall of a house or fence with a little basic pruning. One of the workhorses of the garden, it holds its form beautifully in all weathers, providing dependable structure, stability, consistent foliage color and a touch of drama throughout the seasons. This euphorbia is a great conversation piece and its lovely lyrical name rolls off the tongue when friends inquire about its pedigree.

Where to plant it

Native to open hillsides of warm Mediterranean countries from Portugal to Turkey, *E. c. wulfenii* can be grown in full sun or light shade in average well-drained soil. Thought hardy to several degrees below freezing, it should be protected in the open garden during long cold spells. Protection could be as simple as a wall, fence or burlap screen. Euphorbia performs exceptionally well in a planter box provided it is sheltered from icy winds and not left to dry out in the summer.

How to care for it

Tolerating hot dry spells, *E. c. wulfenii* is undemanding provided it receives routine watering and feeding with a balanced fertilizer in spring and mid-summer. The flowerheads last a long time, but should be cut off once they start to lose their color, turn brown and begin to look messy. Being such a tidy, sculptural plant, it is a shame to allow it not to always look its best. Be very careful when pruning or deadheading or even stripping yellowed leaves since all euphorbias, especially *E. characias*, emit an irritating milky sap that can harm the skin.

Good companions

Euphorbia contrasts well in the perennial border with red hot pokers, lavatera or lavenders and it can be underplanted with lamb's ear, if you don't mind clipping off the flower stalks, or *Artemisia schmidtiana* 'Silver Mound', which can be used to soften the spurge's stiffer, more formal profile.

For your collection

Other euphorbias worth checking out include those below.

- *Euphorbia griffithii* 'Fireglow' has smashing orange-red flowers and red-tinted leaves. There is another very similiar one called 'Dixter'.
- Cushion spurge (*Euphorbia polychroma*) is a drought-tolerant, clumping plant that produces a cushion or dome of light yellow-green flowers in spring.
- *Euphorbia dulcis* 'Chameleon' is one of the newest hybrids. It has the remarkable characteristic of changing color 3 times during the year.
- Donkey-tail spurge (*Euphorbia myrsinites*) is a succulent, evergreen species with blue leaves and yellow flowers in spring. It's a good plant for growing in a sunny spot over a wall or rockery as it is highly drought tolerant.
- Purple wood spurge (*Euphorbia amygdaloides* 'Rubra') has mounding purple foliage and clusters of lime-green flowers. It makes a very useful groundcover in light shaded locations.

*F*oeniculum vulgare 'Purpureum'

Common name: Bronze fennel

Chief characteristics

You might not find bronze fennel terribly attractive if you saw it for the first time on its own in a pot at the garden center. Nor would you be the first person to dismiss it as a gangly, weedy-looking thing. It is one of those plants that doesn't always make a good first impression. However, it will do a first-rate job of providing light, airy color contrast and textural interest to your garden.

Location: Full sun
Type: Perennial
Size: 6 feet (1.8 m)
Conditions: Good, well-drained soil
Flowering time: July to August

Growing 5 or 6 feet (1.5 to 1.8 m) high, *Foeniculum vulgare* 'Purpureum' has feathery bronze-green foliage with a very pleasant anise-like scent. All parts of the plant are edible. Cooks and herbalists have used it for years to give food more flavor and to help the digestive system to work more efficiently. It can also be fun to pinch off a few sprays of the finely textured foliage and invite visitors to your garden to taste it. If they have no idea what the plant is, they tend to hover a little apprehensively. This hesitancy soon passes once they recognize the distinctive licorice flavor of the soft foliage.

In July and August, bronze fennel develops flat dill-like umbels of tiny dull-yellow flowers which make the plant even more decorative and interesting. The seeds that follow will fall and germinate with no assistance.

Where to plant it

Grow bronze fennel in a sunny spot at the back of the perennial border in average, well-drained soil. Once established, it will come back every year, eventually forming a dense clump you will need to split up.

Since you are mainly interested in growing this plant to add foliage texture, it is best to place it so it can mingle with its neighbors without becoming a nuisance. You don't want it to block them out completely.

Don't be afraid to take your pruners and thin out fennel clumps, even in the heart of the season, in order to maintain the look you want. It should be relaxed, breezy and elegant, not weedy, sprawling or overpowering.

How to care for it

Bronze fennel is drought tolerant and needs very little encouragement to revive itself in spring. The sturdy, bamboo-like stems can hold themselves up. Stakes are usually only needed to pull back thickets that are leaning to reach more light.

Fennel is very generous about seeding itself. You'll find seedlings popping up here and there. They are easily pulled and can be transplanted to other sites or given away to friends. Divide clumps to thin or make more plants as desired in mid-September or early March.

Good companions

The white-pink hollyhock flowers of *Lavatera thuringiaca* 'Barnsley' and soft gray leaves of *Stachys byzantina* or *Stachys* 'Countess Helen von Stein' combine well with the smoky purple of bronze fennel. Shrub roses such as 'Ballerina' and 'Mary Rose' also make excellent partners. For more outstanding contrast, combine either the yellow flowers of the evening primrose (*Oenothera*) or verbascum, and the red of *Lobelia cardinalis* or *Lychnis viscaria*. The pure white annual mallow (*Lavatera trimestris* 'Mont Blanc') also can be worked in for a little theatrical lighting.

For your collection

Herbs fulfil a very useful role as decorative plants in the ornamental flower border as well as culinary and medicinal specimens for the physick garden. Here are some others to consider.

- The common fennel (*Foeniculum vulgare*) is also known as sweet or wild fennel and has green leaves that taste like sweet licorice.
- Florence fennel (*Foeniculum vulgare azoricum*), also known as finocchio, has large celerylike stems and green featherlike leaves.
- Angelica (*Angelica archangelica*) is one of the most dramatic herbs for the perennial border. It can rise 8 feet (2.4 m) with wrist-thick hollow stems and magnificent umbels of green-white flowers. These bold flowerheads are very eye-catching. They can be cut and used to great effect in floral arrangements.
- Joe-pye weed (*Eupatorium purpureum*) is a dynamic partner for angelica with its pink flowers and lush foliage. It is also put to best use at the back of the border or in an open area where it can fill ground without restriction. But think twice before getting carried away with angelica or joe-pye weed. Neither plant is really suitable for the small garden.
- The purple-leafed sage (*Salvia officinalis* 'Purpurascens') and the gold-yellow form (*Salvia officinalis* 'Kew Gold') are both useful for creating exciting foliage contrast and interest.
- Chives (*Allium schoenoprasum*) are marvelous in sauces and salads and have fine, pale purple flowerheads.
- Borage (*Borago officinalis*) has coarse, hairy foliage and bright blue flowers.

$\mathscr{F}$uchsia magellanica 'Riccartonii'

Common name: Hardy fuchsia

Chief characteristics

Most people know fuchsias as the large, tropical-looking red and purple flowers they see trailing from hanging baskets or trained into little patio trees grown in containers. But there are also hardy forms of this beautiful native South American plant that can be grown successfully in the garden. They have splendid lanternlike red flowers that appear very natural suspended from arching branches in the light shade border. In the warmer west-country areas of England, hardy fuchsias have been used to make hedges. In gardens here on the coast, they are mostly used as shrubby, background plants for providing a continuity of color through the dog days of summer to the hard frosts of fall.

> **Location:** Sun to semi-shade
> **Type:** Deciduous shrub
> **Size:** 3 to 4 feet (90 to 120 cm)
> **Conditions:** Ordinary, well-
>   drained soil
> **Flowering time:** July to October

The most reliable and hardy species is *Fuchsia magellanica*. The slim flowers are red on the outside and purple on the inside. The two top performers are 'Gracilis' and 'Riccartonii'. They are both capable of growing 5 feet (1.5 m), but rarely get taller than 4 feet (1.2 m) in gardens where they die down every winter and have to regrow in spring. 'Riccartonii', which looks rather like a bush covered with dangling crimson earrings, is also known as lady's eardrops. It is a favorite of many gardeners and was awarded the Royal Horticultural Society award for hardiness in 1966. There are about half a dozen species of hardy fuchsia available. Other forms of *F. magellanica* that have made a name for themselves include the pinkish-white *F. m. molinae* (often listed as 'Alba'), the variegated 'Sharpitor' and 'Tricolor', and 'Aurea', which has golden-yellow foliage.

Where to plant it

Hardy fuchsias make excellent background plants in sunny or light shade spots in the perennial border. They flower best when given morning sun and light shade in the afternoon. They rise slowly back to life in spring and soon expand 3 or 4 feet (90 to 120 cm) before producing their lovely red, waxy lantern-shaped flowers in July. If *Fuchsia magellanica* is planted in well-drained soil in a location where it is sheltered from severe frost, it will perform like any other resilient perennial, returning faithfully year after year.

How to care for it

Plant your hardy fuchsias deeply and add plenty of organic matter. If grown in a cold spot, cover with a light mulch in winter. Don't prune down the woody stems in fall but rather wait until spring and then cut out dead wood after the new buds have broken.

Good companions

The scarlet-violet flowers of 'Riccartonii' can be mixed with blues of veronica, monkshood (*Aconitum*), agapanthus, salvia, nepeta or the Chinese balloon flower (*Platycodon grandiflorus*), all of which flower into the late summer. The yellows of coreopsis or rudbeckia would make a more startling contrast but the white flowers of the Japanese anemone 'Queen Charlotte' or the silvery pink of 'September Charm' fit in quite naturally.

For your collection

- Other hardy fuchsias that have proved themselves winners over the last few years include 'Santa Claus', 'Double Otto', 'Little Giant' and 'Silver Pink'. More and more gardeners are now experimenting with fuchsias and testing the limits of their hardiness. We can expect to find others made available in the future.
- If you are looking for compact fuchsias that grow less than 3 feet (90 cm) for featuring in a container on a patio or balcony, try 'Papoose', 'Tom Thumb' or 'Mrs Popple'.

eranium cinereum 'Ballerina'

Common name: Cranesbill, hardy geranium

Chief characteristics

Cranesbills are real geraniums. The plants many people call geraniums are not geraniums at all—they are pelargoniums. These true geraniums are tough, winter-resistant plants with tiny, exquisite flowers that come in a delicious range of colors from sky blue to candy pink, royal purple to milk white. No garden should be without at least a couple of these versatile plants. They are called cranesbills because the seed heads look something like the beak of the crane. There are several exceptional hardy geraniums to choose from. Two of the best—both great favorites

Location: Full sun
Type: Perennial
Size: 6 inches (15 cm)
Conditions: Ordinary, well-drained soil
Flowering time: May to September

of mine—are *Geranium macrorrhizum* and *G. cinereum* 'Ballerina'.

Geranium macrorrhizum has lovely pink flowers in early spring and doubles as an extremely good, mounding groundcover. Look for 'Ingwersen's Variety' or the white 'Album' or the magenta-pink cultivar, 'Bevan's Variety'. *G. cinereum* 'Ballerina' has exquisite pink flowers with purple veins that keep on coming all summer long. (The cultivar 'Lawrence Flatman' is almost identical to 'Ballerina'.)

Both *G. macrorrhizum* and *G. cinereum* 'Ballerina' are star performers, but 'Ballerina' is the superior garden plant overall because of its compact form, noninvasive habit, decorative foliage, and relentless flower power which makes it a treasure for the sunny rockery.

But do give *G. macrorrhizum* a try, too. Its evergreen foliage has a pleasant pungent aroma when touched and smelled. Not everyone likes it, of course, but the scent does not detract from the intrinsic beauty and general usefulness of the plant.

Where to plant it

Geraniums are so adaptable they can be grown in sun or shade and will perform beautifully. *Geranium cinereum* 'Ballerina' needs to be planted in extremely well-drained soil if you are to get it through a wet winter. Four clumps have survived two dreadful winters in my garden, quite happy in raised terraces on the sunny but protected south-facing side of the house. In summer, they mound and never stop generating their magnificent purple-veined flowers.

The danger in growing geraniums is that you end up with too many. *Geranium macrorrhizum*, for instance, is so easy to propagate. All you have to do is pull off a few of the leggy rhizomatous stems from a mature clump, make a shallow trough and lay them in it, end to end, to create an entirely new colony. New gardeners who don't have money to buy all the plants they need in one fell swoop, can certainly rely on *G. macrorrhizum* to cover the ground and hold the site until they are ready to replace them with more exotic fare.

How to care for it

Hardy geraniums are problem-free plants. The only attention they need is to be clipped back when they get too enthusiastic and tidied up once the flowers have come and gone and the plants start to look a little messy. They can be grown in sun or shade. Most perform best if provided with shade in the afternoon.

Good companions

Cranesbills are the most gregarious of plants. Try them at the feet of lavatera, under climbing hydrangea, skirting shrubs in the mixed border or providing foliage contrast with lady's mantle, variegated or sun-yellow hostas, dicentras and fancy ferns. Columbines make excellent lanky pals to tower over hardy geraniums in the late spring.

Geranium macrorrhizum looks best grown in clumps next to lady's mantle (*Alchemilla mollis*) or in crowded drifts, sweeping down around the bases of rhododendrons or fruit trees in an orchard.

For your collection

When you go to buy hardy geraniums, you will find dozens of superb names besides those just mentioned. Where to begin? None of the following will disappoint.

- *Geranium endressii* 'Wargrave Pink' is a must. It has rich pink flowers from June to September, mounds to 3 feet (90 cm), and is a good-natured mixer in the perennial border.
- 'Johnson's Blue' has lovely sky-blue flowers in spring. It can get a bit leggy but you can easily scissor it back.
- 'Phoebe Noble' is requisite for all coastal gardeners as it bears the name of one of our own, the beloved Victoria, B.C. gardener and former math prof who surely ranks as the world's biggest geranium fan. Phoebe has grown dozens of cultivars for years in her 2-acre (.8 hectare) garden. So it was perhaps predictable that one day a new form of geranium would pop up there. It did, Phoebe spotted it as something quite unique, and it is now named after her and is one of the best new perennials on the market. Its official name is *Geranium × oxonianum* 'Phoebe Noble'.
- *Geranium clarkei* 'Kashmir Purple' and 'Kashmir White' are both other first-rate members of the geranium family, especially the white, which makes a dazzling appearance in late spring. Two other superb whites are *G. sylvaticum* 'Album' and *G. phaeum* 'Album'.
- Mourning widow (*Geranium phaeum*) has dark purple flowers, so dark and brooding they almost look black. It makes a good conversation piece to grow in the cool, moist shade of a woodland setting.
- The meadow cranesbill (*Geranium pratense*) is far more cheerful, producing delightful deep blue flowers. It is attractive and will form a terrific little bush. It needs to be staked to get it to stand upright and look its best.
- *Geranium psilostemon* (Armenian cranesbill): One of the tallest hardy geraniums, this grows 3 to 4 feet (90 to 120 cm) high and produces striking magenta flowers with black centers in early summer. It is one of the best geraniums to use as an accent plant for the middle of a perennial border.

$\mathcal{H}$amamelis × intermedia

Common name: Witch hazel

Chief characteristics

Color in the garden in the dark days of
winter can lift the spirit. It reminds us that
spring is only weeks away. Witch hazel, an
insignificant plant most of the year, comes
into its own in mid-winter when it produces
spidery yellow or copper-red flowers on its
leafless branches. The flowers are sweetly
scented with a fragrance that has been
compared to that of hyacinths or lilies. For some people, witch hazel
brings back childhood memories of astringents used to heal scrapes on
knees and elbows. Witch hazel gets its name from its fork-shaped twigs,
used as divining rods in "water witching"—a way of searching for
underground water sources.

> **Location:** Sun or light shade
> **Type:** Deciduous shrub
> **Size:** 10 feet (3 m)
> **Conditions:** Well-drained,
>   acidic soil
> **Flowering time:** December
>   to February

The two most popular plants for the average-sized garden are
Hamamelis × *intermedia* 'Diane', which has deep red flowers, and *H.* ×
intermedia 'Jelena', which has coppery orange flowers. Both grow 10 feet
(3 m) tall and produce small clusters of flowers in January and February.
These appear attached to bare branches like neatly twisted tufts of
shredded paper in January and February. Chinese witch hazel, *H. mollis*,
one of the parents of the popular hybrids 'Jelena' and 'Diane', has bright
yellow flowers. The top cultivars of *H. mollis* to look for are 'Pallida',
which has fragrant pale yellow flowers, and 'Brevipetala', which has large
dark yellow flowers.

Where to plant it

Witch hazel fits naturally into a woodland part of a garden. It is best
planted where the scent and color of the flowers can be appreciated in
winter. Just keep in mind that the shrub offers very little interest the rest
of the year. It has a valuable, supporting role to play in the border, filling
in gaps between other shrubs, and it is right at home in an out-of-the-
way corner by a gate-entrance, by a driveway or a path, tucked next to a
hedge or under a tall tree. For best effect, 'Diane' should be planted
where the sunlight floods through the bush from behind.

How to care for it

Witch hazel likes rich, moist, acidic soils and it is not bothered by
polluted air. The shrub can be pruned to size, but it will be happier if it

is allowed to expand and fill a sizable corner. Basic pruning involves removing dead or damaged or unwanted branches after flowering but before leaves unfurl in spring. Prune judiciously to keep the shrub within its prescribed boundaries but don't resist the opportunity to take off branches for forcing indoors in early spring.

Good companions

Viburnum × bodnantense 'Pink Dawn' is another shrub with the ability to flower in the dead of winter. It produces heavily scented pink flowers in late January or mid-February. Its pink blooms would clash with the yellow flowers of the witch hazel, but would harmonize with the coppery reds.

Since witch hazels don't have flowers in summer and their oval leaves are not especially attractive, it is necessary to underplant them with spring-flowering bulbs such as dog's tooth violets, *Iris reticulata* and chionodoxa, and groundcovers like sweet woodruff. Your witch hazel can offer support to shrubs like rhododendrons, pieris, magnolia, viburnum and philadelphus.

For your collection

 In the world of witch hazels, *Hamamelis virginiana* is the first to bloom, producing small lemon-yellow flowers in October to November. It is followed by the spring witch hazel (*H. vernalis*) and Japanese witch hazel (*H. japonica*). All three are interesting to plant connoisseurs, although none is as desirable or useful in the home garden as the hybrids 'Diane' and 'Jelena' or the popular forms of *H. mollis*.

Hebe 'Autumn Glory'

Common name: Shrubby veronica

Chief characteristics

Too many gardeners dismiss hebes because they have been told they are too tender and too short-lived to be worth the effort. This is only partly true. There are a few cultivars tough enough to survive our cold winters if planted in a sheltered, free-draining spot. Hebes are worth growing for their great foliage, which can be tight and compact or soft and loose, and for their lovely bushy, cone-shaped flowers that come in a range of colors from pink to lilac,

Location: Full sun

Type: Evergreen shrub

Size: 24 to 30 inches (60 to 75 cm)

Conditions: Ordinary, well-drained soil

Flowering time: July to October

blue to purple. There is one other reason to grow hebes—to break the climatic-zones barrier and prove the experts wrong! Native to New Zealand, hebes at one time were lumped in with veronicas and they are still called that by some long-time gardeners. There are dozens of excellent cultivars of hebe but not all of them are readily available here. The British are very keen on them and it can be disappointing to find so many more mentioned in books than are available at garden centers on the west coast.

'Autumn Glory' is one of the best to start off with. It grows about 30 inches (75 cm) high, has dark green semi-glossy evergreen leaves, and produces violet-blue flower spikes from July to October. What makes 'Autumn Glory' a top performer is its winter toughness, its beautifully compacted foliage, its lovely blue blooms and its prolonged flowering period. To find all these qualities in one plant is impressive.

Another tough species of shrubby veronica is *Hebe buxifolia*, also known as the boxleaf hebe because it looks rather like boxwood. This is both cold and drought tolerant and grows into a neat dome shape that can be easily sheared into an attractive bush. The white flowers are not very significant, but the foliage makes a pleasant contrast to other leafy shrubs.

Where to plant it

Grow hebes in fertile, free-draining soil in a sunny, sheltered position, preferably in a raised bed or planter box close to the house where they can receive some winter protection. Tough as they are, 'Autumn Glory' and *Hebe buxifolia* will not tolerate waterlogging or persistent icy blasts.

The more tender hebes can be grown in pots overwintered in the greenhouse or in a frost-free corner. But the fun is to see how far you can push the hardiness barrier, so you should experiment with growing various hebes in south-facing planters and flower beds.

How to care for it

Hebes are trouble-free plants with only one real enemy—frost. Yet even if knocked back by a cold snap, the hardier hebes can bounce back. Prune lightly to shape and tidy. Good drainage is imperative, so dig deep and add sand to the subsoil to eliminate the risk of waterlogging.

Good companions

Try partnering hebes with hardy fuchsias, daphne, dwarf nandina, lavender, roses and euphorbia. The shorter, rocky types will mingle well with sempervivum, saxifrage, pulsatilla, dianthus, dwarf scabiosas and purple hardy geraniums.

For your collection

- *Hebe speciosa*, also known as the "showy hebe," is a beautiful specimen, producing 3- to 4-inch (7.5- to 10-cm) long reddish-purple flowers on stout stems from July to September. The dark green foliage with a purple tinge is also very attractive. The rule of thumb with hebes is that the smaller the leaves the hardier the plant. *H. speciosa* has survived successfully two winters outdoors in my garden in a sheltered planter box, facing south, close to the house.
- *Hebe* 'Patty's Purple' is a compact plant that grows about 3 feet (90 cm) high and has light lilac-purple flowers in early summer.
- *Hebe ochracea* 'James Stirling', which looks more like a heather or a dwarf conifer than a hebe, is known as one of the "whipcord hebes." You will find it sometimes labeled *H. armstrongii* because both species are very similar in appearance.
- *Hebe albicans* 'Red Edge', a compact form with red-tipped leaves in winter and early spring, has pale lilac flowers in summer.
- Other top cultivar names include 'Midsummer Beauty' (lavender), 'Great Orme' (pink), 'Boughton Dome' (white), 'Bowles Hybrid' (mauve) and 'Carl Teschner' (purple).
- Some of the popular veronicas have hebe-like flowers and it's worth finding a place for them in your garden. Three of the best kinds are the woolly speedwell (*Veronica incana*), which has compact silver-gray foliage and purple-blue flowers; *V. spicata* 'Red Fox', which has rose-pink flowers, and *V. spicata* 'Blue Carpet', which has deep blue flowers. For the sunny, well-drained rockery you could try *V. allionii*, the alpine speedwell, which has compact violet-blue spikes and grows about 6 inches (15 cm) high.

$\mathcal{H}$elictotrichon sempervirens

Common name: Blue oat grass

Chief characteristics

What makes ornamental grasses so special is not just their color and shape but the way they can catch the barest breeze and bring sound and movement to the garden. The gentle swaying of the rose-red plumes of purple fountain grass (*Pennisetum setaceum* 'Rubrum') or the rustle of the distinctive blades of zebra grass (*Miscanthus sinensis*

Location: Full sun
Type: Ornamental grass
Size: 18 to 20 inches (45 to 50 cm)
Conditions: Ordinary, well-drained soil
Flowering time: July to August

'Zebrinus') brings a whole new dimension to the beauty of a summer garden. Ornamental grasses contribute to the color and design of a garden. Grasses also remind us of open meadows and country footpaths and carefree childhood days when we would pull up a stem of grass and amble along a lane with pals and not have a care in the world.

Many grasses deserve a place in the coastal garden but few are as versatile or as easy to grow as blue oat grass, *Helictotrichon sempervirens*. It has a fabulous mounding form, outstanding intense silvery blue blades, and long, arching stalks which slowly turn to straw by the end of summer. In mild areas it also stays evergreen, which brings much valued color to the garden in winter.

Where to plant it

Blue oat grass is not a small grass. It needs room to be seen at its best. It will grow 2 feet high (60 cm), send pale blue flower stalks up another 2 feet (60 cm), and form a round, compact mound at least 2 feet (60 cm) wide. Blue oat grass may be used as an accent plant or planted in groups for greater drama. Perfect for the sunny perennial border, its color contrasts well with silver-leafed plants such as artemisia or dark-leafed plants like *Heuchera micrantha* 'Bressingham Bronze' or *Cimicifuga* 'Brunette'.

Plant blue oat grass in fertile, well-drained, average soil in a sunny location. Make sure it gets good air circulation. If the drainage is poor, especially if the soil is wet clay, it will die from root rot. In my garden, blue oat grass flourishes beautifully next to a path on the west side of the house where it is sheltered from the hot afternoon sun by a cedar hedge, yet still gets plenty of morning sun and daylight. In a simple unadorned pot on a balcony, it can be very attractive.

How to care for it

Too much shade will lead to fungal problems. Too much sun will make your blue oat grass go into an early dormancy and quit performing. Cut down the spent flower stems in fall. Divide and replace every three years.

Good companions

The succulent foliage of *Sedum* 'Autumn Joy' with its heavy broccoli-like flowerheads and the silver leaves of either *Stachys byzantina* 'Silver Carpet' or *Artemisia ludoviciana* 'Valerie Finnis' will all add to the beauty of blue oat grass. The rose-red flowers of *Lychnis coronaria* and the bright red flowers of the cape fuchsia, *Phygelius* 'Devil's Tears', would also make a striking combination. Annuals like the purple-flowering cherry-pie plant (*Heliotropium arborescens*) and the spidery pink or lavender flowers of *Cleome spinosa* would add excitement. Shrub roses, particularly any of David Austin's top English roses like 'Mary Rose' or 'Gertrude Jekyll', would make fine companions for *Helictotrichon sempervirens*.

For your collection

If you fall in love with blue grasses, there are plenty more for your garden. Here are two of the best.

- *Festuca cinerea* 'Elijah Blue': This has powdery blue evergreen leaves and grows only 18 inches (45 cm) high. It is rated by nursery experts as one of the brightest and best of the blue grasses. It also goes under the name *F. ovina glauca* 'Elijah Blue'.
- Lyme grass (*Elymus racemosus*): This favorite blue grass of the illustrious 19th-century English garden designer Gertrude Jekyll can be used as an accent plant or as a groundcover.

*H*eliotropium arborescens

Common name: Heliotrope, cherry-pie plant

Chief characteristics

An old-fashioned summer annual, heliotrope has it all: great color, memorable fragrance and a lyrical common name, cherry-pie plant. It is called that because some people think the remarkable scent of the purple flowers is reminiscent of a baked cherry pie, fresh out of the oven. Others think the fragrance is more like baby powder or licorice. It is a strong, but not offensive aroma. You may catch a whiff of it as you breeze by but most of the time you need to put your nose quite close to the large purple flowerheads to catch the fragrance's full strength.

Location: Full sun
Type: Annual
Size: 8 to 24 inches (20 to 60 cm)
Conditions: Fertile, well-drained soil
Flowering time: June to September

Native to South America, where Europeans first encountered it in Peru toward the end of the 18th century, heliotrope is now a firm favorite of container gardeners, who like to use it in pots and hanging baskets. It is also listed as *Heliotropium peruvianum*. An easy plant to care for, it flowers nonstop from June to September. In addition to its dense flowerheads, composed of tight clusters of tiny individual mauve-purple flowers, it also has very attractive, dark green, corrugated leaves.

Where to plant it

Heliotrope performs superbly in patio pots, window boxes, hanging baskets and planter boxes. Or it can be grown in a sunny, well-drained site in the open garden. It is not invasive and is rarely troubled by pests or disease.

How to care for it

Two golden rules for growing heliotrope: 1) Don't overwater. It hates having its roots waterlogged and perpetually damp soil will cause the leaves to turn brown and fall off; 2) Remember to feed it, especially if it is planted in a pot, with a half-strength solution of 20-20-20 at least twice a week.

Good companions

Heliotrope contrasts well with silver foliage plants such as dusty miller, white petunias, the two-tone yellow-maroon heads of French marigolds, and yellow argyranthemum.

For your collection

There is a white heliotrope (*Heliotropium arborescens* 'Alba'), which has a slightly more powerful vanilla scent. Other scented plants that can be grown in pots on the patio include scented geraniums, mints and chocolate cosmos.

elleborus orientalis

Common name: Lenten rose

Chief characteristics

There are fads and trends in gardening just as there are in fashion and the arts. For a time, the winter/early spring-flowering hellebores were the "must-have" plants of the moment. Avid gardeners still talk of how remarkable hellebores are and how it is a major oversight not to have at least 2 or 3 types in the garden.

Location: Semi-shade
Type: Perennial
Size: 18 to 24 inches (45 to 60 cm)
Conditions: Good, well-drained soil
Flowering time: February to March

In reality, while they are robust, reliable plants with charming, open cup-shaped flowers, they are actually rather modest performers, not at all showy or attention-grabbing in the way roses or daylilies are. This makes hellebores something of an acquired taste. But once you like them, you will probably grow to love them. If, on the other hand, you don't see what all the fuss is about, that is also perfectly understandable.

Two of the most popular kinds are *Helleborus orientalis*, the Lenten rose, which comes in a range of flower colors from red to pink, maroon to white; and *H. niger*, the Christmas rose, which has flowers ranging from pure white to blush green. I think it's worth finding a place for both, but if I had to choose between them I would pick the Lenten rose because of its exquisite plum-colored flowers. They each form low-mounding clumps of firm, leathery, evergreen leaves. The Christmas rose (rarely ever in bloom at Christmas) flowers usually in mid- to late January. It is still a major asset in the winter garden, while the Lenten rose flowers in February or March.

Where to plant it

The Lenten rose and Christmas rose flourish in rich soil that is moist but well drained, in light to full shade. A dappled woodland-type setting is the perfect location for showing hellebores. In too much sun, the leaves tend to scorch and look tatty.

The flowers rise 10 to 12 inches (25 to 30 cm) above the foliage and nod downward. You sometimes have to lift the shy flower's face up to see it, something that only adds to its charm. Both these hellebores make good underplanting for rhododendrons, deciduous trees and shrubs.

How to care for it

When the Lenten rose and Christmas rose are in full bloom you will probably want to cut a few and bring them indoors. They look very good in a small glass vase but they don't last very long unless they are cut and put in water immediately. Some gardeners say adding a nip of vodka or gin to the water seems to make these flowers last longer. Grow hellebores toward the front of the shade border, where the flowers won't be hidden and can be easily reached. When flowers have faded, allow them to go to seed. Cut out old, dead and decaying leaves back to the base clump of healthy green foliage.

Clumps can be divided in spring or fall, but hellebores prefer not to be disturbed and have a tendency to recover slowly and refuse to flower for a couple of seasons after being messed with. If you cut away the foliage of *Helleborus niger* as the buds expand, the flowers tend to be more showy.

Good companions

Surrounded by spring-flowering bulbs like muscari and erythronium, the Lenten rose and Christmas rose both fit well under trees and shrubs. They won't object to sharing ground with hostas, hardy geraniums, barrenwort, lungwort, jack-in-the-pulpit, lily-of-the-valley, maidenhair fern, rhododendrons and deciduous shrubs like hydrangea and *Edgeworthia chrysantha*.

For your collection

There are other important hellebores you should consider.

- The Corsican hellebore (*Helleborus argutifolius*): This grows about 3 feet (90 cm) tall and has tough, glossy leaves with serrated edges. It has dense bunches of lime-green flowers in early spring. It may require staking to hold up the weighty flowerheads. Prune out the old flower stalks after it has bloomed and it will produce new healthy foliage.
- The stinking hellebore (*Helleborus foetidus*): This is not really stinky at all unless you put your nose very close to the flowers, which are pale yellow-green and have a vaguely skunky aroma. The foliage is deeply cut and is useful in the shade border for creating textural contrasts.

  The Corsican hellebore and the stinking hellebore are both first-rate plants but they are generally valued more by plant connoisseurs than average weekend gardeners, partly because the flowers and foliage are not especially showy and partly because you mostly find these plants at specialty nurseries that cater to knowledgeable plant-lovers.
- *Helleborus vesicarius*, native to the oak scrub and rocky limestone outcrops of Turkey, has lovely deep-cut oaklike leaves and nodding maroon flowers. Tests have found that it is a lot hardier than was originally thought. Another hellebore worth seeking out is 'Bulmer's Blush', which is a new pink-flowered version of the standard Corsican hellebore. It caused quite a stir when it was showcased for the first time at the Chelsea Flower Show.

ℋemerocallis 'Stella de Oro'

Common name: Daylily

Chief characteristics

The daylily has two major assets: superb trumpet-shaped flowers that now come in a grand range of colors, and handsome strap-like leaves that rise and fall in cascading mounds. Both flowers and foliage play an indispensable decorative role in the summer garden.

Location: Full sun to light shade
Type: Perennial
Size: 18 inches (45 cm)
Conditions: Good, moist, well-drained soil
Flowering time: May to September

One of the easiest and most reliable performing perennials to grow, the daylily gets its botanical name, *Hemerocallis*, from two Greek words—*hemero* for day and *kallos* for beauty. The delicate flowers—more water than substance—last for only a day, two at most, depending how much sun and shade they receive. A major compensation for the shockingly brief lifespan of such a beautiful flower is that a mature clump of daylilies is perfectly capable of producing dozens of exquisite blooms in a single season. A 3-year-old plant can produce in excess of 600 blooms in just 8 weeks. Over the last few decades, hybridizers have been astonishingly busy, with the result that today there are at least 38,000 registered hybrids, covering a vast range of colors in virtually every shade of pink, orange, yellow and red imaginable.

Like roses, daylilies all have marvelous names: 'Fairy Tale Pink', 'Pandora's Box', 'Pardon Me', 'Holly Herrema', 'Pineapple Frost', 'Velveteen', 'Daquiri', and on and on. Most gardeners, however, have not the foggiest idea what they actually have growing in their garden. The fight to rectify the daylily's identity crisis is a cause célèbre for many daylily breeders. They campaign with almost evangelical zeal to persuade nurseries and garden centers to call daylilies by their full botanical name instead of dumping them into nonspecific, generic color categories.

There are a few classic top performers that over the years have earned a special place of honor. Top of the class is 'Stella de Oro', a long-time favorite, loved for its short 12- to 18-inch (30- to 45-cm) form and its lightly ruffled orange-gold flowers that bloom continuously from spring to fall. 'Catherine Woodbury' is another classic, producing lovely, fragrant, pale orchid-pink blooms with a lime-green throat. 'Happy Returns' is similar to 'Stella de Oro', with canary-yellow flowers. It blooms from early summer into autumn.

'Frans Hals' is a plain golden-yellow and dark orange bicolor with an elegant simplicity to it—like work of the Dutch artist for whom it is named. 'Hyperion' is an established star performer with international appeal. It produces highly scented lemon-yellow flowers. 'Kwanso' is one of the most well-known cultivars, with rusty-orange flowers. 'Janice Brown' is one of the rising-star daylilies for coastal gardens. It has rose-pink flowers with a dark center. It flowers for a long period, at least 10 weeks.

Where to plant it

Daylilies thrive in full sun or light shade. They flower best if, like roses, they get at least 6 hours of sun a day. They are marvelous mass-planted in deep drifts by the side of a path or to edge the front of a raised bed. They can also perform very successfully in large single clumps in the perennial border or even in containers, provided they are well watered. Moisture is essential: They need at least an inch (2.5 cm) a week in order to produce quality flowers that won't shrivel the first moment the sun touches them. For this reason, make sure you plant daylilies in rich, moisture-retentive soil. Although they are sun-lovers, they benefit from being located where they get light, dappled shade in the afternoon.

When buying daylilies, look not only at the quality of the flower, but also for healthy, vigorous foliage. Daylily connoisseurs also look closely at the part where the flowers are formed. The wider the flower junctions, the less likelihood there is of blooms becoming congested and failing to appear at their best.

How to care for it

There is no need to spray daylilies. They will thrive in fertile soil that has been well amended with fully aged compost or manure. Slugs and snails can be a nuisance, especially when young daylily foliage is developing. This is a time to be extra vigilant, although most daylilies seem quite capable of compensating for any damage inflicted by slugs by producing even more flowering stems. A healthy daylily will grow at an astonishing rate, almost doubling itself in a year. You can deadhead your daylilies— pulling off the spent blooms each day—but do it only for the sake of tidiness. It makes no difference to the plant.

Division is very easy. Large clumps can be pulled apart to make many new colonies. This is what often drives gardeners to be very selective in the first place. They know one day they will end up with hundreds of plants of whatever form they have chosen.

Good companions

Daylilies combine effortlessly with many summer-flowering perennials. Phlox and beebalm, crocosmia and lavatera are all good candidates. Ornamental grasses, artemisia and bronze fennel can provide interesting foliage contrast while yarrow, liatris and daisies offer stimulating color combinations in sunny locations. In light shade, late-flowering astilbe and ligularia offer pleasant companionship along with hostas and astrantia and the blue flowers of *Geranium pratense*. Deciduous shrubs like the variegated dogwood (*Cornus alba* 'Elegantissima') or the purple-leafed smoke bush (*Cotinus coggygria*) can also provide creative backdrops to the expressive foliage and elegant flowers of daylilies.

For your collection

You can spend a fortune if you really get bitten by the daylily bug. Some plants can sell for more than $200 each. You could concentrate on collecting collections. For example, there is the Siloam series, hybrids produced by Pauline Henry in Arkansas and each named after her hometown, Siloam. There are at least 27 daylilies named Siloam something-or-other. There's 'Siloam Rose Queen', 'Siloam Red Toy', 'Siloam Little Fairy' and 'Siloam Ethel Smith'.

Daylily specialist Pam Erikson, who lives in Langley, B.C., has also started her own series. You can get 'Langley Big Top', 'Langley Red Devil', 'Langley Autumn Princess', 'Langley Bull's-eye', 'Langley Rose Explosion' and 'Langley Lady'. There are more on the way.

*H*euchera micrantha 'Bressingham Bronze'

Common name: Coral bells, purple-leafed heuchera

Chief characteristics

Heuchera can be used as a groundcover or as an edging plant beside a path or as a texture plant in the flower border. It also looks good grown in a pot on its own or combined with colorful summer annuals. The delicate sprays of white, red or pink flowers look particularly attractive in flower arrangements and heuchera's foliage is most useful as a counterpoint to the bright blooms of lavender, salvia, achillea, coreopsis, corydalis and blue and gold ornamental grasses.

Location: Full sun to part shade
Type: Perennial
Size: 9 inches (23 cm)
Conditions: Good, moist, well-drained soil
Flowering time: June to July

Heuchera wasn't always so popular. But over the last few decades, hybridizers have been very busy with the result that today there are many new, outstanding cultivars. They are available in a wide range of foliage and flower colors.

Some of the most impressive heucheras are the Bressingham hybrids, raised by the Blooms Nursery of Bressingham in Norfolk, England. One of the best of the new hybrids is 'Bressingham Bronze', which gets its name from its distinctive crinkly, bronzy red foliage. It has tiny white flowers on thin stems in summer, but the main reason for getting this plant is to create exciting color contrasts by combining it with blue grasses and plants with silver leaves. 'Bressingham Bronze' is actually an improved version of another very popular heuchera called 'Palace Purple', which was so impressive when it came on the market it was voted Perennial Plant of the Year in 1991 by the Perennial Plant Association of North America. 'Palace Purple' has white flowers and dark purple-brown, maple-shaped leaves that have an almost metallic look to them. However, 'Bressingham Bronze' now routinely outperforms 'Palace Purple' in European and North American gardens, partly because its creators insist that it be propagated vegetatively (by division or from cuttings) rather than from seed, which tends to produce inferior plants that lack the all-important foliage characteristic for which the plant is famous. "Once you've seen 'Bressingham Bronze'," says Adrian Bloom, of Blooms Nursery, "you won't want 'Palace Purple'."

Where to plant it

Grow heuchera in full sun or semi-shade in well-drained soil. Don't let the ground become too dry, especially in blazing afternoon sun. Create a tapestry of contrasting foliage by planting different heucheras together. The light sprays of flowers also command attention, frothing up in mass plantings. Or you can employ heuchera to edge a path, or try out new exciting color associations in the perennial border. The semi-shaded rockery is another place heuchera will thrive provided it is well watered.

How to care for it

Once settled in the right place, heucheras are easy plants to care for. Simply improve the soil by mulching around them with an enriching well-rotted manure or compost mulch in spring. Cut off the faded flower stalks in summer to keep the plants looking tidy. Divide clumps every few years. You may think you have selected precisely the right spot for your heuchera, but it will sulk if given too much sun and too little water. Watch it for the first season; if it performs well and the leaves look crisp and healthy and attractive, you know you have it in the right spot.

Good companions

Some of the best companions for heucheras are other heucheras. The foliage of 'Palace Purple' can be contrasted with 'Snow Storm' or 'Chocolate Ruffles'. Not hugely creative but it does work.

The pale lemon–tinted leaves of *Stachys byzantina* 'Primrose Heron' and the white flowers of *Geranium clarkei* 'Kashmir White' would give *Heuchera micrantha* 'Palace Purple' two quality neighbors. The small, clumping grass, *Festuca glauca*, could also be tossed into the mix to add a blue note. Other possible associates: *Allium christophii*, with its silver-purple starlike blooms; black mondo grass (*Ophiopogon planiscapus* 'Nigrescens'); *Euphorbia polychroma*; and *Scabiosa columbaria* 'Pink Mist'.

For your collection

The list of heuchera hybrids now in commercial production is staggering. Other top names to look out for include the following.

- 'Chocolate Ruffles': You can't miss the large, dark chocolate-brown leaves with ruffled edges. It produces white flowers.
- 'Persian Carpet': It has dark green and silver-blue foliage.
- 'Pewter Moon': This has cool pink flowers on tall maroon stems but it is loved mostly for its oustanding silver-gray foliage with pewter-gray veins.
- 'Brandon Pink': One of the biggest heucheras, growing 18 to 24 inches (45 to 60 cm), it produces coral-pink flowers. It is also exceptionally hardy.
- 'Northern Fire': This is another admirably hardy cultivar. It has variegated white-green foliage and scarlet-red flowers.
- The first coral bells to flower are the *Heuchera sanguinea* hybrids, which are now well-established favorites and still pretty hard to beat. They send up pink or bright red flowers from May to July. Look for 'Splish Splash', which has variegated green-white foliage with veins that turn red at the first chill of fall; 'Splendens', a compact plant with scarlet-red flowers; and 'Snow Storm', which has pink flowers and ruffled white leaves edged with green.
- Two other plants with bronzy foliage worth having are purple sage (*Salvia officinalis* 'Purpurascens') and *Euphorbia amygdaloides* 'Rubra'.

Hosta 'Frances Williams'

Common name: Frances Williams hosta

Chief characteristics

Hostas are so dependable, versatile and long lasting, it is no surprise so many gardeners regard them as the perfect perennial. They are certainly one of the indispensable, structural, workhorse plants of the shade garden. Once settled, they can have a formidable presence either in a large group planting or alone as a solitary feature. Hostas can be large and lush or diminutive and delicate. They come in an astonishing diversity of color and form.

Location: Light shade
Type: Perennial
Size: 2 to 3 feet (60 to 90 cm)
Conditions: Moist, well-drained soil
Flowering time: July

For all-round beauty and reliability, however, one of the best hostas is 'Frances Williams', an old favorite with pale lavender flowers and variegated heart-shaped blue-green leaves trimmed with gold. The foliage variegation is consistent and not sick- or anemic-looking. This hosta has a reputation for being more slug resistant. It can also tolerate more sun than other hostas.

Other fine variegated hostas include 'Francee', 'Wide Brim' and 'Brim Cup'. Another top performer is the urn-shaped 'Krossa Regal', which has frosty blue leaves, pale lavender flowers and an ability to handle more sun than a lot of other hostas. 'Krossa Regal' also forms an attractive vase-shaped clump.

There are marvelous blue hostas such as 'Hadspen Blue', 'Blue Moon', 'Blue Cadet', 'Halcyon' and 'Blue Boy'; delicious yellow forms like 'Piedmont Gold', 'Sun Power', 'Midas Touch' and 'August Moon'; classy, large-leafed cultivars like 'Sum and Substance' and 'Elegans'; and rich green plants like 'Devon Green', 'Canadian Shield', 'Green Acres', 'Honeybells' and 'Royal Standard'.

Where to plant it

Hostas thrive in light shade or full shade in moist, well-drained soil. They need at least 4 hours of sunshine to flower properly, so it is best to place them in light shade rather than total shade.

Some gardeners do not like the flowers, which top long, stiff stalks. They cut the stalks the moment they appear. It is the hosta's broad, handsome leaves they want, not the lilac or white flowers. However, the flowers of some—'Honeybells' and 'Royal Standard', for example—have a delightful fragrance and it would be a pity to lose them.

Grow hostas in a mass planting as a groundcover or to contrast their fabulous leaf texture against the leaves of other plants. Hostas can also look very good grown in pots to decorate decks, balconies and patios or held in the wings and used as fill-in plants to plug gaps in the shade border in summer. Good candidates for containers include 'Wide Brim', 'Gold Standard', 'Francee', 'Krossa Regal', 'Halcyon' and 'Snowden'.

Try growing the larger-leafed forms as a dramatic focal point in the herbaceous border or by the side of a stream or pond. The golden-yellow cultivars can be used to brighten dark corners, while the blue cultivars are exceptional, almost a novelty to show off to visitors.

How to care for it

All hostas are prone to slugs. Some, like 'Frances Williams', 'Krossa Regal' and 'Sum and Substance', seem to be more resistant than others. There are numerous strategies for dealing with them. Sprinkle diatomaceous earth around the new leaves as they emerge from the ground in spring. This material has sharp, microscopic edges that makes it unpleasant for slugs to slither over and deters them. Beer in a plastic container sunk into the ground is supposed to lure the slimy mollusks to a boozy last night. The chemical slug killer, metaldehyde, works, but its use is frowned upon because of the risk of poisoning birds and household pets. You could get your own pet toad—toads eat slugs and snails. Pity we don't have hedgehogs in this part of the world: they also eat slugs. The best way—perhaps only way—to deal with slugs is to regularly patrol your hosta patch. Look for them, especially after rain. You may find them sitting munching on the top of leaves or lurking in folds of as-yet-uncurled leaves or hiding under pieces of wood or close to the ground in the cool crevices of large stones.

What to do with them once you have found them? Snip them with a pair of scissors or toss them into a plastic bag bound for the garbage or drop them into a bucket of hot water or sprinkle them with salt. I have heard there are people who collect slugs and walk them a mile or two down the road and release them into a friendly wood. This sounds so fantastic, I think these people should go directly to heaven or get a sainthood. How do they bring themselves to cut flowers? Hostas like to be left to settle down and form large clumps, but they are easily divided when clumps become too large or when you want more hostas.

Good companions

Combine hostas with other shade-loving perennials like ligularia, *Hydrangea aspera*, polygonatum, hellebores, astilbes, dicentra, *Alchemilla mollis*, epimedium and rhododendrons.

Don't be a slave to the shade rule, however. Hostas, especially the variegated kinds, often appreciate more sun. It is all trial and error. But it is worth trying to grow hostas in more exposed, sunny locations where the soil is moist and combine them with daylilies and astilbes. Where the ground is perpetually boggy, you can mix hostas with the water-loving *Iris laevigata*.

For your collection

🐾 There are several novel hostas worth having just for the fun of their names. 'Hosta La Vista' is one. 'Wrinkles and Crinkles' is another. 'Raspberry Sorbet' has red flower stems while 'Canadian Shield' has very strong, firm, metallic leaves that look like they could be used to do some steel-plating. 'Gold Standard' is 'Frances Williams' in reverse—it has gold-yellow leaves with green edges and grows 2 feet (60 cm) high.

*H*ydrangea petiolaris

Common name: Climbing hydrangea

Chief characteristics

If you have only a small wall or fence or garden shed you want covered, a climbing hydrangea is probably not the right choice. It is a slow starter but is a vigorous climber capable of reaching 30 feet (9 m) once it gets going. In the ideal spot, and left unpruned, it has been known to soar 50 feet (15 m) or more. This is also one of its great strengths. Its energetic

Location: Semi-shade
Type: Deciduous vine
Size: 30 feet (9 m) plus
Conditions: Good, well-drained soil
Flowering time: May to June

growth habit makes it a magnificent plant for covering large walls or long fences or growing into sturdy big trees. It leafs out quickly in early spring with handsome green foliage and goes on to produce large white lacecap flowers. These can measure as much as 9 inches (23 cm) across.

The vine is self-supporting, climbing by means of tiny aerial roots that attach themselves firmly to any available surface. It likes to grow outward as well as upward, but it does not object to being firmly pruned or clipped and trained in the way you want it to go. It can be clipped neatly into shape once it has lost its leaves in fall and will resume its normal growth pattern in spring. As years go by, it will thicken out, become woodier and eventually form a massive, majestic spectacle. Some of the older gardens in England have made extremely good use of the climbing hydrangea to cover walls that separate different areas of a garden. In one case, the vine was allowed to swarm and completely overwhelm a long, tall brick wall. But it was also carefully pruned to leave a narrow doorway in the thick barrier of leaves. The bright opening, leading from the shade into a sunny flower garden, looked exceptionally elegant and inviting.

Where to plant it

The climbing hydrangea grows best in rich, moist but well-drained soil in semi-shade. In too much sun, the leaves scorch and the vine becomes tatty and unattractive. It reaches the peak of performance in late spring when its leaves layer themselves in glorious patterns and the handsome white lacecap flowers open up against the solid backdrop of lustrous green foliage.

If you grow it against the house you should realize that it is a tenacious clinger and won't let go without a fight. This is exactly what you want if you are looking for a long-lasting vine that will form a solid, structured framework. It can be made to clamber up brick chimneys or into trees or against garages or over sheds and fences in the shade of west- or east- or north-facing locations. It is also an excellent vine for screening.

In my garden, it covers a high and wide wall on the little used west side of the house in a shady space that faces a neighbor's deck. In summer, when the vine is fully leafed out, my neighbors have a much more pleasant view from their deck than looking at an unadorned flat wall. The vine also forms a softer, more attractive side to a stepping-stone path that leads down that side of the house and on through an arbor into the main garden.

How to care for it

Prune your climbing hydrangea in late fall or winter to keep it within bounds and to form a nicely structured shape. Branches that grow outward can easily be pruned to maintain the vine's symmetry and to prevent lower branches suffering because they are too shaded.

Don't be fooled if your newly planted vine doesn't grow at rocket speed. It is very deceptive at the beginning, taking its time to put in a good root system before it launches off. Have your secateurs on hand once it gets going.

Good companions

You can underplant a climbing hydrangea with *Geranium macrorrhizum* (white and pink) or corydalis (yellow or white).

For your collection

❧ The Persian ivy (*Hedera colchica* 'Dentata Variegata') is another vigorous climber that, like the climbing hydrangea, is capable of growing to 30 feet (9 m). It is another excellent choice for decorating a large wall or covering an unsightly garage or garden shed.

❧ Three other powerful climbers that are useful in the right location are the Virginia creeper (*Parthenocissus quinquefolia*), with brilliant red leaves turning to orange in fall; Boston ivy (*Parthenocissus tricuspidata*), with leaves that turn a striking red color in fall; and the purple-leafed grape vine (*Vitis vinifera* 'Purpurea'), with red-purple foliage.

ℋydrangea serrata 'Bluebird'

Common name: Lacecap hydrangea

Chief characteristics

Location: Light shade to full sun
Type: Deciduous shrub
Size: 4 to 6 feet (1.2 to 1.8 m)
Conditions: Ordinary, moist soil
Flowering time: June to September

The envy of all prairie gardeners, blue hydrangeas have been called the "queen of flowering shrubs." Some garden snobs consider them coarse and boring. But even a snob can't deny the glory of a hydrangea in full bloom. To my mind, they are magnificent plants, an indispensable part of the botanical backbone of a garden.

There are two main kinds of hydrangea: mopheads (also called hortensias), which have large, globular flowerheads, and lacecaps, which have slightly more decorative flowerheads with dense centers skirted by a light garland of single, flat flowers. Both types are extremely popular. You tend to see more mophead hydrangeas in the general urban landscape, but more and more gardeners are now finding room for slightly more decorative lacecap cultivars.

Easily the most outstanding is *Hydrangea serrata* 'Bluebird', which produces lovely blue lacecap flowers that will fade to a delicate pink if the soil is allowed to become more alkaline. The beauty of 'Bluebird' is also its compact nature—it grows only 4 to 6 feet (1.2 to 1.8 m), which makes it very easy to accommodate in the semi-shady mixed shrub border. The cultivar *H. macrophylla* 'Blue Wave' is very similar but is harder to find at garden centers. It also has blue flowers ringed by a lacecap-like border of pinkish-blue florets.

Top cultivars of the more familiar mopheads include 'Nikko Blue', 'Teller's Blue', 'Merritt's Beauty' and 'Merritt's Supreme'.

Where to plant it

Hydrangeas are versatile shrubs that fit into almost any kind of garden scheme. They look most natural in woodland settings where they enjoy the protection of high trees that allow in plenty of dappled sunshine. Hydrangeas thrive in light shade, but they are frequently grown in full sun. They won't object provided they are well watered. They also need to be well fed or they will starve. Keep the soil amended by adding compost or nutrient-rich mulches in spring. Also, consider growing hydrangeas in half barrels; they don't seem to mind having limited space for root development and they flower just as profusely.

How to care for it

Hydrangeas require good soil and plenty of water, especially during hot, dry spells. Grow them in a location that protects them from heavy frosts. The more acidic the soil, the more blue the flowers; the more limey or alkaline the soil, the more pink the flowers will be. To make hydrangea flowers more blue add aluminum sulfate to the soil; to make them more pink, add lime.

Faded flowerheads can be cut after flowering or you can leave the dead flowerheads on throughout winter if you like the look of them and then snip them off in early spring when you do your routine cleanup pruning. There is no evidence that leaving the faded flowers on over winter has any benefit other than providing decorative textural interest.

Good companions

Good partners for hydrangeas include rhododendrons, evergreen azaleas, *Enkianthus campanulatus*, *Edgeworthia chrysantha*, *Cornus alba* 'Elegantissima' and *Viburnum opulus*, a deciduous shrub that produces large bunches of bright red berries in winter.

For your collecton

Here are a few other kinds of hydrangea you should know about.

- The climbing hydrangea (*H. petiolaris*) produces 10-inch (25-cm) white lacecap-type blooms in June and is useful for dressing up large boring expanses of wallcovering.
- The hills of snow hydrangea (*H. arborescens* 'Grandiflora') grows 5 to 10 feet (1.5 to 3 m) and produces large white trusses of flowers from July to September. The cultivar 'Annabelle' grows only 4 feet high (1.2 m) but is equally prolific.

- ❧ The peegee hydrangea (*H. paniculata* 'Grandiflora') grows 8 feet (2.4 m) high and produces masses of large, cascading, creamy white or light pink cone-shaped flowers from August until frost. This can be trained into a small tree.
- ❧ *Hydrangea aspera* is a larger, shrubby hydrangea with a more natural, uncultivated, jungle-bush look to it. *H. sargentiana* is another species with an exotic jungle look.
- ❧ The oakleaf hydrangea (*H. quercifolia*) is an unusual plant that has white flowers and large leaves resembling those of an oak tree.
- ❧ *Hydrangea macrophylla* 'Winning Edge' is a dwarf mophead with deep pink flowers. It grows only about 2 feet (60 cm). 'Tovelit', 'Forever Pink' and 'Elf' are 3 other compact mophead-type hydrangeas that are ideal for growing in the semi-shade in a pot on a deck, balcony or patio.

*I*ris sibirica

Common name: Siberian iris, water iris, Siberian flag

Chief characteristics

You can easily get lost in the jungle of irises. There are more than 200 species and thousands of cultivars. Some classifications have been so broken down into subcategories, it can be quite overwhelming to sort it all out. Of course, you don't have to. You will be more than content growing a clump or two of Siberian irises, a few bearded iris, and some of the little early spring–flowering irises.

Location: Full sun to light shade
Type: Perennial
Size: 3 feet (90 cm)
Conditions: Moist soil
Flowering time: May to June

The Siberian iris (*Iris sibirica*) is a marvelous clumping plant with thin, upright leaves and superb purple or blue flowers in May to June. Sadly, the flowers don't bloom for very long, 2 or 3 weeks at most, but the foliage stays green and attractive all summer. Like old garden roses, the beauty of the Siberian iris is in the exquisite delicacy of the blooms. Top named cultivars include 'Caesar's Brother' (deep purple), 'Eric the Red' (wine-purple), 'Orville Fay' (medium blue), 'Sky Wings' (light blue), 'Teal Velvet' (deep purple), 'Papillon' (light blue) and 'Persimmon' (mid-blue).

Longer flowering, and generally a more familiar sight in coastal gardens, are the bearded irises. They bloom in June and are a lot more showy. They have a very distinctive flower, formed by 3 upright petals and 3 drooping petals, which have hairy turfs on their ridges—hence the "beard" name. Bearded irises have very solid, sword-shaped leaves and the flowers come in a remarkable range of colors from blue to peach, pink to yellow, purple to black. There are many bicolor variations. It really all comes down to picking the size and color you like.

It helps to know irises come in six basic sizes—dwarf (less than 10 inches/25 cm), standard dwarf (10 to 15 inches/25 to 38 cm), intermediate (15 to 28 inches/38 to 70 cm), miniature tall, (18 to 26 inches/45 to 65 cm), border (up to 28 inches/70 cm), and standard tall (more than 28 inches/70 cm). The border and tall bearded irises are the most popular.

Top bearded irises include: 'Beverly Sills' (coral pink), 'Blue Staccato' (bright blue with white edges), 'Cherub's Smile' (pink) and 'Dusky Challenger' (black-purple). The ones not in flower at garden centers now mostly come with an attached color photo, designed to eliminate guesswork.

Where to plant it

Grow Siberian irises in ordinary, moist soil in full sun or light shade. Make sure the rhizome is not planted too deep or too shallow. It likes to bake in the sun while its roots stay cool and moist.

Grow your tall bearded irises in fertile, moist but well-drained soil in full sun. The rhizomes need to be positioned so that they get full sun on their tops while their rooted undersides are able to draw water from the soil. Bearded irises will thrive in large groups or alone, scattered in the perennial border.

How to care for it

Irises need to be well fed and watered to bloom properly. They can be fertilized in spring just before they bloom and again when they have finished flowering in preparation for their second flush in late summer. Moist, well-drained soil is a must for bearded irises, so they need to be watered well, especially during their flowering stint.

Clumps can be lifted and divided using a sharp knife. Each new rhizome must have at least one fan (thick leaf-blade) in order to establish itself and flower. A sign that Siberian irises need to be divided is when there is a bald spot in the center of a clump.

Good companions

Mix irises with shrub roses, peonies and hardy geraniums. The color of the flowers packs a powerful punch. Other good companions include the blue flowers of *Campanula glomerata* 'Superba', herbs such as rosemary, mint and fennel, and bold leafy plants like *Helleborus corsicus* and *Euphorbia characias*. Yellow bearded irises look outstanding placed in front of the yellow flowers of a *Viburnum plicatum* 'Summer Snowflake'.

For your collection

- There are two cultivars of sweet iris (*Iris pallida*) that have interesting variegated foliage—'Aureo Variegata' and 'Variegata'. Both are good for edging or creating a bright focal point of foliage interest. They both have lavender-blue flowers.
- There are two tiny spring-flowering irises worth getting—*Iris reticulata* (various blues) and *Iris danfordiae* (yellow). They both grow 4 to 6 inches (10 to 15 cm) high and make a cheerful showing in April.
- If you have a pond or stream or lake on your property, you could use Japanese iris (*Iris ensata*, also known as *I. kaempferi*) or the yellow flag iris (*I. pseudacorus*), which has canary-yellow flowers, on the banks.

niphofia

Common name: Red-hot poker, torch lily

Chief characteristics

Red-hot pokers are exotic, architectural plants. Kniphofia 'Royal Castle Hybrids' is one of the best. It has attractive mounds of evergreen, daylily-like foliage and sends up tall two-tone, yellow flowers tipped with orangey red in June. The tops of the stiff, 3-foot-long (90-cm), "poker" stems are composed of dozens of tiny tubular flowers. The plant gets its common name from the look of the thick stems, which appear like hot pokers just drawn from the fire of a forge. Sensational for about a month, the flowers slowly lose their color, at which time the pokers need to be cut out.

Location: Full sun
Type: Perennial
Size: 3 feet (90 cm)
Conditions: Moist, well-drained soil
Flowering time: June to August

Native to South Africa, kniphofia is a moderately drought-tolerant plant. It will flourish in a hot, sunny border in average soil that is reasonably moisture retentive. There are many good cultivars available. Some bloom in early summer, some in the middle of summer, others at the end of summer and into fall. When buying kniphofia, you need to decide what time of the year you want to see the torchlike flowers. Colors range from lemon-yellow to orange to rose-red to the popular two-tones.

For spring/early summer flowering, look for 'Alcazar' (orange), 'Bressingham Torch' (orange-yellow), 'Earliest of All' (coral-red) and 'Royal Castle Hybrids' (yellow-orange). For mid-summer flowering, look for 'Jenny Bloom' (yellow-orange), 'Firefly' (orange-red), 'Shining Sceptre' (golden orange), 'Primrose Beauty' (yellow), 'Royal Standard' (brilliant red and yellow), 'Bressingham Comet' (yellow and orange) and 'Little Maid' (ivory and light yellow). For late summer/early fall, look for 'Bee's Lemon', 'Ice Queen', 'Cobra', 'Wayside Flame', 'Underway' and 'Fiery Fred'.

Most easily available on the west coast are: 'Bressingham Comet', 'Royal Castle Hybrids', 'Shining Sceptre', 'Primrose Beauty', 'Little Maid' and 'Alcazar'.

Where to plant it

The perfect plant for the sunny perennial border, kniphofia needs to be supported at the front and the rear by plants that can take over when the poker flowers have gone. The mound of green leaves that is left is not particularly unattractive but neither does it add much to the garden once the flowers are over. So it is best placed a little back from the front of the border to allow for suitable companion planting.

How to care for it

Kniphofia is supposed to hate wet winters, yet it survives very well through the wettest winters in coastal gardens. The secret is to plant in well-drained soil in a spot where it also is protected from severe frosts. The leaves can be tied up over winter to reduce the amount of water and cold getting into the central crown. Just untie and clean them up in early spring. Clumps can be divided in March every few years.

Good companions

Liatris will send up spikes of purple or white flowers after kniphofia has finished flowering. Daylilies also combine nicely, compensating for the kniphofia's loss of flowers with their own tall flower stems. The daylily leaves also blend perfectly with kniphofia's foliage. Other possible companions include the sulphur-yellow flowers of *Achillea* 'Moonshine', the red and orange blooms of *Crocosmia* 'Lucifer', 'Bressingham Beacon' and 'Firebird' and the blues of globe thistle (*Echinops ritro*) or sea holly (*Eryngium alpinum*). Late summer–flowering grasses like the purple-leafed fountain grass (*Pennisetum setaceum* 'Rubra') and late summer–flowering perennials like black-eyed susan and *Aster* × *frikartii* 'Monch' would also make good companions.

For your collection

🐾 Orange is not the easiest color to place in the garden, but if you wanted to create an orange monocolor garden there are lots of suitable kniphofia cultivars. One of the best is 'Orange Torch', which was cultivated by the famous English plantswoman Beth Chatto, a lover of kniphofia, especially the yellow-green 'Little Maid', one of her own selections.

*L*avandula angustifolia

Common name: English lavender

Chief characteristics

Location: Full sun
Type: Evergreen, aromatic shrub
Size: 18 to 24 inches (45 to 60 cm)
Conditions: Well-drained soil
Flowering time: June to August

You don't have to grow heaps of lavender in your garden, but you probably should grow a clump or two. Lavender has been a mainstay in gardens for as long as gardens have existed. Over the centuries, it has transcended mere popularity and entrenched itself as much more than an aromatic herb. It has risen to a place of honor accorded few plants in horticulture. Today, it has almost a defining presence, giving a garden, large or small, the stamp of authenticity and credibility. A favorite in the organized floral chaos of English cottage gardens for generations, lavender has a long history of supplying its powerful fragrance for use in sachets to freshen fusty closets and wardrobes and as a key ingredient in potpourris for sweetening the air in stuffy rooms. It is now used in aromatherapy where its old nickname, the "herb of devotion," is taking on a whole new meaning.

Lavender's primary scent is located in the dense clusters of tiny light blue or purple flowers. These are tightly bound together at the top of slender grasslike stalks that rise up above thick clumps of grayish-green foliage. One of the most intense and familiar of all garden aromas, the fragrance is most effectively released by brushing the flower stalks or foliage with your hand.

There are more than 25 different types of lavender. The best are two cultivars of *Lavandula angustifolia*—'Hidcote', which has bluish-purple flowers on long, tumbling stalks; and 'Munstead', which has violet-blue flowers. 'Sarah' is very similar to 'Munstead' but grows a little taller and has larger flowers that bloom longer. There are also pink forms: 'Loddon Pink' and 'Jean Davies'. One of the very best new lavender cultivars is

L. angustifolia 'Lady', an All-American Selections winner in 1994. 'Lady' can be grown from seed and will produce beautiful lavender spikes the first year.

Where to plant it

Drainage is crucial. Nothing kills lavender faster than boggy, waterlogged soil. Native to the Mediterranean region, it thrives in full sun in well-drained soil. Its love for dry places makes it very useful for covering drought-prone slopes and exposed sunny sides of paths. You can plant it as a special feature or in rows to form a low hedge or to edge driveways. It will also grow very happily in a pot.

How to care for it

Plant lavender properly and forget about it. There is very little to do but clip the flower stalks once the blooms have faded. Plants should be pruned to tidy them up at the end of summer and give a slightly harder pruning in mid-spring after the buds have started to break. Whatever you do, however, the plants will eventually become woody and ragged. Pruning back into the old wood rarely works as buds have a difficult time breaking from old wood. So you usually end up having to replace plants with new ones.

You may find "cuckoo spit" on the flower spikes in damp springs. The "spit" is home to a little green insect called a froghopper. You can wash it away or squish it between your fingers or ignore it because it doesn't do too much harm anyway.

Good companions

Lavender fits in beautifully around roses and looks good sharing ground with blue ornamental grasses. *Sedum spectabile, Hebe buxifolia, Coreopsis grandiflora* 'Early Sunrise', *Scabiosa columbaria* 'Butterfly Blue' or 'Pink Mint' all offer worthwhile partnerships. The bright blue flowers of 'Munstead' lavender can be used to bring out the subtle blue tone in the magnificent leaves of *Euphorbia characias*. The soft purple heads of chives (*Allium schoenoprasum*) will also combine very attractively with the deeper violet-blue of the 'Hidcote' lavender.

For your collection

- Spanish lavender (*Lavandula stoechas*) is very beautiful. It has attractive violet butterflylike ears at the top of deeper purple, pineapple-shaped flowers. The blooms have a pleasant scent reminiscent of varnish. It is a lovely plant to grow in a pot, but needs to be brought into a frost-free place in winter, not being hardy enough to survive outside.

🐦 French lavender (*L. dentata*) is also a good container plant with fragrant flowers. It needs to be brought indoors in winter.

$\mathcal{L}$avatera thuringiaca 'Barnsley'

Common name: Tree mallow, Barnsley lavatera

Chief characteristics

With its lovely white-pink hollyhock-like flowers, 'Barnsley' has rightfully earned a respected place in the hearts of gardeners everywhere. It is a particularly charming, attractive perennial that brings a cheerful,

Location: Full sun to light shade
Type: Perennial
Size: 4 to 5 feet (1.2 to 1.5 m)
Conditions: Rich, well-drained soil
Flowering time: July to August

relaxed, cottage garden look to the summer border. In a gallon pot at the garden center, it may not impress. You can be forgiven for dismissing it as insignificant and walking on to examine more exciting plant material. But once it gets growing in a sunny spot in your garden, it soon swells up to become a substantial bush, reaching 6 or even 8 feet (1.8 to 2.4 m).

In early July, it will start to flower and it will continue to produce masses of outstanding white-pink blooms with bright strawberry centers right up to the end of summer. 'Barnsley' looks like a tough shrub in the garden at the height of summer yet it is sensitive to frost and chilling winds. It needs to rejuvenate itself with new growth every spring. This is why it is more usually grown in the herbaceous border with peonies and phlox and euphorbia.

'Barnsley' gets its name from Barnsley House, the home and garden in Gloucester, England, of one of Britain's most respected garden experts, Rosemary Verey. The plant first surfaced in 1985 and has since become an international favorite. You will also have no difficulty finding 'Candy Floss', which grows to about the same size as Barnsley but has pale full-pink flowers.

Lavatera trimestris, the annual mallow, is also very popular. It is grown as a bedding plant. The two fine cultivars are 'Mont Blanc', which has pure trumpet-shaped white flowers, and 'Silver Cup', which has rose-pink flowers. Both grow to about 2 or 3 feet (60 to 90 cm) and are easily propagated from seed indoors and transplanted in spring.

Where to plant it

Grow 'Barnsley' in well-drained, fertile soil in a sunny, sheltered location where it will be protected from severe frosts in winter. Its flower power is quite awesome. It mixes well in the perennial border and will flower repeatedly and reliably all summer.

How to care for it

Leave your 'Barnsley' untouched to go through the winter. Wait until after the buds break in spring to see what damage has been done by icy winds and frosts and then decide how much pruning you need to do. It can be pruned back hard, close to the ground, but often this is not necessary and by being less severe you end up with a much more substantial shrub in summer. There is also less risk of the plant reverting back to the pink flowers of one of its parents. Take out all dead stems to tidy up the plant in summer before the flowers appear. In fall, you can lightly trim back the ends of branches to make the plant less prone to wind damage.

After a few years, you will find the plant becomes very woody and it will eventually need to be replaced. Take cuttings after the first year or so and grow a few plants so they are ready in the wings when the old ones need to be replaced.

Good companions

There is no shortage of partners for lavatera. Lamb's ear (*Stachys byzantina*), *Lavandula angustifolia*, *Phlox paniculata*, red-hot pokers and the flowering tobacco plant (*Nicotiana*) all make excellent companions. Other possibilities include Russian sage (*Perovskia atriplicifolia*), catmint (*Nepeta*) and *Penstemon digitalis* 'Husker's Red'.

For your collection

🐾 There are a few other notable cultivars of *Lavatera thuringiaca*: 'Kew Rose' has deep pink flowers; 'Burgundy Wine' has purplish-red flowers; 'Ice Cool', which also goes under the name 'Peppermint Ice', has pure white flowers with attractive green centers; 'Bredon Springs' has rose-pink blooms with shallow-notched petals that give the flowers an unusual hexagonal shape; and 'Candy Floss' has bright pink flowers.

$\mathcal{L}$iatris spicata

Common name: *Gay feather, blazing star*

Chief characteristics

Location: Full sun to light
  shade
Type: Perennial
Size: 2 to 3 feet (60 to 90 cm)
Conditions: Ordinary, moist,
  well-drained soil
Flowering time: July to
  August

Many new gardeners are astonished to discover they can actually grow liatris in their own garden. They are so used to seeing the slender, pokerlike, pinkish-purple flower spikes in florist shops and exotic flower arrangements, it comes as a surprise to learn the plant will thrive very nicely in sunny, well-drained sites in the open garden. Native to North America, liatris grows naturally in moist meadows and on the edges of marshes in sunny, open areas. Liatris is a welcome sight in the late summer garden. It brings a fresh burst of color and provides exciting vertical architecture to the flagging perennial border or cutflower garden. The most popular form is *Liatris spicata*, which has 2- to 3-foot (60- to 90-cm) soft, spiky-leafed stems and pinkish-purple, bottlebrush flowers. There is a cultivar named 'Floristan Violet' but you will mostly find this plant labeled simply *Liatris spicata*.

Where to plant it

Everyone talks about how liatris is so drought tolerant, yet it really grows best in free-draining soil that is able to retain moisture while allowing the plant to enjoy a full-sun exposure. This can pose a challenge when it comes time to choosing an appropriate site. Liatris can easily be overwhelmed by more aggressive neighbors like shasta daisies, asters, daylilies and bee balm. So it is also important to plant it where it can be seen and enjoyed when it finally blooms in mid-July. It is an exceptional cut flower, if you can bear to leave the garden empty of its royal spikes.

How to care for it

Cold winters are no threat to *Liatris spicata*. It can endure temperatures several degrees below freezing. But it won't tolerate waterlogged soil. Good drainage is essential.

Once the flowers appear, you want them to be seen, so you may have to clear away the foliage of other perennials to give liatris its day. When flowers fade, cut the stems down for neatness.

The plant will disappear completely in winter, which can be a problem. It is easy to forget it was ever there and dig it up accidentally in the spring while finding slots for new perennials. Since it is also not a fast plant out of the ground in spring, it is best to mark its place in the garden at the end of summer. Clumps can be divided every few years.

Good companions

The spectacular blue spheres of globe thistle (*Echinops ritro*) and steel-blue flowers of sea holly (*Eryngium alpinum*) both come into flower around the same time as liatris in July and are even more drought tolerant. Other good partners for liatris include *Phlox paniculata* 'David' or 'Elizabeth Arden', *Crocosmia* 'Lucifer', black-eyed susans, *Kniphofia* 'Primrose Beauty' or 'Bressingham Comet', *Aster dumosus* 'Lady in Blue' or *A.* × *frikartii* 'Monch'.

For your collection

- ❧ A dwarf purple form of liatris, *Liatris spicata* 'Kobold', grows only 15 inches (38 cm) tall.
- ❧ There is a white form of liatris, *L. spicata* 'Floristan Weiss', which is now also easy to obtain and has been used very nicely to combine with ornamental grasses.

*L*igularia stenocephala 'The Rocket'

Common name: Ligularia

Chief characteristics

Ligularia is a magnificent plant with spectacular flowers. The challenge is to get it to maturity without having it chewed to pieces by slugs.

Location: Shade to semi-shade
Type: Perennial
Size: 4 to 6 feet (1.2 to 1.8 m)
Conditions: Good, moist soil
Flowering time: June to July

There are two first-rate species you should get: *Ligularia stenocephala* ('The Rocket') and *L. dentata* ('Desdemona' or 'Othello'). Your garden will be all the richer for them. 'The Rocket' has soaring yellow-gold flower spikes similar in shape to foxgloves or foxtail lilies while 'Othello' and 'Desdemona' have golden-yellow star-shaped flowers. All three have great foliage, but 'Desdemona' and 'Othello' are noted for their exceptional, big purple-black leaves. Both species are summer flowering. 'The Rocket' blooms slightly earlier than 'Desdemona' or 'Othello', which flower at the end of July and continue into August. Yellow can be a difficult color to place, but the warm golden-yellow flowers of 'The Rocket' are easy on the eye. They also bring architectural strength and height to the summer garden.

Where to plant it

Grow 'The Rocket' in the bog garden or at the back of the shade border in a spot where it has plenty of room to spread sideways. It also needs open space above so nothing interferes with its soaring yellow flower spires. It flourishes nicely in dappled shade beside a stream in a woodland setting. In bright shade it will look healthy and happy until the warm late-morning sun touches its large foot-wide leaves. Then it will slump and look wilty and miserable even if the ground is watered copiously. However, once the sun has slipped by and 'The Rocket' is again in the shade, it will perk up and resume its previous splendid form. The lesson in all of this is to locate 'The Rocket' in a shady spot where it gets light but not a lot of heat, and in soil that never dries out.

How to care for it

Slugs are the biggest problem with growing ligularia. They simply cannot resist its leaves, which have been described as "cheesecake for slugs." The young leaves of both kinds of ligularia need to be diligently inspected and protected from the moment they appear. Slugs are so intent on eating the tasty leaves, they will find a way over the sharpest and most threatening of obstacles. The only real defence is to patrol at night with a flashlight and a pair of sharp scissors.

Heavy rain can knock over the flower spikes of 'The Rocket', leaving them looking rather disheveled. Staking is not always necessary but not a bad idea if it can be done unobtrusively. A lot of the time the flowers get adequate support from the plant's own muscular, rough-cut leaves.

Good companions

The umbrella plant (*Peltiphyllum peltatum*) and *Rodgersia pinnata* are two robust companions for 'The Rocket'. Astilbes, ferns, hostas, primroses, lysimachia, astrantia and polygonum also all make content partners.

For your collection

- If you are interested in collecting big, bold plants, you might also like to check out ornamental rhubarb (*Rheum palmatum* 'Atrosanguineum'). In addition to having gigantic leaves, it also has bright crimson flower plumes.
- You will also want a plume poppy (*Macleaya cordata*), which has gray-green leaves and can jump up 7 feet (2.1 m). It produces white flowers.
- The grand-daddy of all bog plants is *Gunnera manicata*, which can drink a lake by itself. It is the perfect plant for setting on the edge of a sizable pond or the edge of a stream.

Geranium psilostemon: Masses of magenta
flowers in early summer, page 89.

Helictotrichon sempervirens: One of the
most striking blue ornamental grasses,
page 93–95.

***Hosta* 'Frances Williams':** Lovely variegated
leaves and good slug resistance, page 104–6.

Kniphofia 'Royal Castle Hybrids':
Unbeatable red-hot poker with
impressive two-tone flower stems,
page 112–13.

Lavandula angustifolia 'Lady': One of
the best tried-and-tested varieties of
lavender, page 114–15.

Muscari armeniacum: Clusters of deep blue appear like bunches of grapes, page 135–37.

***Lilium* 'Casa Blanca':** Giant, fragrant, pure white flowers in summer, page 121–22.

Rhododendron augustinii: Deep blue to lavender flowers in spring, page 172–74.

Robinia pseudoacacia 'Frisia': Graceful tree with bright, golden yellow leaves, page 175–76.

***Rosa* 'Ballerina':** Dainty shrub
rose noted for its free-flowering
habit, page 177–78.

Tulipa 'Queen of the Night': Black tulip looks dynamic in spring when combined with red or white tulips, page 176.

Verbena canadensis 'Homestead Purple': Drought-tolerant, reliable summer performer, page 193.

***Viburnum plicatum* 'Summer Snowflake':** Ideal for
a low-maintenance garden, page 205.

Lilium 'Casa Blanca'

Common name: Casa Blanca lily

Chief characteristics

There are almost as many types of lily as there are roses. It is an enormous family. If you get into a conversation with a lily expert, you are going to hear about American hybrids, Harlequin hybrids, Aurelian hybrids. It is perfectly understandable if you feel over-whelmed. The lily family is vast and full of exotic specimens, producing some of the most dazzling, fragrant, exotic and tropical-looking flowers in the summer garden.

Location: Full sun to light shade
Type: Bulb
Size: 4 feet (1.2 m)
Conditions: Good, deep, well-drained soil
Flowering time: June to September

Selection usually comes down to a matter of color and style. Height can also be a factor. Lilies can be tiny and delicate, or gigantic. Most of the popular ones range in size from 3 to 6 feet (90 to 180 cm). There are 3 main flower forms: trumpet-shaped, bowl-shaped (with petals curved slightly back) and turk's-cap (petals curved fully back on themselves). Colors range from orange to pink, from white to purple. Some lilies have 2-tone speckled flowers like the familiar tiger lily (*Lilium lancifolium*), which has orange petals with black spots. (It is also known as *L. tigrinum*.)

Increasingly popular are the Oriental hybrids, of which the pure white 'Casa Blanca' lily is one of the best. It is fragrant, grows 4 feet (120 cm) high, and is a very easy color to place in the garden. It is one of the show-stopping bloomers that gives the garden a much needed lift of color and scent in late summer.

Other outstanding cultivars include 'Stargazer' (fragrant, strawberry-pink throat with a creamy white edge), 'Mona Lisa', (fragrant pink flowers), 'Acapulco' (watermelon-red), 'Arena' (white with red and yellow markings) and 'Montreal' (white with yellow stripes). Asiatic hybrids, the first of the family to bloom, usually by the end of June, include 'Citronella' (yellow), 'Paprika' (red), 'Cote d'Azur' (pink) and 'Apollo' (white).

Trumpet lilies (Aurelians) are mid-summer bloomers with large flowers that can easily stretch to 8 inches (20 cm) long. One of the best is 'African Queen' (apricot-orange). Other quality performers include 'Pink Perfection', 'Golden Splendour' (pure yellow), and *Lilium regale* (wine-red buds becoming white).

Where to plant it

Grow lilies among perennials or alone in pots on the patio. They are
one of the plants that really should be used more to add color to the
mid-summer garden.

They will tolerate average soil, but always need good drainage. For
the best effect, plant in large groups in the middle or at the back of the
perennial border in full sun or light shade. Like clematis, lilies prefer
to have their heads in the sun and their roots in the shade. You will
keep your lilies happy if they are shielded at the base from the hot
afternoon sun.

How to care for it

Plant bulbs 6 to 9 inches (15 to 23 cm) deep. The rule of thumb is to
put them down to a depth 3 times the thickness of the bulb. Lilies are
not bothered by cold, wet winters, but they will rot in poorly drained
ground. However, they will also not do well if left without moisture in
fast-draining dry, sandy soil.

Taller plants need to be staked or they will flop over the moment the
flowers appear. They are really not as temperamental as all this sounds
and can be used to make a spectacular showing throughout the growing
season.

Good companions

Contrast is the name of the game with lilies. They can be planted to
provide striking color combinations with roses, hydrangeas, red-hot
pokers, peonies, and perennials such as late-flowering astilbes, white
gooseneck loosestrife (*Lysimachia clethroides*), *Echinacea purpurea*,
Monarda 'Marshall's Delight', 'Prairie' Night' or 'Gardenview Scarlet'. Use
lilies to inject color into those areas of the perennial border that need a
lift in mid-summer.

For your collection

- Lily connoisseurs delight in the reasonably hard-to-find Martagon
  hybrids because of their distinctive turk's cap flowers that are
  displayed in graceful, nodding clusters. Look for the pure white
  Lilium martagon album, which has escaped the family curse of rank
  odor and has a very pleasant smell.
- The Madonna lily (*Lilium candidum*) has very fragrant white flowers
  with yellow stamens in the center. It grows 4 or 5 feet (1.2 to 1.5 m)
  high and thrives in soil sweetened by wood ashes. You can also
  achieve a similar scent by growing *Hosta plantaginea*, which has
  fragrant white flowers in late summer.

❦ Calla lilies have the name "lily" but they are not lilies at all. Their botanical name is *Zantedeschia*. Native to South Africa, they thrive in full sun to light shade and grow 18 to 24 inches (45 to 60 cm). Names to look for include 'Flame' (red), 'Gem' (rosy-mauve) and 'Crystal Blush' (ivory).

*L*onicera japonica 'Halliana'

Common name: *Hall's honeysuckle*

Chief characteristics

Every English-style garden has honeysuckle. It is as important to the total garden picture as roses, clematis, shrubs or perennials. Without a freewheeling tangle of bright-flowered honeysuckle, a summer garden seems somehow incomplete. The vine not

Location: Sun or part shade
Type: Deciduous vine
Size: 15 feet (4.5 m)
Conditions: Ordinary, well-drained soil
Flowering time: June to August

only saturates the air with delectable perfume, it brings a relaxed balance to the stiffer, more formal structures of the garden. Honeysuckle is a reliable worker, vigorously smothering walls or fences, trellises and arbors with attractive soft green foliage. The heavily scented flowers, ranging from creamy white to reddish-purple to pale yellow, are a wonderful added bonus.

The most popular is *Lonicera japonica* 'Halliana', better known as Hall's honeysuckle. It is the best all-purpose honeysuckle, quickly scampering to 15 feet (4.5 m) high by 10 feet (3 m) wide and producing extremely fragrant white flowers that eventually turn a golden yellow. There are other species, such as the yellow-flowering *L.* × *tellmanniana* and red-flowering *L.* × *brownii*, that have excellent flower color, but no scent.

Other top forms of honeysuckle include the scarlet-trumpet honeysuckle (*Lonicera* × *brownii* 'Dropmore Scarlet'), which has rich red blooms; *L.* × *heckrottii* 'Goldflame', which has yellow-pink flowers; the purple-leafed Japanese honeysuckle (*L. japonica* 'Purpurea'), a semi-evergreen cultivar valued for its foliage rather than its purple-red flowers; and the late-blooming Dutch honeysuckle (*L. periclymenum* 'Serotina'), which produces blooms that are red-purple on the outside and pinkish yellow on the inside. Any of these attractive vines will do well in coastal gardens.

Where to plant it

Ideal for covering fences, trellises, arbors and arches, honeysuckle can also be used to cover banks and as a groundcover. Plant vines in spring to early summer. Honeysuckle needs 6 hours of sun but, like clematis, they also prefer to have shaded roots. The sugary scent of honeysuckle can travel on the night air right across the garden, so there is no need to have the vine situated directly under windows or next to doorways.

How to care for it

Young shoots of a new plant need support to get started up a trellis or fence. You can use canes or wires or sturdy black thread. Prune severely in spring and lightly in summer to keep it in bounds. Left unpruned, honeysuckle will suffer dieback in the center because of the lack of air flow and light. Aphids can be a problem, particularly in hot, dry summers. Use a strong jet of water to knock them off or bring in some ladybugs. Frequent visits by hummingbirds are a major compensation.

Good companions

Early flowering clematis, *Clematis alpina* 'Jacqueline du Pre' or 'Pamela Jackman', or *C. macropetala* 'Bluebird', can be encouraged to intermingle with honeysuckle and put on an early spring flowering, leading into the honeysuckle's summer performance. To provide shade for roots, you could use *Geranium macrorrhizum* or *Corydalis lutea* as a groundcover.

For your collection

There are many types of honeysuckles worth trying.

- *Lonicera pericylmenum* 'Graham Thomas'—another late-blooming Dutch honeysuckle—has yellow blooms and a spicy fragrance.
- The creamy white flowers of the winter honeysuckle (*L. fragrantissima*) have been known to bloom at the same time as the heavily scented evergreen shrub *Daphne odora*, creating a memorable combination.
- The Chinese honeysuckle (*L. tragophylla*) is also highly regarded as one of the most outstanding, producing extra large golden-yellow flowers in June and July.

*L*upinus Russell hybrids

Common name: Russell lupins

Chief characteristics

There was a time when lupins were regarded as coarse, wild flowers, not suitable for the civilized flower garden. That changed with George Russell, a patient Yorkshire gardener who earlier this century took time to grow all kinds of wild lupins, allowing them to freely mix and mingle. That experiment resulted in a whole new generation of exciting hybrids. Today, many gardeners consider lupins indispensable to their planting scheme.

Location: Sun or semi-shade
Type: Perennial
Size: 3 feet (90 cm)
Conditions: Moist, well-drained, neutral soil
Flowering time: June to July

Lupins do a similar job to delphiniums and foxgloves. They add height, color and attractive architectural form to the perennial border. Planted in large, sweeping drifts, they are particularly outstanding. Their tall, distinctive, tapering spikes of tightly clustered flowers have a classical, good-humored elegance that makes them the very model of a well-behaved border plant. The range of colors extends from rose, pink and red to white, yellow and assorted vibrant bicolors. The Russell hybrids are still among the best and most reliable. Top hybrids include 'Mrs. Micklethwaite' (named after the woman whose garden George Russell tended), 'Elsie Waters', 'La Chatelaine', 'Magnificence', 'My Castle' and 'Limelight'.

Where to plant it

Grow lupins in neutral to slightly acidic, well-drained, sandy soil in clumps at the front or the middle of the perennial border or in dense sweeping drifts.

How to care for it

Short lived, lupins last no longer than a couple of seasons. To ensure you always have a few in the garden it is usually necessary to grow standby plants from seed or get into the habit of picking up new plants every spring.

Slugs and snails can be a nuisance, so you need to watch for them, especially when the plants are emerging in spring. Mildew can also be a problem, especially in hot, humid summers. You can minimize it by not allowing the soil to dry out and by thinning the foliage to improve air circulation.

Cut off the flower stems before the seed pods develop and you can often stimulate a second flush of blooms later in the summer.

Good companions

A generous clump of lupins can share ground with poppies and phlox, penstemon and campanulas. They mix well with the blue flowers of baptista and contrast warmly against the blue-green foliage of *Euphorbia characias* or behind the silver leaves of lamb's ears.

For your collection

🦋 The lupin is native to the coast, so you may want to find room for our own indigenous species, *Lupinus polyphyllus*, which was one of the plants George Russell (and other top hybridizers) used to raise some of his best modern hybrids. This lupin has deep blue to reddish-purple flowers and can grow as high as 5 feet (1.5 m).

🦋 The tree lupin (*Lupinus arboreus*) is a short-lived semi-evergreen shrub that grows between 5 and 7 feet (1.5 to 2.1 m) high and produces fragrant primrose-yellow blooms from July to October.

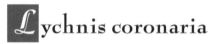 ychnis coronaria

Common name: Rose campion, catchfly

Chief characteristics

New gardeners always fall in love with *Lychnis coronaria* when they see it for the first time. What they like best are the lovely rose-magenta or white flowers, displayed in loose sprays at the ends of slender pale gray stems. The word *Lychnis* is derived from the Greek *lychnos*, which means lamp and refers to the brightness of the flowers. The plant is now as common in many gardens as foxgloves and roses. In a mass planting scheme, lychnis's silver-gray foliage provides a pleasing canvas of color on which to exhibit the red flowers. A relative of the carnations (*Dianthus*), the best known campion is the Maltese cross or cross of Jerusalem (*Lychnis chalcedonica*), which has dazzling scarlet flowers. But *L. coronaria*, especially the white version, 'Alba', is now seen more often in private gardens.

Location: Full sun or light shade

Type: Perennial

Size: 2 feet (60 cm)

Conditions: Ordinary or poor soil

Flowering time: June to August

Where to plant it

The dainty red-magenta flowers of *Lychnis coronaria* catch the eye wherever they appear. The plant looks best tucked behind other things in the perennial border, such as short forms of achillea, blue centaurea or lavender, or popping up from behind a low boxwood hedge or dotted among the green foliage of still-developing perennials.

How to care for it

Lychnis needs to be regularly deadheaded in order to keep it blooming. It grows best in full sun and prefers ordinary, or even poor soil, as long as it is well drained. It will also flourish reasonably well in light shade. It is easy to propagate from seed. Not a long-lived plant, it often self-sows and succeeds in propagating itself around the garden. If you don't want it to self-sow, you need to snip off the dead flowerheads before they turn to seed. Cut the stems down once flowering has finished.

Good companions

The vivid blue spikes of *Salvia farinacea* or *Nepeta* 'Dropmore Blue' offer an interesting contrast to lychnis's small red-magenta flowers. The blooms also look striking set against the burgundy-plum–colored leaves of a smoke bush (*Cotinus coggygria*) or mingled with the feathery silver foliage of *Artemisia ludoviciana* 'Valerie Finnis' or 'Silver King'. It can also be harmonized with penstemons and shrub roses.

For your collection

- *Lychnis × arkwrightii* 'Vesuvius' has red-orange flowers, grows 18 inches (45 cm) tall and is a good cut flower.
- Jove's flower (*Lychnis flos-jovis*) has small clusters of purple or red flowers. It grows 24 inches (60 cm) high, quickly naturalizes and combines well with mock orange and hydrangeas.
- The arctic campion (*Lychnis alpina*) is ideal for the spring rockery, growing only 6 inches (15 cm) high and producing tufts of green leaves and pink flowers from May to June.

$\mathcal{L}$ ysimachia clethroides

Common name: *Gooseneck loosestrife, Chinese loosestrife*

Chief characteristics

Location: Sun or part shade
Type: Perennial
Size: 3 feet (90 cm)
Conditions: Ordinary, moist soil
Flowering time: July to August

A superb cut flower, *Lysimachia clethroides* is admired for its distinctive white blooms which resemble the head and neck of a goose. A substantial clump in the summer garden can be quite dramatic, especially when there is a slight breeze that causes the shapely goosenecks to nod gently in unison in the same direction. The spectacle is enchanting.

Lysimachia clethroides should not be confused with purple loosestrife (*Lythrum*), which is a terrible imported weed that has taken over many of our lake and marsh areas. The cheerful gooseneck loosestrife does, however, have one downside. It is an incorrigible colonizer. But it can also be restrained in the most basic way—dig the clump back into bounds the same way you do with a rampant clump of mint when it starts to get out of hand. Gooseneck loosestrife first appears in spring as tiny red shoots in the ground. It quickly jumps up 2 or 3 feet (60 to 90 cm) to form a lush patch of leaves. The white flowers, which are actually composed of hundreds of smaller star-shaped flowers with black centers, appear from early July to the end of September. A native of China and Japan, *L. clethroides* found its way to Europe many years ago and has now become a part of the natural landscape.

Where to plant it

Grow *Lysimachia clethroides* in fertile, moist garden soil in full or partial shade. It has even been used in water gardens but it probably prefers being on the banks of a stream, pond or brook.

How to care for it

It will reward you if you dig in lots of compost when you plant it. Divide clumps every 3 or 4 years or whenever you feel your loosestrife is getting carried away with itself. The flowers can be cut any time. They do look exquisite indoors mixed with hosta leaves, liatris, summer phlox, roses and daylilies. In the fall, the leaves will die back and you will know it is time to clean up. But what a fun party it was.

Good companions

Whatever plants you pick to mix with *Lysimachia clethroides* will need to have height and solid form if they are going to hold their own. The lovely white flowering *Campanula latifolia* 'Alba' will blend nicely, flower earlier while the lysimachia is still developing and disappear before the gooseneck flowers appear. This gives you continuity of color. Blue bellflower (*Campanula persicifolia*), *Helleborus corsicus* and peonies will do the same. For direct contrast, use the blue flowers of aconitum or yellow blooms of rudbeckia or pink flowers of *Lavatera thuringiaca* 'Bredon Springs' or 'Kew Rose'. The solid form of *Sedum spectabile* 'Brilliant' or *Sedum* 'Autumn Joy' can be used to provide structure and also as a cover for the uninteresting lower part of lysimachia's flower stems.

For your collection

- *Lysimachia punctata* is a bushy plant that produces masses of yellow flowers from June to August and grows about 2 feet (60 cm) high. It also likes moist soil and is an excellent choice for growing in sunny spots at the side of a pond or stream, although it will also perform perfectly well in light shade.
- Moneywort or creeping jenny (*Lysimachia nummularia*) is a trailing, groundcovering plant that can also be used in window boxes and hanging baskets. It is also natural cover for moist, light shade areas.

Magnolia × soulangiana

Common name: Saucer magnolia

Chief characteristics

English garden guru Christopher Lloyd called magnolias "the most glamorous and effective of all shrubs or trees." He added: "There is room for at least one specimen in every garden." There is no arguing with that. Magnolias have long been regarded by garden authorities everywhere as classy, aristocratic plants with exquisite flowers and handsome foliage. There is a record of magnolias being grown extensively in gardens as early as 650 A.D. when Buddhist monks planted *Magnolia denudata*, with its striking white flowers, at temples to symbolize purity.

There are many popular magnolias. We all have our favorite. The

Location: Sun or light shade
Type: Deciduous tree or shrub
Size: 15 to 25 feet (4.5 to 7.5 m)
Conditions: Ordinary, well-drained soil
Flowering time: May to June

saucer magnolia (*M.* × *soulangiana*) is one of the most reliable. It flowers for 4 weeks in late spring with creamy white, goblet-shaped blooms, flushed with purplish-pink. It can be grown as a bush in the mixed border or as a stand-alone tree. The foliage, which is a lush and pleasant green, comes after the flowers. It is sometimes wrongly called a "tulip tree" because of the shape and color of the flowers. Popular names include 'Alexandrina', 'Lennei', 'San Jose' and 'Rustica Rubra'.

Where to plant it

Magnolia × *soulangiana* grows happily in moisture-retentive, well-drained soil, where it can enjoy full sun in the mornings and semi-shade after lunch. Once established, magnolias can be difficult to relocate, so it is important to take your time picking the right spot. The flowers of *M.* × *soulangiana* are beautiful against the dark background of a yew or cedar hedge. They last longer if given some protection from wind and driving rains. *M.* × *soulangiana* can be worked into a mixed border or planted as a special feature in a formal lawn.

How to care for it

Grow magnolias in fast-draining soil and water well in the summer. They also like to be fed well, so add enriching organic material— fertilizer or well-rotted compost—to the soil every spring but be sure not to disturb the magnolia's roots. Heavy pruning is discouraged because magnolias bleed and have a problem bouncing back, but light pruning can be done after flowering in mid-summer.

Good companions

Underplant magnolias with blue-flowering ajuga or hardy geraniums. In the mixed border, they will harmonize with rhododendrons and evergreen azaleas, photinias and pieris.

For your collection

- The star magnolia (*Magnolia stellata*): It has a profusion of pure white, multi-petaled flowers in early spring. A small tree, it grows 10 feet (3 m) and is a good choice for gardens where space is limited.
- *Magnolia sieboldii*: Loved by plant connoisseurs because of its classy pure white, fragrant, cup-shaped blooms, it also has delicately colored green leaves. You can grow it as a tree or a shrub but since it has a spread of 15 feet (4.5 m) high and wide, you need a fair amount of space in your garden to accommodate it properly. The fragrance of the flowers has been described as like a flavorsome bouquet of pineapple-orange lilies.

- The giant southern magnolia (*M. grandiflora*): A broadleaf evergreen tree, this can ultimately reach 50 feet (15 m) tall and spread 15 feet (4.5 m) wide. It is noted for its exceptional, lemon-scented blooms which are the size of a breakfast bowl. They sporadically appear throughout summer. It is one of the few magnolias to survive the ice age in North America; none survived in Europe. Good cultivars include 'Saint Mary', 'Edith Bogue', Majestic Beauty' and 'Victoria'. There is a dwarf form, 'Little Gem', probably more suitable for the medium-sized garden. It is very compact and grows to about 25 feet (7.5 m) high. It is also rather tender, so it needs to be planted in a warm, protected spot.
- For something completely different, consider *M. hypoleuca*, which has massive 16-inch (40-cm) long leaves and short-lived, creamy white flowers with a distinct fruity scent in summer.
- Other magnolias with bright white starlike flowers include the Kobus magnolia (*M. kobus*), which produces slightly more substantial flowers, although they have been described as "dirty white" compared to the clear white blooms of the more familiar *M. stellata* and the graceful anise magnolia (*M. salicifolia*). The cultivar 'Wada's Memory' also has a very high rating for the whiteness and abundance of its blooms.

*M*iscanthus sinensis 'Gracillimus'

Common name: Maiden grass

Chief characteristics

Location: Full sun to light shade
Type: Ornamental grass
Size: 4 to 6 feet (1.2 to 1.8 m)
Conditions: Good, moist soil
Flowering time: August to September

Miscanthus is not an ornamental grass to trifle with. It can be big and bold and dramatic and you need to find the right spot for it to look its best. In the right place, this very expressive grass will make a powerful architectural statement. One of the tidiest and most versatile forms is *Miscanthus sinensis* 'Gracillimus', also known as maiden grass. It can be easily accommodated in a medium-sized garden and will quickly proceed to form a magnificent cascading clump of thin, straplike blades. The dwarf form, 'Yaku Jima', grows only 3 or 4 feet (90 to 120 cm) and has silvery plumes in late summer. This is a good choice for gardens where space is limited.

Other top cultivars of *Miscanthus sinensis* include the novel 'Zebrinus' (zebra grass), which has bright green leaves with golden, horizontal zebralike stripes; 'Silver Feather' (silver feather grass), which has tall, white plumes, very much like pampas grass; and 'Variegatus' (Japanese silver grass), which forms a striking fountain of silver-green cascading leaves. All these are worth experimenting with, although you will probably only want one.

Where to plant it

'Gracillimus' is best used to give the garden a special accent or focal point. It can punctuate the flow in a perennial border. Or it can be placed at measured intervals to create a recurring theme. It would also be useful for screening less attractive corners of the garden. The idea of incorporating ornamental grasses into your planting scheme is primarily to provide visual and textural relief. Grasses bring movement as they sway in the breeze. They can also refract sunlight in ways that add unexpected dimensions to the overall look and atmosphere of the garden.

How to care for it

Maiden grass can grow over 6 feet tall (1.8 m) but it is quite capable of standing without support. Grow it in full sun or semi-shade in moist soil and it will flourish. Leave it untouched at the end of summer and allow it to go into winter, by which time many of the cascading blades will be the color of straw. After a heavy frost or light snowfall, it will look astonishingly ethereal with a pale, ghostly beauty.

Good companions

Maiden grass combines well with kniphofias like 'Primrose Beauty', 'Little Maid', 'Bee's Lemon' and 'Bressingham Torch'. Shorter red asters like 'Royal Ruby' and 'Winston Churchill' or the lavender blue *Aster × frikartii* 'Monch' can be planted in front of the taller grass for color accents. The bold, swordlike leaves of *Crocosmia* 'Lucifer' make an exciting foliage contrast and the bright red flowers add an engaging theatrical touch. Also, consider using big-leafed hostas like 'Sum and Substance' or vase-shaped forms like 'Krossa Regal', again for textural tension and focal interest.

For color, red canna lilies or yellow rudbeckia make interesting partners. For more subtle colors, try the blues of *Iris sibirica* 'Caesar's Brother' or the purples of liatris or the gentle hues of late-flowering Japanese anemones like 'September Charm', 'Honorine Jobert' or 'Prince Henry'.

For your collection

🦞 Other excellent cultivars of *Miscanthus sinensis* include 'Strictus' (porcupine grass); 'Silberpfeil' (silver arrow miscanthus); 'Morning Light' (variegated maiden grass), which has silvery plumes in October; and 'Variegatus', which has distinctive green-and-white-striped, arching foliage.

🦞 The giant Chinese silver grass (*Miscanthus floridulus*) produces a massive towering fountain of leaves that can form a very effective screen or large grassy hedge if mass planted. If you have acreage, this is an awesome plant to have.

🦞 A particularly striking grass to try in a pot is *Hakonechloa macra* 'Aureola'. It is slow growing, with two-tone green-yellow leaves that turn reddish-brown in fall.

Monarda 'Gardenview Scarlet'

Common name: Bee balm, bergamot

Chief characteristics

The flowers of monarda—bright red, candy pink or purplish-blue—are extraordinary works of art. They are displayed, very confidently, at the top of sturdy, 3- or 4-foot (90- to 120-cm) stems. The plant's leaves are mildly aromatic when rubbed and have been used for generations in potpourris. But the main reason you should grow monarda is for the flowers that add much color and verve to the garden in July and August. A mature clump of monarda looks fantastic, especially contrasted with other spectacular summer-flowering perennials such as shasta daisies or phlox or lavatera or blue globe thistles. The flower clusters of bee balm first begin to appear in early to mid-July. They continue blooming into September. Each bloom is a masterpiece of creative design. Each flower is formed by more than a dozen smaller, open-throated, tubular flowers that look rather like snapping (or singing) crocodiles. These individual flowers form a cluster and explode in a fountain of color from a central crown that has small, downward-pointed leaves forming a decorative collar.

There are several fine cultivars available but *Monarda* 'Gardenview Scarlet' is an old tried-and-tested favorite with bright scarlet-red flowers.

Location: Full to part sun
Type: Perennial
Size: 3 to 4 feet (90 to 120 cm)
Conditions: Good, moist, well-drained soil
Flowering time: July to September

There is a similar form called 'Cambridge Scarlet', also an established favorite, but 'Gardenview Scarlet' is considered the superior performer. Two other top cultivars are 'Marshall's Delight', a Canadian hybrid with handsome candy pink flowers, and 'Prairie Night', which has dark purple flowers.

All the blooms make fine cut flowers and look rather exotic and tropical when combined with liatris, echinops and ligularia. Put the four together in a vase and you have brilliant red (bee balm), lilac-purple (*Liatris spicata*), steel blue (*Echinops ritro*) and golden yellow (*Ligularia stenocephala*). It may sound like a jarring clash of colors, but each flower has the strength to maintain its own presence and individuality without detracting from that of the others, in a remarkable example of harmony and diversity.

Where to plant it

Grow monarda in large clumps in good, moist, well-drained soil, in full or part sun along with other sun-loving mid- to late summer–flowering perennials. It will flourish very happily in full sun next to a stream or on the edge of a bog garden.

Since the flower stems themselves are not immensely attractive, it is best to plant bee balm in the middle of the border. As they are not tall enough to go right at the back, and are far too tall for the front, the middle of the border is the ideal location. This also allows you to grow shorter perennials or shrubs in front to hide bee balm's spindly stems.

As its name suggests, bee balm attracts bees. It also will catch the eye of butterflies and hummingbirds. Herbalists used the leaves of the plant to treat sore throats and bronchitis and to make a soothing tea. Bergamot is what gives Earl Grey tea its distinctive smell.

How to care for it

Don't let your monarda go without water, especially in the hot days of summer. Make sure you mulch around the plants in spring as a moisture-conserving device and water copiously during dry spells. Bee balm is also notorious for gobbling up all the nutrients in the soil. The solution is to remember to mulch with well-rotted compost or manure in spring and again in late fall as a way of enriching the soil. Monarda is a good plant for reminding us that soil needs to be repeatedly amended and nourished with new organic material. So the plant's greedy feeding habit can actually work for the good of all the other plants in the flower bed if it gets us into a routine of regular soil amendment.

Like *Phlox paniculata* and delphiniums, monarda can be prone to mildew in late summer after a spell of hot weather. The problem is made much worse if the plants are not watered adequately at soil level and if there is poor air circulation. You can also spray with a fungicide but you may find mildew will only be a minor problem if you water carefully and plentifully and if you take a little time to thin out clumps to allow greater air flow. Cut down stems at the end of the season. Clumps can be easily divided every few years.

Good companions

In full bloom in July and August, monarda combines well with delphiniums, echinops and eryngium, echinacea, daylilies, crocosmia and shasta daisies, all of which like similar conditions—lots of sun and soil that is well drained without drying out completely. The red flowers of 'Gardenview Scarlet' can be heightened by combining them with the blues of *Salvia farinacea*, *Nepeta* 'Six Hills Giant', *Scabiosa columbaria* 'Butterfly Blue' or *Aster dumosus* 'Lady-in-Blue'. The bright yellows of rudbeckia would be too harsh but the soft pale yellow of *Coreopsis verticillata* 'Moonbeam' would work. For a safe and successful partnership, plant bee balm with silvery artemisias like 'Powis Castle' or 'Valerie Finnis'.

For your collection

Other very good monarda cultivars for your collection include 'Snow White' (creamy white flowers), 'Violet Queen' (purple-blue flowers), 'Mahogany' (purple-brown), 'Kardinal' (bright red), 'Blue Stocking' (purple-blue) and 'Adam' (bright red).

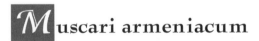 uscari armeniacum

Common name: Grape hyacinth

Chief characteristics

After winter, we crave color in the garden. Snowdrops, the traditional harbingers of spring, are a welcome sight. But few early spring–flowering bulbs are as long lasting or as useful throughout the garden as the simple grape hyacinth. Its lack of complexity and pretension makes it all the more likeable. It is without doubt a true garden classic with a subtle sophistication many of the showier stars of the garden somehow lack.

Location: Full sun
Type: Spring-flowering bulb
Size: 6 to 8 inches (15 to 20 cm)
Conditions: Moist but well-drained soil
Flowering time: March to April

Muscari gets its common name, grape hyacinth, because its tiny blue flowers are tightly gathered in grapelike clusters at the top of the short 6-inch (15-cm) stems. The faintly fragrant flowers last a long time. They can usually be found in the garden from early March through to the middle of May.

Native to southeast Europe and western Asia where it flourishes on grassy hillsides, muscari naturalizes effortlessly when scattered throughout the garden under trees and shrubs and in clumps intermingled in the perennial border. It does particularly well in rockeries, probably because of the sunshine and good drainage. A member of the lily family, muscari is indifferent to frost, being able to cope with temperatures several degrees below freezing.

Where to plant it

Where not to plant grape hyacinths? There's the question. They fit in every corner of the garden and are especially useful for providing color while other perennials are waking up from winter.

Grow muscari in full sun or light shade in average, well-drained soil. The bulbs should be planted to a depth of 3 times their height—3 to 4 inches (7.5 to 10 cm)—any time from September to October. They are not expensive, so plant lots of them and watch them multiply as the years go by. You can also grow muscari in pots. They are impressive mass-planted in a simple terracotta pot or shallow dish. Bring the pot into a warm room in the middle of winter and you can have a colorful show in January or February to whet your appetite for the coming season.

How to care for it

Muscari is a reasonably rapid self-propagator. Thick clumps should be divided every few years and replanted immediately. When the flowers fade and the straplike leaves turn yellow, mow or shear them to the ground. They will bounce back as good as new the following spring.

Good companions

Violas and primulas combine well with muscari, which are usually up and out of the ground long before most perennials have begun to stir. This is really one of their great attributes. While hostas and astilbes, bleeding hearts and daylilies are slow risers, grape hyacinths can cover the ground with their rich green leaves and brighten the earth with their vivid blue flowers. They should be mixed with other spring-flowering bulbs like *Iris reticulata*, snowflakes (*Leucojum vernum*), bluebells (*Scilla non-scripta*) and the yellow flowers of the trout lily (*Erythronium*

'Pagoda'), all of which flower around the same time. An excellent combination involves marrying up the pale blues of *Puschkinia scilloides* with chionodoxa and muscari.

For your collection

🐾 The white-flowering *Muscari azureum* 'Album' or *Muscari botryoides* 'Album' provide a nice change of pace to the popular deep blue 'Blue Spike'. You can also buy a 'Sky Blue' cultivar.

icotiana alata

Common name: Tobacco plant

Chief characteristics

When you first discover this remarkable plant (and there has to be a first time, even though it has been in gardens for generations) you are bound to be impressed by its perpetual and reliable flowering habit

Location: Full sun to part shade
Type: Annual
Size: 2 feet (60 cm)
Conditions: Good, well-drained soil
Flowering time: June to September

and the exceptional fragrance of its blooms at twilight. The trumpet-shaped flowers not only come in great colors—warm reds, clear whites and a classy lime-green—they also have the knack of attracting hummingbirds. Native to South America, *Nicotiana alata* is also structurally impressive. The taller forms may need staking, but the more popular, shorter hybrids are perfectly able to stand upright without support in a border or flower pot. That is a quality much appreciated by gardeners who like plants that behave themselves and do not interfere too much with their neighbors.

Outstanding cultivars to seek out include 'Havana Appleblossom', the bushy 'Nikki' series and the dwarf 'Starship', 'Domino' and 'Merlin' series, ideal for using in tubs, pots and window boxes. When you start to garden, it is satisfying (and necessary) to have some undisputed successes. Nicotiana lets you express a certain amount of creativity and also put on a great show of color on your patio or deck. When gaps appear in the perennial border, the sweetly scented tobacco plant is the plant you can rely on to restore harmony without losing respect.

Where to plant it

You will see "nicki" mass-planted in city parks. That might put you off doing the same in your own garden, but it can be great fun to "paint" with it. There are tasteful white and lime-green forms, and a solid clump of red nicki can be exceptionally vibrant and eye catching. Use nicotiana in pots on your deck or patio where the sweet scent can be enjoyed when you sit out with friends on a summer's evening.

How to care for it

Nicotiana grows best in rich, well-drained soil in a sunny location. Deadheading the spent flowers will encourage plants to keep on blooming. Leaves are slightly sticky with sap, so this is best done with a pair of scissors. Watch out for aphids. Nicotiana produces tiny brown seeds in tiny baked pods at the end of summer. Collect the seeds in an envelope. They germinate very easily indoors in February and will provide you with a massive crop of new plants for the next season.

Good companions

Nicotiana has many and varied uses. Use it in combination with any other annuals in tubs and pots. You could trim a pot, for example, with lobelia or alyssum, verbena and dusty miller (*Cineraria maritima*) for a touch of soft gray. The best companions for nicotiana in the open garden are plain, green-leafed perennials like lady's mantle (*Alchemilla mollis*) or hardy geraniums or a backdrop of peony foliage. For color contrasts, try white *Cosmos bipinnatus* 'Sonata', or the orange-yellow flowers of California poppies (*Eschscholzia californica*) or the purple, fragrant flowers of *Heliotropium peruvianum*.

For your collection

- If you fancy trying your hand at growing the true tobacco plant you need to pick up *Nicotiana tabacum*. It will grow 5 feet (1.5 m) tall with a strong stem, large leaves and rose-pink flowers at the top. Quite a talking point for your next garden party.
- Better bets are *Nicotiana sylvestris*, which is also somewhat towering, but has exceptionally perfumed white trumpet-shaped flowers, or *N. langsdorffii*, which produces apple-green flowers and is a particular favorite of floral artists. Both of these are praised to the hilt by plant connoisseurs, but weekend gardeners are not so easily impressed. These more obscure nicotiana are an acquired taste.

*N*ymphaea pygmaea 'Helvola'

Common name: Yellow water lily

Chief characteristics

There is always room in a garden, no matter how small, for a water feature and a few water plants. It doesn't matter if you live in an apartment with a short balcony or a townhouse with a tiny patio, you can still have at least a ceramic pot or half-barrel with a few well-chosen water plants and a small fountain or bubbler. The look and sound of a water feature is immensely relaxing. Water features are easy to install, take no time at all to maintain, and can make a world of difference to the atmosphere of your outdoor living space.

Location: Full sun to light shade
Type: Water plant
Size: 3-foot spread (90 cm)
Conditions: Water
Flowering time: June to July

If you have plenty of room, consider installing a simple rectangular trough or a small oval-shaped pond. Forget fish. Keeping fish means you have to worry about raccoons and herons and filtration systems. No, what we are thinking about here is a small water garden containing a few plants and a pump to create a gentle little fountain or the sound of water trickling or spouting. You don't need a lot of plants, but you should probably start with a water lily. They are, after all, the quintessential pond plant. They also need 5 or 6 hours of sun to bloom properly, though the flat, floating lily pad has charm with or without flowers.

Water lilies are not cheap. There are thousands from which to chose. There are tropical and hardy water lilies, so you need to be sure which kind you are buying. One will overwinter, the other won't. Water lilies can be separated into 3 basic sizes: large, medium and small. For a tub or trough or small pond, look at the miniature plants which spread only a few feet and don't require deep water.

An outstanding all-round specimen for formal or informal ponds and water features in average-sized gardens is *Nymphaea pygmaea* 'Helvola'. This has compact 2-inch (5-cm) canary-yellow flowers. It is regarded as a miniature but it looks perfectly at home in the small pond and is the ideal size to create a cluster without covering the entire water surface. The added bonus of 'Helvola' is that unlike most water lilies it is reasonably tolerant of shade and will still flower beautifully even if it doesn't get at least 6 hours of sun a day. 'Alba' is another dwarfish form that has white flowers.

You will also need some oxygenators—plants that float on the surface or sink under the water and help to keep the water clean. The water violet (*Hottonia paulstris*) is an excellent oxygenator. It has pale lilac flowers and bright green feathery leaves. Other easy-to-find oxygenators include hornwort (*Ceratophyllum demersum*), parrot's feather (*Myriophyllum aquaticum*) and Canadian pondweed (*Elodea canadensis*).

Where to plant it

Grow your lilies in a small pond or rectangular pool or even in a 3-foot (90-cm) square planter box or large ceramic pot with black plastic liner to make it water tight. Water lilies are not the least expensive of plants. You might be surprised how much one costs. So, it is important to think about the color you want when you go to buy one. The more water surface you have the bigger the lily you can place. In a small pond you probably don't need more than a couple. In a tub or barrel, you definitely need only one.

How to care for it

Water lilies are heavy feeders. They need to be well fertilized before being plonked into the water. The way to do this without polluting the water is to use heavy clay to sandwich slow-release fertilizer in the soil in the pot. You can also get water lily food in powdered tablets or sachets. The same technique can be used for other plants that will be standing in the water all the time. Dead and decaying leaves should be removed to prevent any buildup of rotting vegetation in the water.

The oxygenators will do a great job of keeping the water clean and free of algae but you should also change the water in small tubs and troughs regularly. Water pumped into the air through a fountain or a spouting ornament will also add oxygen to the water, which is a way to keep it fresh and clear.

Good companions

Other great pond plants include pickerel weed (*Pontederia*), which has blue flower spikes, and marsh marigold (*Caltha*). Both of these make excellent companions for water lilies and irises. There are many moisture-loving perennials such as astilbes and hostas, *Iris ensata*, polygonum, rodgersia and ligularia. They can all be grown in the moist soil at the edge of a pond.

For your collection

🐌 Other top performers to look for include: 'Indiana' (orange-red), fragrant 'Chromatella' (creamy yellow), 'Rose Arey' (fragrant rose), 'Albida' (white with pale-pink petals), 'Attraction' (garnet-red) and

'Madame Wilfron Gonnere' (large pink blooms). You will find dozens more. If you have a large pond, the sky's the limit.

🐾 If you really fall in love with water gardening, you will want more and more water lilies. The flowers can be exquisite. There are people who have collected hundreds of cultivars because they find the flowers so exotic and tropical-looking. Once you reach this stage, 'Gladstoniana', 'Charles de Meurville', 'Bob Trickett', Conqueror', 'Colonel A.J. Welch' and 'Richardsonii' will be names you want for your pond.

🐾 For those looking simply to expand their range of water plants, zebra rush (*Scirpus* 'Zebrinus') or cattail (*Typha minima*) are two interesting additions.

🐾 Irises are another excellent pick for your small pond because of their bold, upright, broad swordlike leaves. The yellow flag iris, *Iris pseudacorus*, is very popular, producing a bright yellow flower at the top of a stem that can reach 4 or 5 feet (1.2 to 1.5 m) high. A more manageable option is the blue flag iris, *Iris versicolor*, which grows only 3 feet (90 cm) high. The variegated iris, *Iris laevigata* 'Variegata', is another good choice.

🐾 Sweet flag (*Acorus*) is another attractive pond plant. Look for *A. calamus* or the two-tone cultivar, *A. calamus* 'Variegatus'.

🐾 Water hyacinths (*Eichhornia crassipes*) make an excellent floating plant with thick succulent-like leaves, while arrowheads (*Sagittaria*) and umbrella sedges (*Cyperus*) can also be added for heightened interest.

Ophiopogon planiscapus 'Nigrescens'

Common name: Black mondo grass, black lilyturf, black spider grass

Chief characteristics

Black is a fun color to play with in the garden. It adds a sense of drama, novelty and curiosity, and it allows you to show the dark side of your imagination. There is really no true black in nature. What appears black to our eyes is actually the deepest shade of purple. But why spoil the fun? If it looks black, let's call it black.

Location: Part shade
Type: Ornamental grass
Size: 6 to 8 inches (15 to 20 cm)
Conditions: Fertile, moist soil
Flowering time: July to August

One of the best black plants is black mondo grass (*Ophiopogon planiscapus* 'Nigrescens'). Its botanical name, *Ophiopogon*, roughly translated means "snake beard." Originating in Japan, it produces a spidery clump of thin, jet black, straplike leaves. In late summer, it has tiny mauve flowers, which are soon followed by minute, rather insignificant black berries that last most of winter. The leaves are actually evergreen (everblack?) and keep their color all winter.

Mondo grass is especially useful for creating bold contrasts. For shockingly effective results marry it up with the yellow leaves of creeping jenny (*Lysimachia nummularia*) or the silver foliage of *Lamium maculatum*, or allow it to creep up through white fairy thimble bellflowers (*Campanula cochleariifolia*). The grass is often planted under birch trees to contrast against the white bark. My son has made use of it in his black-and-purple garden along with purple ajuga, black hollyhocks, purple sage, black daylily, purple liatris, black pansies (*Viola cornuta* 'Black Magic') and purple-black–leafed *Euphorbia dulcis* 'Chameleon'. You can have even more fun with black mondo grass by using it to give "hair" to a Greek-styled terracotta wall sconce.

You also might also like to experiment with *Liriope muscari*, another compact, grasslike perennial with blackish tones. It has dark, grassy leaves and short, spiky, violet flowers.

Where to plant it

Grow black mondo grass in moist, well-drained soil in partial shade, although it will tolerate full sun if kept reasonably well watered. It is best used as an accent plant. It may look like a useful groundcover but it doesn't spread rapidly enough to provide extensive cover. Like its spidery nature, it tends to creep here and there and turn up in unexpected places. It does, however, work well as an edging plant next to paths and it can be very effective planted between stepping stones or next to the pure white bark of a birch tree.

How to care for it

Mondo grass is trouble-free and indifferent to wet winters provided it has good drainage. Thick clumps can be divided in spring.

Good companions

There is no shortage of good companions for *Ophiopogon planiscapus* 'Nigrescens'. It contrasts beautifully with any of the following: Japanese blood grass (*Imperata cylindrica* 'Red Baron'), blue grass (*Festuca glauca*), spurge (*Euphorbia myrsinites*), dead nettle (*Lamium maculatum*), creeping jenny (*Lysimachia nummularia*) and *Ajuga reptans* 'Purpurea'.

For your collection

🐾 Other black plants worth pursuing include the black snapdragon, *Antirrhinum* 'Black Prince', black sweet william (*Dianthus barbatus* 'Nigrescens') and the hardy geranium, *Geranium phaeum* (mourning widow), which has small black flowers.

*P*aeonia lactiflora 'Karl Rosenfeld'

Common name: Peony

Chief characteristics

We all know and admire peonies; they have been firm favorites in gardens for years. They are a plant even nongardeners have little difficulty identifying. We love them for their large, fragrant flowers, which

Location: Full sun
Type: Perennial
Size: 3 to 4 feet (90 to 120 cm)
Conditions: Fertile, well-drained soil
Flowering time: May to June

appear from May to June, and for their lush foliage, which stays a pleasant, restful shade of green all summer long. Yet how many of us can name the peony we are besotted with?

Not all garden centers can be bothered to label them with their full name, preferring to tag them by color. They have great names like 'Hot Chocolate', 'Moonrise', 'Butterbowl', 'Petticoat Flounce', 'Raspberry Sundae' and 'Marshmallow Puff'. But most people wouldn't know them by those names if they saw them. Even some expert gardeners, when pressed, can do no better than describe a peony by its color. This is a dishonor peonies share with daylilies, which are also extremely useful in the garden landscape and universally loved, but which are rarely referred to by their proper and complete botanical name.

Peonies also have a reputation for sulking when moved or messed with. They flower their best after being left undisturbed for several years. And they don't bloom for very long. Their magnificent multipetaled blooms, some with a fragrance that rivals that of old garden roses, appear in the middle of spring and are over and done within a month. By the time we start to notice them, they have run their course and our attention quickly gets diverted to other showy early summer performers. Despite all of this, peonies are still superb plants and no garden can afford to be without them.

There are 3 key groups: early flowering hybrids; Japanese or anemone-form peonies which have large, graceful blooms; and double peonies which have tightly packed multipetaled, chrysanthemum-like flowers or cup-shaped blooms like roses that are wide open.

The basic garden peony is *Paeonia lactiflora*. It comes in a wide range of colors including assorted shades and combinations of pink, red, white and yellow. One of the most reliable all-round performers is 'Karl Rosenfeld', which produces brilliant, fragrant red flowers in June. It has handsome foliage and is a trouble-free plant with excellent resistance to pests and diseases.

Where to plant it

Grow peonies in full sun in fertile, well-drained soil with a mixture of other perennials and flowering shrubs. Peonies are best combined with other plant material rather than grown in mass groups. Once flowering is over, peonies form a great backdrop with their soft, shapely leaves. Before planting your new peony, think carefully about where you are placing it. Once it is in the ground, it does not like to be disturbed. Plant in late September, then leave it alone to establish itself. This could take more than one season. Don't be alarmed if you see weak or few flowers the first year after planting.

How to care for it

There are a few rules about looking after peonies that if followed make them a lot more enjoyable to grow. Peonies hold themselves up perfectly well while they are developing in early spring, but once they start to flower, especially if they get hit by heavy rain, the stems can topple sideways and the bush will begin to look ragged and unkempt. The secret is to set link-stakes around the emerging stems to give the bush the support it will need later on when it reaches its peak blooming period.

Ants can seem like a problem. They can often be found running all over the plant, especially over unopened flower buds. Some gardeners say this actually stimulates the buds to open more rapidly. The consensus of opinion, however, is that ants do neither harm nor good; they just busy themselves and disappear.

The most important thing to remember about peonies is that they should not be disturbed. They don't like being moved or having their roots interfered with in any way. If you divide a clump, expect the plants to sulk for a season.

Good companions

Since peonies vanish completely back into the ground over winter, the space they occupied can look very barren in early spring. Surround the peony crown with various spring-flowering bulbs. Bluebells (scillas), grape hyacinth (*Muscari*), crocus, glory-of-the-snow (*Chionodoxa*) and dwarf narcissi are all good choices. They will provide color and cover while the new pink-red peony shoots are slowly rising. Once the leaves have formed, the bush will need some supporting neighbors. Try campanulas, centaurea, euphorbia, aquilegia, salvia, lupins, foxgloves, shrub roses, lychnis and alliums. Peonies fit in well between lavateras and alongside daphne.

For your collection

- Other star peonies to look out for are 'Sarah Bernhardt (apple-blossom pink), 'Bowl of Beauty' (pale pink with white center), 'Okinawa' (red with yellow center), 'Laura Dessert' (white petals surrounding soft lemon-yellow petals), 'Lady Alexandra Duff' (pale pink) and 'Duchesse de Nemours' (pure white).
- Coastal gardeners looking for more unusual colors have been particularly impressed by early flowering hybrids such as 'Cytherea' (cherry-peach mix), 'Red Charm' (rich red), 'Coral 'n' Gold' and 'Coral Charm' (coral-peach).
- Also growing in popularity are the Japanese peonies, notably 'Leto' (pure white), 'Snow Swan' (ivory) and 'White Cap' (raspberry). Doubles with outstanding color include 'Angel Cheeks' (pink with red freckles), 'Dinner Plate' (shell-pink), 'Jeannot' (rose-pink) and 'Mary Eddy Jones' (light pink).
- The fernleaf peony (*Paeonia tenuifolia*) is unlike any other peony. It has elegant, finely cut, fernlike leaves and produces dark crimson flowers in May. Another very popular peony is *Paeonia lutea*, which has single, vivid yellow flowers and attractive foliage. It grows to 6 feet (1.8 m).

*P*apaver orientale 'Mrs. Perry'

Common name: Oriental poppy

Chief characteristics

Poppies are like cherries on a cake. They don't add a lot of substance, but they inject a special beauty and charm. In the early summer garden, poppies hover like butterflies, their delicate flower petals appearing as fragile as tissue paper. Think of poppies as a garden's jewelry and you will immediately understand how to use them

Location: Full sun
Type: Perennial
Size: 2 to 3 feet (60 to 90 cm)
Conditions: Light, well-drained soil
Flowering time: May to June

to the best effect—as decorative finishing touches, decadent indulgences, the carnation in the buttonhole. The opposite of hostas and rhododendrons, they are flowers we flirt with—just don't expect a long-term relationship from them. They are full of frivolity and gaiety and have nothing to offer in terms of structural longevity.

The Oriental poppy (*Papaver orientale*) is one of the most popular kinds. It has rough, hairy foliage and soft, satinlike flowers that come in a wide range of colors from blood-red to salmon-pink to pure white. The peachy pink 'Mrs. Perry' is an old-fashioned hybrid, a favorite of cottage gardeners. Other top Oriental poppies include: 'Perry's White' (white with black spot), 'Goliath' (deep red with dark center), 'Allegro' (scarlet), 'Brilliant' (red), 'Carneum' (salmon-pink) and 'Picotee' (salmon-pink with white edges). They all grow 2 and 3 feet (60 to 90 cm) high.

Where to plant it

Grow Oriental poppies mixed with perennials in full sun in well-drained, light soil. They won't flourish in heavy, clay soils and will die even faster in waterlogged or overly wet soil. The main drawback to growing poppies is that they leave gaping holes in your garden once they have finished flowering. The solution is to plant them among late-flowering perennials that will rise up once the poppies are done and fill the gaps. Another idea is to have perennials standing by in pots that can be moved into gaps. This is not a bad idea to use throughout the garden to keep it looking in great shape all year. You would be amazed how many gardeners do this and no one knows because their borders always look so seamless.

How to care for it

Make sure you grow poppies in well-drained, fertile soil. Pick the seed pods and sow seed where you would like flowers the following year. Once plants have finished flowering, don't allow the foliage to become an eyesore. Cut it down or take it out completely and replace with perennials in pots or use fill-in annuals like nicotiana, pelargoniums or red salvia.

Good companions

Grow Oriental poppies along with perennials that flower from July to September. Good choices are *Phlox paniculata*, ornamental grasses, daylilies, veronica, fall asters and Japanese anemones. For companions in late spring/early summer, think about lupins, alliums, forget-me-nots, campanulas, hardy geraniums and shrub roses.

For your collection

- The poppy that most new gardeners fall in love with is the California poppy (*Eschscholzia californica*), which has yellow to deep orange flowers and distinctive feathery foliage. It grows 8 to 15 inches (20 to 38 cm) high on sunny, well-drained hillsides or banks. Easy to grow from seed, the California poppy will self-sow and return year after year. Efforts to transplant rarely succeed, even when the poppies are lifted in a whole clump of earth.

- Two other poppies, the passion of plant connoisseurs, are the Himalayan blue poppy (*Meconopsis betonicifolia*) and the Welsh poppy (*M. cambrica*). The Himalayan poppy grows 3 to 4 feet (90 to 120 cm) high in cool, semi-shade and has light, sky-blue flowers. The Welsh poppy has small yellow or orange flowers atop 12-inch (30-cm) stems.

  If you do grow the Himalayan blue poppy, be aware of the popular belief that you should prevent it flowering the first year. This seems to have some truth in it as the plant will put out more foliage growth if it is not putting energy into flower production—and a more robust plant is better able to survive winter.

- The famous Flander's field poppy (*Papaver rhoeas*) is also known as the Shirley poppy. It grows 12 inches (30 cm) high in a range of colors. It is grown as an annual, being sown in early spring.

- The atlas poppy (*Papaver atlanticum*) grows 12 inches (30 cm) and has soft orange flowers.

- The infamous opium poppy (*Papaver somniferum*) is grown in many gardens on the coast, but is not sold commercially. It grows 30 inches (75 cm) high and has gray-green foliage and pink, red, white or purple flowers.

- The Iceland poppy (*Papaver nudicaule*) comes in shades of yellow, red, pink and white and grows 18 inches (45 cm). It is a biennial, growing leaves one year, flowering the next.

*P*assiflora caerulea

Common name: Blue passion vine

Chief characteristics

Everyone who sees the extraordinary flowers of a blue passion vine immediately falls in love with them. They are quite unique. Each flower has 10 petals, which provide a decorative backdrop for a skirt, or fringe, of purple-blue bristles. Above the bristles, there are 5 green stamens with 3 more purple-colored stamens above them. The whole complex construction is superb. It is called the passion vine because Christians see symbols of Christ's passion in the flower: the petals (10 faithful apostles), bristles (crown of thorns), 5 stamens (5 wounds). All of which makes the vine an interesting conversation piece for the garden as well as an outstanding plant with gloriously glossy foliage.

Location: Full sun
Type: Semi-evergreen vine
Size: 20 feet (6 m)
Conditions: Rich, well-drained soil
Flowering time: July to September

Flowers first appear in July. They do not crop up in exuberant flushes, but singularly and sporadically, here and there, usually not more than half a dozen on the vine at any given moment throughout the summer. The biggest disappointment is that the flowers are not fragrant. Exotic-looking, they measure 3 inches (7.5 cm) across and can be cut and floated in water in a rose bowl indoors. They certainly look like they should be fragrant but perhaps they put so much effort into their design, they neglected their scent.

The vine also has fabulous, glossy green foliage, which in mild areas will stay green all winter. At the end of summer, flowers give way to yellow passion fruits. They are not edible. *Passiflora caerulea* is the most viable species to grow in coastal gardens. Native to Brazil, it is vigorous and can easily cover a large wall 15 by 20 feet (4.5 by 6 m). New stems flop down, rather than clinging and climbing upward.

Where to plant it

The secret to growing the blue passion vine successfully is to plant it against a south- or west-facing wall in a frost-free location. If it is protected from heavy frost and the blast of icy winds in winter, it will survive and thrive magnificently. The radiant heat it gets from a house will help it overcome even the most frigid days in winter. It stands less chance in a completely exposed location.

How to care for it

Grow *Passiflora caerulea* in ordinary, well-drained soil in a sunny, frost-free location. There are microclimates like this in most gardens, so there is usually the ideal place for it somewhere in your garden, too. The vine needs a trellis or guides of black thread to which it may attach its curly tendrils in order to climb without becoming tangled. It is easy to train and will go where you place it. Prune out dead foliage and stems at the end of winter. Even if it is pruned to the ground, it will spring back again. Offshoots will pop up in the most unexpected places.

Good companions

Perennial nightshade (*Solanum crispum*) or the purple-pink–leafed ornamental grape (*Vitis vinifera* 'Purpurea') make interesting companions. The danger of growing clematis or roses into the vine is that you could end up obscuring the exquisite flowers. But you could do this and take extra care to prune away parts that look like they are interfering.

For your collection

- There is a white flowering cultivar of *Passiflora caerulea* called 'Constance Elliott', which some say is even hardier than the blue form. It was given a first-class certificate by the British Royal Horticultural Society in 1884 and has been observed to survive in mild areas provided it is protected from heavy frost.
- There are also some tender species such as the purple grenadilla (*P. edulis*) or the scarlet-flowered banana passion fruit, *P. antioquiensis*, grown for its fruit in Australia and New Zealand. In our climate they need to be grown in a conservatory or hothouse.

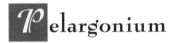

Pelargonium

Common name: Geranium, zonal geranium

Chief characteristics

Most people, even those who don't garden, know the name of these plants. Or at least they think they do. Pelargoniums are a standard in all summer gardens. You see them everywhere, adding cheerful, long-lasting color to patios and decks,

Location: Full sun
Type: Annual
Size: 12 to 18 inches (30 to 45 cm)
Conditions: Fertile soil
Flowering time: Spring, early summer

window boxes and hanging baskets. They are also used to inject a festive splash of color into large-scale planting schemes in public parks. The majority of people call them geraniums. This is technically (botanically) incorrect. True geraniums are equally wonderful plants, actually hardy perennials, commonly called in informed horticultural circles, "cranesbills."

Unlike the true geranium, pelargoniums are tender, summer annuals. Although native to South Africa, they are not considered rare or terribly exotic. Unfortunately, like the lowly marigold, they are sometimes rejected as loud and common. Nevertheless, they are a vital player in the summer garden. Drought tolerant and pest-free, they are marvelously dependable and forgiving plants. They are certainly among the world's most loved flowers. All gardeners should find a place for at least a pot or two on their patio or porch.

The most familiar pelargoniums are the ones known as zonal geraniums. They come in a wide variety of colors from deep red to hot pink, to bright white, to salmon, to orange. There are far too many to mention by name here. It really comes down to picking out what you like most when you visit the garden center in April.

Within this category, you will also find "fancy-leaf" types, which literally have fancy, decorative leaves, most variegated creamy yellows and purplish maroons.

There are a few other types of pelargoniums worth knowing. Ivy-leafed geraniums (cultivars of *Pelargonium peltatum*) have ivy-shaped leaves and a cascading habit. They are especially useful for hanging baskets or for trailing over the edges of large pots. Angel pelargoniums (*Pelargonium* × *dumosum*), with lovely delicate flowers that resemble angel wings, are great for hanging baskets and window boxes. These are immensely popular in England, thanks to the work of hybridizers who have produced exciting new cultivars that have caught the eye of gardeners at the Chelsea Flower Show. Regal geraniums (*Pelargonium* × *domesticum*) are also known as Martha Washington pelargoniums. They have large, showy flowers with ruffled, overlapping petals. Colors range from soft white to raspberry-red, to dark purple, to magenta-pink.

Where to plant it

Pelargoniums like rich, porous soil. They like heat, so they should be planted where they will get full sun. They'll tolerate some shade, but too much shade will produce leggy growth and feeble flowers. They don't like to be watered too generously. In fact, overwatering is one way to kill them. But they have no objection to being potted with other annuals. They like it when their roots are somewhat restricted by space.

How to care for it

Feed pelargoniums every couple of weeks during their flowering period with a half-strength solution of 20-20-20. Water regularly but sparingly. Pinch prune the tops of the plant to make them bushier and more floriferous. Remove faded flowerheads regularly to keep the plant tidy and to encourage blooming. If you like, take cuttings in late summer to maintain a supply of your favorite plants, but don't bother to overwinter whole plants. In most cases, all you end up overwintering is fungal or viral diseases. The cost and effort is not really worth the trouble, especially when you know inexpensive plants are available every spring.

Good companions

The beauty of pelargoniums is that they provide a stable foundation for imaginative container-planting schemes. Trailing verbena, petunia, alyssum, diascia, brachycome, anagallis, argyranthemums all make excellent companions for pelargoniums in pots. Red salvia and lime-green nicotiana can also be combined with canna lilies and red or white pelargoniums for outstanding container plantings.

For your collection

🐾 Scented geraniums are always fun to have around in the summer. Grown for their aromatic leaves, which need to be touched or brushed to release their scent, these collectible geraniums offer a surprising range of fragrances including lemon (*Pelargonium crispum*), apple (*P. odoratissimum*) or peppermint (*P. tomentosum*). While ordinary pelargoniums are not worth overwintering—it is best to grow new plants from seed or cuttings or buy new plants in spring—scented geraniums are a little more special and can be kept for many years by bringing them into a frost-free environment during winter.

𝒫 eltiphyllum peltatum

Common name: Umbrella plant

Chief characteristics

Sometimes you need to make a dramatic statement in the garden. You have the room, so why not grow something big, bold and beautiful? *Peltiphyllym peltatum* (now called *Darmera peltata*) is a marvelous foliage plant for growing in

Location: Full sun to part shade
Type: Perennial
Size: 4 feet (1.2 m)
Conditions: Good, moist soil
Flowering time: April to May

moist soil. It thrives in boggy ground next to a pond or stream. In spring, it has quirky white/pale-pink flowers that are clustered in a bunch at the top of a hairy stem and come shooting out of the ground like seedlings from Mars. These are eye-catching but they are only the prelude to the plant's main business, which is to produce large, attractive, rhubarblike leaves. The leaves unfold precisely and form a large mound that looks solid and confident and provides a beautiful background for showing the more delicate flowers of such plants as astrantia, candelabra primulas and sweet-scented white-flowering hostas.

Where to plant it

Grow *Peltiphyllum peltatum* in sun or light shade but make sure it has plenty of moisture at its roots. It thrives next to a pond or stream but will do well in average soil in a variety of locations. Don't be afraid to grow it alongside other plants, as it is capable of sharing space.

How to care for it

Peltiphyllum doesn't require a lot of care. Give it water and space to grow and it is happy. The leaves die down naturally at the end of the season and need to be cleaned away when the rest of the garden is put to bed in late fall. Fertilizing is probably unwise as this plant is capable of reaching 4 feet (1.2 m) high by 4 or 5 feet (1.2 to 1.5 m) wide without much help.

Good companions

Astilbe, hostas, ligularia and primulas all make viable partners. They all enjoy moist soil conditions and prefer shade to full sun.

For your collection

If you are looking for other bold, space-filling, dramatic specimen plants, consider one of the following.

- *Rodgersia podophylla*: This has large, rugged, fan-shaped leaves that are broken into 5 segments that make it very easy to identify. The pale, creamy white flowers are somewhat like astilbe plumes. The cultivar *R. pinnata* 'Superba' is not so wide-spreading and has red flower plumes. *Rodgersia* also likes damp, boggy ground.
- Ornamental rhubarb (*Rheum palmatum* 'Atrosanguineum'): Its large, sharply cut leaves will cover 6 feet (1.8 m) while its plumes of flaming red flowers will leap just as high into the air. Grow it in full sun.
- Pampas grass (*Cortaderia selloana*): This has giant fountains of razor-shape straplike leaves and tall, graceful plumes that are extremely elegant in the late-summer, early fall garden. Plant it on a fast-

draining bank in full sun, but not near a path or sidewalk where the leaves can be unpleasant for passersby. The plumes will last long into winter and can look outstanding drooping with frost or rising out of snowbanks. By the spring, they will look very tatty and will need to be cut out. A good new cultivar is 'Ivory Feathers', which is perfect for smaller gardens since it grows only 3 feet (90 cm) high and sends plumes up another 3 feet (90 cm).

* *Crambe cordifolia*: A member of the cabbage family, it has mounds of hairy, crinkled dark green leaves and is mostly loved for the great clouds of fragrant white flowers it produces in summer. Grow it in full sun in fast-draining soil. It will reach 6 feet (1.8 m) high by 5 feet (1.5 m) wide.

* Bear's breech (*Acanthus mollis*): The leaves, which inspired the architects of ancient Greece, are pure classicism. The purple-pink hooded flowers are no less wonderful, stacked on top of one another like seashells on tall stems. Grow bear's breech in full sun or light shade. Be prepared to cut it back if it tries to take over too much of the dappled shade of trees and tall shrubs. It grows 4 feet (1.2 m) high by 3 1/2 feet (1 m) wide.

* The grand-daddy of all bold foliage plants, of course, is *Gunnera manicata*. It can reach 10 feet (3 m) tall and produce gigantic, prickly, junglelike leaves big enough to shelter half a dozen people in a rain storm. It is quite astonishing how popular this plant is despite the space it consumes and its tenderness in winter (it needs protection from frost and icy winds to survive). The most popular position for it is by the edge of a pond. Spectacular.

*P*ennisetum alopecuroides

Common name: Fountain grass

Chief characteristics

Fountain grass produces a generous cascade of foxtails at the end of long arching stems in late summer. It gets its name because it resembles water splashing out from a fountain. It can be used as a feature plant to create a focal point or to add foliage interest to the perennial border. Planted in substantial drifts or alone in a container, it will still perform outstandingly, growing about 2 feet (60 cm) high.

Location: Full sun
Type: Ornamental grass
Size: 2 to 3 feet (60 to 90 cm)
Conditions: Fertile, moist soil
Flowering time: July to September

Pennisetum's main function, however, is to provide a light, airy textural contrast to neighboring plants. Starting out green, *Pennisetum alopecuroides* slowly turns yellow at the end of summer and becomes a delightful barnyard-tan color in fall. The graceful bottlebrush-like foxtails start out creamy white and turn more almond as the season progresses.

The cultivar 'Hameln' is a more compact, early flowering, dwarf form that grows about 2 feet (60 cm) high, while the slightly taller 'Moudry' produces dark, almost black, bottlebrush spikes. A miniature cultivar called 'Little Bunny' grows 10 to 12 inches (25 to 30 cm), which makes it quite suitable for use in a rockery.

Oriental fountain grass (*Pennisetum orientale*) is hardier and is considered by some to be the most handsome of all the fountain grasses because of its glossy, blue-green, compact leaves and its silky soft pink plumes which last a long time and gradually fade to gray. It grows about 18 inches (45 cm) high.

Where to plant it

Fountain grass grows naturally in open meadows and beside streams in open woodland areas. It is best planted in the middle or back of the perennial border, although the shorter forms can be located more to the front. Use fountain grass to soften the hard edges of rock walls or to provide some textural relief to hard brick or slate patios.

How to care for it

Fountain grass has no pest or disease problems. To thrive, it needs plenty of sun. Plant it in moist, well-drained soil. If you can find a sunny, sheltered, frost-free part of the garden in which to plant it, all the better. Divide the clumps in spring.

Good companions

Angel's fishing rod (*Dierama pulcherrimum*) has a similar habit to fountain grass, producing long, arching grasslike stems—but it also has exquisite flowers at the tips. The pink, broccoli-like heads of stonecrop (*Sedum spectabile*) in the fall also make an attractive architectural contrast to the almond-colored late-summer plumes of fountain grass. The butterfly gaura (*Gaura lindheimeri*), which produces a myriad of pinkish-white flowers at the end of tall waving stems, makes a good partner for pennisetum and does not mind if the grass takes more of the available water. The red-magenta flowers of *Lychnis coronaria* could also be mixed in for fun and the dark moody blues of *Caryopteris* × *clandonensis* 'Dark Knight' are worth experimenting with.

For your collection

🐾 The ornamental grass everyone falls in love with each summer is the purple-leafed fountain grass (*Pennisetum setaceum* 'Rubrum'). It has warm, burgundy foliage and striking wine-colored foxtail plumes. Unfortunately, it is not hardy, which means it won't survive winter in a coastal garden, so you have to grow it as an annual. Even though you often can't get it into the garden before the beginning of July, it still makes a superb feature plant right up to the first frosts of October. It is spectacular combined with silver artemisias or pink petunias or on its own in a pot. There is a dwarf form of 'Rubrum', specially created for balcony gardeners, called 'Eaton Canyon', which grows about 2 feet (60 cm) and is just as tender-hearted as its cousin.

🐾 If you have plenty of room in your garden, try growing *Pennisetum* 'Burgundy Giant' which will soar 5 feet (1.5 m) and produce thick tropical-looking beet-colored, straplike leaves. It is also tender— officially designated a Zone 9 to 10 plant. Even the mildest frost will kill it in coastal gardens, but gardeners always like to test the limits of hardiness and this grass certainly makes a striking back-of-the-border specimen.

*P*hiladelphus coronarius 'Aureus'

Common name: Mock orange

Chief characteristics

Location: Full sun to light shade
Type: Deciduous shrub
Size: 10 feet (3 m)
Conditions: Ordinary soil
Flowering time: June to July

The great value of having a mock orange in the garden is that it has masses of white flowers in July. This helps to bridge the gap at the critical time of mid-summer and provides a smooth transition in the shrub border between spring and autumn. The other marvelous attribute of a mock orange bush is its highly scented blooms, which have a clear, refreshing orange-blossom perfume. There are many cultivars to choose from. One of my favorites is the golden-yellow–leafed *P. coronarius* 'Aureus', which provides excellent foliage contrast, especially alongside the purple-leafed smoke bush. 'Aureus' is a medium-sized shrub that grows about 6 to 8 feet (1.8 to 2.4 m) high and produces abundant clusters of fragrant creamy white flowers in early summer.

The most planted mock orange in the Pacific Northwest is *Philadelphus × virginalis*, which has large, pure white flowers in late spring with excellent fragrance and attractive green foliage. Its outstanding cultivars are the dwarfish 'Snowflake', which grows only 4 feet (1.2 m) high and has very fragrant double white blooms, and 'Innocence', which has variegated white and gray foliage and fragrant white flowers. Other cultivars grow 6 to 8 feet (1.8 to 2.4 m) high. One of the best is 'Beauclerk'. The real stars of the shorter plants, however, are 'Belle Etoile', which grows only 5 to 7 feet (1.5 to 2.1 m), and 'Sybille', which grows 4 to 5 feet (1.2 to 1.5 m). Both of these produce white flowers with purple markings in the center that look rather like blotches or smudges.

Where to plant it

An excellent choice for the back of the mixed shrub border, the golden-leafed *Philadelphus coronarius* 'Aureus' is good for foliage contrast. Place it in a spot where the fruity orange scent can be appreciated and permitted to mingle with the other pleasant aromas of the summer garden. Mock orange can be grown close to a back gate or next to an arbor or gazebo. The smaller forms will fit very nicely in the garden where space is limited.

How to care for it

An easy-care shrub, mock orange likes sun. Although it will tolerate light shade, it does not like it when it is given too much shade. The soil does not have to be exceptional but it should be well drained without drying out in summer. Prune philadelphus in late summer after flowering or in spring before flowers appear. A third of old stems can be comfortably snipped out, especially in the taller shrubs. This will keep the bush from becoming too dense and it will also promote new growth.

Good companions

Dark backgrounds are best to bring out the foliage color of *Philadelphus coronarius*. A bank of conifers or yew or cedar hedging will also accent the shrub's white flower. The lily-of-the-valley shrub (*Pieris japonica* 'Temple Bells') makes a good partner since it will kick off the season with impressive clusters of white flowers in spring, paving the way for philadelphus in the summer. *Pieris japonica* 'Valley Valentine' does a similar job, growing 7 feet (2.1 m) tall at maturity and producing deep red flowers. These are both, however, slightly less hardy than *Pieris japonica* 'Forest Flame', which has flame-red new foliage in spring that turns green with maturity.

Other suitable partners for philadelphus include magnolias, rhododendrons, old garden roses, peonies, the purple smoke bush (*Cotinus coggygria*) and buddleia. The rose of Sharon (*Hibiscus syriacus*) is another good choice. Top cultivars include 'Blue Bird', 'Diana' (white), 'Aphrodite' (rose-pink), 'Blushing Bride' (rich pink), Collie Mullens' (lavender-purple), 'Helene' (white with red eye) and 'Minerva' (lavender-pink with reddish-purple eye). They all grow about 10 feet (3 m).

For your collection

🌿 *Philadelphus coronarius* 'Variegatus' has white flowers and light white and green leaves that add striking foliage interest to the shrub border. It is a medium-sized shrub, growing about 8 feet (2.4 m).

𝒫hlox paniculata 'Mount Fujiama'

Common name: Phlox

Chief characteristics

Location: Full sun
Type: Perennial
Size: 3 to 4 feet (90 to 120 cm)
Conditions: Good, moisture-retentive soil
Flowering time: July to August

You don't need a wall calender or a digital watch to know what time of year it is. Your garden is just as accurate a guide to the seasons. You know, for instance, that summer is definitely at its peak when you see tall, majestic clumps of *Phlox paniculata* holding up spectacular panicles of bright red, white, pink, and purple, sweetly scented flowers. It is an understatement to say phlox is a stalwart of the summer garden or even to describe it as a workhorse or a popular perennial. It is much more. It is one of the plants you cannot do without if you want to lift your garden in July and August to the zenith of its glory. Before people torment you with tall tales of how prone phlox is to mildew and aphids, scorched leaves and leaf-munching snails, hold on to this: whatever the problems, you can overcome them, and you will be glad you didn't turn your back on phlox. The rewards far outweigh the piddling drawbacks.

There are several excellent cultivars of *Phlox paniculata* to consider. One of the best white forms is 'Mount Fujiama'. It has pure white flowers in mid- to late summer, grows 3 feet (90 cm) tall and is much more disease resistant than most other garden phlox. Its flowers are slightly smaller than those of other cultivars but they last a lot longer. Other top performers include 'Starfire' (cherry-red), 'Amethyst' (lavender-violet), 'Elizabeth Arden' (pink), 'Eva Cullum' (pink with purple eye) and 'Bright Eyes' (pink with a cerise eye).

Where to plant it

Phlox paniculata looks its best grown in large groups in full sun in the middle or the back of the flower bed. It flourishes in soil that is free-draining but also capable of retaining moisture. Top names like 'Mount Fujiama' and 'David' are sturdy plants that hold themselves perfectly erect and do not require staking. Other kinds may need a helping hand to look their best and should be carefully staked as they rise from the ground in spring. Color preferences are personal. You may find the single-color cultivars form less jarring associations. They can also present the most striking image. If you are going to use the more vivid two-tone or orange phlox, you will need to give much more thought to potential color clashes.

How to care for it

Put down a good layer of mulch, either well-rotted compost or manure, in spring as the plants reappear and start their climb upward. Water copiously in dry spells. Thin out clumps to improve air circulation to prevent mildew and leaf rot closer to the ground. As a last resort, spray with a mild solution of fungicide. You can do your delphiniums and bee balm at the same time. But keeping the soil moist, the air flowing and the plants healthy are your three best forms of defense against mildew. It is not nearly as big a problem as some people say.

Good companions

There is no shortage of partners for phlox. Try bee balm, echinops, shasta daisies, hemerocallis, stachys, liatris, crocosmia, penstemon, ornamental grasses, perovskia (Russian sage), gypsophilia, lavatera, alliums, asters, rudbeckia and second-flush campanulas and delphiniums.

For your collection

The phlox family also offers some excellent low-growing, evergreen plants for the sunny rockery garden or for tumbling over a low retaining wall.

- The creeping type, *Phlox subulata*, is very worth getting to know. Look for 'Emerald Blue' (pale lilac), 'Emerald Pink' (soft pink), 'Benita' (lavender-pink) or 'Atropurpurea' (rose-red).
- Another kind is *Phlox douglasii*, which is so similar to the cultivars just mentioned, it is hard to tell them apart. They flower around the same time. Top performers are 'Red Admiral' (soft red), 'Crackerjack' (bright red), and 'Rose Cushion' (pink). All are very useful as mat-forming plants for filling spaces in the rockery or edging or softening the sharp corners of walls.

🐌 There are some lovely forms of meadow phlox (*Phlox maculata*) worth trying. They are supposed to be slightly more mildew resistant than some of the more popular summer phlox. *P. maculata* 'Alpha' has lilac-pink flowers with a darker pink eye in the center; 'Omega' and 'Miss Lingard' have white flowers; and 'Rosalinde' has bright pink blooms.

ℙicea pungens 'Hoopsii'

Common name: *Colorado blue spruce, Hoop's blue spruce*

Chief characteristics

Conifers are not essential in a garden, but they are useful for structure and winter color. The Colorado blue spruce is exceptional in January against white snow or with frost on its bright steel-blue needles. There are many different cultivars

Location: Full sun to part shade
Type: Evergreen tree
Size: 25 feet (7.5 m)
Conditions: Ordinary, well-drained soil

from which to choose but Hoop's blue spruce (*Picea pungens* 'Hoopsii'), is the bluest of the spruces. With stiff horizontal branches, it has dense silvery blue needles. It is also one of the most desirable. It is relatively slow growing, reaching only 8 feet (2.4 m) after 10 years, and its growth can be somewhat irregular for the first few years, but the spectacular bright blue needles easily make up for any perceived flaws.

Other popular forms of *Picea pungens* to look out for include 'Fat Albert', which is a compact, upright pyramidal tree; 'Koster', which is one of the most widely grown cultivars of blue spruce, easily reaching 10 feet (3 m) in 10 years; and 'Thomsen', which, with its pale silver-blue needles, is one of the brightest of the group. You can also find a weeping form of blue spruce, *Picea pungens* 'Glauca Pendula', which has blue-green needles and can be used to add special architectural interest to your garden. *Picea pungens* 'Glauca Globosa' is a dwarf, compact bush, ideal for the rockery since it grows only 2 to 3 feet (60 to 90 cm) in 10 years. The new growth in spring is an impressive blue-gray.

Where to plant it

Grow blue spruces in the mixed shrub border as contrast foliage plants or alone as a special specimen. The role of conifers is to provide structural "bones" in the garden and year-round color. Use them to tie together your garden landscape so that there is some structure even in the dead of winter.

How to care for it

Blue spruces get their color from a powder that is formed on the outside of the needles. If you rub a needle, it will lose its blueness and turn green. Iron trace elements in the soil are very important in the formation of the powder. A trick to keep your blue spruce blue is to add some aluminum sulfate—the same chemical used to keep hydrangeas blue—to the soil. This makes the soil more acidic and helps the plant to absorb more iron, which helps the spruce produce more blue powder.

Conifers need to be well watered when they are establishing themselves. They require routine pruning the rest of the time to maintain their shape. Some of the forms of blue spruce—'Koster', for example—are not always willing to grow a single leader shoot, so you may have to prune carefully to achieve the shape you want. The other popular cultivars, 'Hoopsii', 'Thomsen' and 'Fat Albert', are less demanding.

Good companions

Rhododendrons, azaleas, magnolias, pieris, mahonia, corkscrew hazel, heathers, hollies, yellow- and red-twig dogwoods, ornamental grasses, especially yellow and variegated forms, and witch hazels are all good companions. Groundcover ideas include yucca, euonymus, hebes, euphorbia, cotoneaster, sedums, creeping phlox, junipers and potentilla.

For your collection

These popular evergreens also perform well in coastal gardens.

- If you have a stream or pond and you would like to have a graceful conifer to arch over it in a romantic fashion, you could try the weeping form of the blue Atlas cedar, *Cedrus atlantica* 'Glauca Pendula', which has a distinctive arching habit.
- The monkey puzzle tree (*Araucaria araucana*): It is slow growing, reaching 40 to 60 feet (12 to 18 m) at maturity, and has extremely decorative, spiky "monkey-tail" branches.
- Maidenhair tree (*Ginkgo biloba*): This is one of the world's oldest trees. There is fossil evidence of it dating back to dinosaur times. It has lovely yellow butterflylike leaves in fall. It stays a teenager for the longest time, growing slowly to 25 feet (7.5 m) after 20 years or more. It has the potential to go higher.
- English yew (*Taxus baccata*): This cedar-shaped conifer has a brooding presence in the formal landscape. People love it or hate it. English yew grows slowly and is capable of reaching 30 to 50 feet (9 to 15 m) but is usually pruned to a more manageable height. It bounces back from being pruned with little effort.

- Golden English yew (*Taxus baccata* 'Aurea'): You might perfer this one, which has cheerful, golden-yellow foliage and is just as neat and tidy as its moody cousin. It grows 15 feet (4.5 m) high by 10 feet (3 m) wide. A particularly fine form of yew is *T. b.* 'Fastigiata Aurea', which stands beautifully erect and has needles with golden edges. It will grow 30 feet (9 m) high by 15 feet (4.5 m) wide in time.

- Umbrella pine (*Sciadopitys verticillata*): This is a lovely tree to touch. The dense whorls of needles resemble the spokes of an umbrella. They are long, soft and pleasant to touch. It is a slow-growing tree, reaching 15 feet (4.5 m) after 10 years, by which time it looks magnificent. Feed it lots of nitrogen and it will stay green rather than turning anemic yellow.

- *Thuja occidentalis* 'Rheingold': This popular, slow-growing, dwarf conifer has golden-yellow foliage that turns bronze in winter. It combines well with heathers, especially the winter-flowering species. It grows 10 feet (3 m) high by 6 feet (1.8 m) wide in 10 to 12 years.

*P*olemonium caeruleum 'Brise d'Anjou'

Common name: Variegated Jacob's ladder

Chief characteristics

Location: Part sun to light shade
Type: Perennial
Size: 18 to 24 inches (45 to 60 cm)
Conditions: Well-drained, moist soil
Flowering time: May to June

It is always fun to walk with friends around the garden and point to a plant that has an interesting story to tell. The variegated Jacob's ladder, *Polemonium caeruleum* 'Brise d'Anjou', is just such a plant. The story goes that the plant vanished for almost a century before resurfacing in a small nursery in France. It was spotted by an alert plantsperson and has since been propagated and circulated around the world. The beauty of this handsome cultivar of Jacob's ladder is its striking, stripy, cream and green foliage. It also has delicate blue flowers which are produced at the top of erect stems. The plant gets its name from the ladderlike appearance of its leaves. 'Brise d'Anjou' looks good in the perennial border but really grabs the attention when it is combined in a pot with *Scabiosa columbaria* 'Butterfly Blue'. The two shades of blue flowers interact very well together and the more rigid structure of the Jacob's ladder contrasts effectively with the looser foliage of the scabiosa.

The more common form of Jacob's ladder is the plain green-leafed, cottage-garden inhabitant, *Polemonium caeruleum*, which, like the variegated 'Brise d'Anjou', also produces rosettes of small blue flowers on tall, erect stems in June. A beautiful fragrant white-flowering variety, *P.c.* 'Album', is also available, as well as a more compact plant called 'Blue Pearl'.

Where to plant it

Grow Jacob's ladder in sunny or semi-shaded sites in good, slightly moist soil. It will perform better if given some shade in the afternoon. The middle of a mixed perennial border is a good place for it. The calm, cool blue flowers look spectacular above the warmer, purple-blue crownlike flowers of *Centaurea montana*. 'Brise d'Anjou' looks splendid in a pot on a patio and can be used as a feature plant in the garden.

How to care for it

Polemonium has a reputation for seeding itself here, there and everywhere. To eliminate the problem, clip the flowerheads before they get into full seed production. Keep plants well watered in the dry days of summer. If the leaves show signs of scorching, move them into a shadier site. Divide clumps in fall or early spring.

Good companions

The busy cream-and-green striped foliage of 'Brise d'Anjou' makes it stand out, but it also means you have to be careful about what you put with it or you could end up with a riotous scene. Surround it with the foliage of plants like *Astrantia major* and *Aconitum napellus*. Blue hostas like 'Halcyon', 'Hadspen Blue' and 'Blue Belle' will echo the soft blue flowers of the Jacob's ladder. The white plumes of such astilbe as 'Snowdrift', 'Bridal Veil' or 'Washington' would not cause too much alarm, and dark flowers of the mourning widow cranesbill (*Geranium phaeum*) could be thrown in behind.

'Brise d'Anjou' is still a new plant in the Pacific Northwest and the experimenting continues to find how best to display it.

For your collection

Other fine blue-flowering perennials include the following.

🐾 *Polemonium carneum* has pink flowers and grows about 15 inches (38 cm) tall while *P. pulcherrimum*, the skunkleaf Jacob's ladder, gets only 12 inches (30 cm) high and has blue flowers with a yellow throat.

- Another outstanding blue-flowering perennial worth getting to know is the Chinese balloon flower (*Platycodon grandiflorus*).
- *Caryopteris* × *clandonensis* 'Dark Knight' will flower from August to October in a full-sun location.
- *Corydalis flexuosa* 'Blue Panda', 'China Blue' and 'Purple Leaf are 3 exciting blue-flowering plants that caused quite a fuss when they first became available. They are still very much admired for their blue blooms.
- *Aconitum carmichaelii* 'Arendsii' is a fall-blooming monkshood, with clusters of deep violet-blue blooms displayed on sturdy stems about 3 feet (90 cm) tall.

Polygonum bistorta 'Superbum'

Common name: Fleece flower, knotweed

Chief characteristics

Location: Full sun to part shade
Type: Perennial
Size: 24 to 30 inches (60 to 75 cm)
Conditions: Ordinary, moist, well-drained soil
Flowering time: May to June

'Superbum' produces pink, bottlebrush flowers for about a month starting around the middle of May. The flowers are formed at the top of slender, 2-foot (60-cm) stems. Insignificant on their own, the flowers become an impressive spectacle, especially when combined with purple alliums. The blooms of 'Superbum' make an excellent cut flower, combining well in tall vases with blue or lilac aquilegias, purple-speckled foxgloves, pale blue bearded irises, red peonies and coral bells to form a natural, seasonally correct bouquet. The only drawback to 'Superbum' is that it flowers in spring and has little to offer in the summer months. With thoughtful planting this need not be a problem.

Botanists changed the name of the plant a while ago. You'll now find it labeled *Persicaria bistorta* 'Superba', although a lot of garden centers have stayed with the old name. By the way, the name 'Superbum' is pronounced "Superb-um," although some people have fun pronouncing it "Super-bum." Either way is perfectly acceptable.

Another popular cultivar is *Polygonum amplexicaule* 'Atrosanguineum' (now *Persicaria amplexicaulis*), a taller, bushier plant with crimson poker-like flowers from late summer to early fall. 'Firetail' has salmon-red flowers, while 'Taurus' has scarlet-red flowers.

Where to plant it

The key to placing 'Superbum' in the right spot is to remember that once it has finished flowering and you have cut down the faded flower spikes, all that is left is the low carpet of green leaves. So you need to think about what to plant with it to create a sequence of color. It thrives in full sun or light shade in ordinary soil that is moist but not always saturated. It will fit nicely under trees or shrubs that have a couple of feet of open space at their base. It can also be used in pots. Knotweed grows best in rich, moist soil in full sun or light shade. The ideal spot for it is where it receives morning sun and afternoon shade.

How to care for it

Cut flower stalks to tidy the plant. Divide clumps every few years. Water in dry summers. If the plant starts to become invasive, simply take a shovel and dig it back to its boundaries or give the excess away to friends and neighbors. Leaves will scorch badly in direct afternoon sun.

Good companions

The ball-headed, purple ornamental onion (*Allium aflatunense*) makes an excellent partner for 'Superbum'. The allium's purple cricket-ball heads harmonize perfectly with knotweed's pink bottlebrush spikes. Astilbe, astrantia and hostas are all excellent partners for maintaining a sequence of blooms.

For your collection

Other species worth checking out include the following.

- The Japanese fleece flower (*Polygonum cuspidatum,* now *Fallopia japonica*): This is a somewhat invasive groundcover for mass planting around trees and shrubs.
- The dwarf knotweed (*Polygonum affine,* now *Persicaria affinis*): This is considered by some to be the most useful of the lot because it is compact and mat-forming, growing only 9 inches (23 cm) high and producing dainty pink flowers for a long period. It thrives in semi-shade.

Primula japonica 'Miller's Crimson'

Common name: Candelabra primula

Chief characteristics

There are really only two kinds of primula: the garish, multicolored hybrids you see for sale outside supermarkets in spring, and the rest, which are generally far more beautiful, elegant, simple-flowered plants that are a joy to have in the garden. It is all in the eye of the beholder, of course, but once you have

Location: Full shade to semi-shade
Type: Perennial
Size: 2 to 3 feet (60 to 90 cm)
Conditions: Fertile, moist, well-drained soil
Flowering time: March to May

seen an exhibition of the subtle, soft pastel shades of primula, you will never go back to the jarring "supermarket specials." These supermarket plants seem to escape criticism because they are marketed as the chosen "cheerful" heralds of spring and have been deemed the appropriate symbol for displaying in pots on doorsteps to signal the end of winter.

You can do a lot better. There is, for example, the common English primrose (*Primula vulgaris*), which has superbly simple, soft yellow flowers on modest 6-inch (15-cm) stems in March to April. Or how about one of the oldest and most enduring primulas of all, 'Wanda', which has plain purple flowers and has since been used to produce a wide range of colorful hybrids? There are many other classy performers such as 'Gold Laced', which has dark maroon flowers with golden-yellow edges, making it look rather like a stylish necklace. This was bred by British Columbia primula expert Dr. John Kerridge, of Saltspring Island. 'Mahogany Sunrise' is very similar, with each petal edged with gold. He has also introduced a number of other worthy primulas, including 'Velvet Moon' (red with yellow center). The drumstick primrose (*P. denticulata*) is among the first to appear in spring and is also very lovely, growing only 12 inches (30 cm) high and coming in a range of subdued colors from blue to lilac, white to pink. It gets its name "drumstick" from the shape of the tightly clustered flowerhead. Names to look for include 'Alba' (white), 'Rubin' (rose) and 'Blue Selection' (lilac to deep blue). You will easily spot them because of their distinctive shape.

But of all the primulas, the most classy to my mind are the candelabra primulas (*Primula japonica*), which also just happen to be among the easiest to grow. In moist soil, especially by the banks of streams or ponds, they will quickly colonize to present a magnificent picture in late spring. The flowers are beautifully arranged in neat tiers (hence candelabra) along stems that can stretch 18 to 24 inches (45 to 60 cm) high. Colors range from white to pink, red to apricot. Despite being next to one another in mass plantings, the colors never jar. 'Miller's Crimson' is sensational. It has intense crimson-pink flowers and large leaves. It is especially attractive when mass planted. 'Postford White' is one of the most famous candelabra primulas, not only because of its pure white flowers but because it comes true from seed.

The old-fashioned double English primroses, which have multi-petaled, roselike flowers, are also now more available. They thrive in moist, rich soil, and must be protected from scorching sun. Top names include 'Alan Robb' (pale apricot), 'April Rose' (deep red), 'Dawn Ansel' (white), 'Lilian Harvey' (rose-pink), 'Sunshine Susie' (golden-yellow), 'Sue Jervis' (muted peach), 'Miss Indigo' (purple with white edges) and 'Quaker's Bonnet' (lavender-violet).

Where to plant it

The primula family is enormous. Some like wet, boggy ground; others like growing in cool rockeries. *Primula japonica* 'Miller's Crimson' is happiest in moist soil. The ideal location to grow most primulas is on the east side of the house in a cool, shady spot, perhaps under rhododendrons, deciduous trees and shrubs, where they can flower safely in spring and enjoy foliage protected from the sun in summer. In the spring, primulas will take all the sun you can give them. In the summer, the morning sun won't hurt them, but the midday or afternoon sun will burn them. They are not as long lived as other perennials, but in the right location, they usually manage to self-seed.

How to care for it

Primulas need moist shade. Give them a shot of 20-20-20 liquid fertilizer to wake them up in spring and 0-10-10 to put them to bed in fall. They like moist soil but good drainage. When you plant them, dig in some sand or crushed rock or peat moss to get the soil right. Don't make your soil too rich in organic matter or it can become compact and soggy in winter and your primulas will rot. Watch for slugs, snails, cutworms, weevils and aphids—they can all be a problem.

Good companions

Primulas are happiest tucked under rhododendrons or deciduous shrubs and trees. They combine well with spring-flowering bulbs like muscari, scillas, chionodoxa, leucojum and narcissus as well as spring-flowering perennials like *Helleborus orientalis*. To achieve a sequence of blooms, put *Primula florindae* together with *Primula japonica*.

For your collection

🐾 If you're lucky enough to have a woodland brook or stream or pond in your garden, you could grow the giant cowslip (*Primula florindae*), which is summer flowering and has fragrant yellow blooms on stems 2 to 3 feet (60 to 90 cm) high. Everything about these primulas is oversized. Their perfume is heavy rather than delicate, and the leaves grow bigger according to the degree of moisture in the soil. There are also red and orange shades of *P. florindae* available.

🐾 Everyone falls in love with the Chinese pagoda primrose (*Primula vialii*) when they see it for the first time. It has short pink bottlebrush flower spikes with a distinctive red cone on top that makes it look rather like a miniature red-hot poker plant (*Kniphofia*). It does self-seed and if you get it in the right spot—a cool, well-drained, semi-shaded, woodland-type setting—you might have it for years to come.

🐾 The Japanese star primrose (*Primula sieboldii*) is another collector's item, growing 9 inches (23 cm) tall and producing fabulous white or pink, magenta or purple flowers. Top names are 'Geisha Girl' (shocking pink), 'Mikado' (purple) and 'Snowflakes' (pure white). One other important group of primulas is the Auricula hybrids, regarded by some as the "aristocrats of the primrose world" because of their showy, decorative flowers. Names to look for include 'The Baron' (yellow), 'Matthew Yates' (deep red), 'Camelot' (purple) and 'Chorister' (white).

*P*runus subhirtella 'Pendula Rubra'

Common name: Japanese cherry, ornamental cherry

Chief characteristics

There are dozens of types of Japanese cherry trees. The big question is which one is the right one for your garden. For form and color, you can't go wrong with a weeping cherry. My favorite is *Prunus subhirtella* 'Pendula Rubra'. This has a graceful umbrella form and

Location: Full sun
Type: Deciduous tree
Size: 25 to 30 feet (7.5 to 9 m)
Conditions: Average, well-drained soil
Flowering time: March to April

produces masses of deep pink flowers in April before the dark green, oval-shaped leaves appear. When it is mature it has something of the look of a small weeping willow. It grows 25 to 30 feet (7.5 to 9 m) high and the leaves turn gold-yellow in fall.

Prunus subhirtella 'Pendula', known as the single weeping cherry, is also suitable for the home garden. It has a flat top and a graceful, cascading, mushroom shape. It produces rose-pink flowers in late March or early April.

Where to plant it

The ornamental Japanese cherry tree is one of the great symbols of spring. Some call it the "queen of trees" and the "champion of spring bloomers." Plant your tree in March or late September.

If you are unsure of what kind you want, it is a good idea to take time in spring to look around and then pick out the one you like best. If you buy in late summer for fall planting you need to know what the tree will perform like in spring.

Ornamental cherries thrive in a sunny location in well-drained soil. They look particularly lovely next to a pond where the pink blossoms can be reflected in the water. The weeping cherries also look very handsome placed in a strategic place next to a lawn or against a dark hedge.

How to care for it

Japanese cherries require little maintenance. Prune them for shape when young, taking out crossing branches and routinely removing any branches left dead or damaged by winter. Once trees are more mature, prune as soon as they finish flowering or wait until early winter. It is best not to touch them in the dead of winter for fear of creating wounds that could be open to disease.

Good companions

Underplant your weeping cherry trees with spring-flowering bulbs to contrast with the pink blossoms. It can be a lot of fun trying to get the timing right and working out suitable color combinations. Early tulips are a good choice.

The foliage of the cherry tree is not exceptional, so think about planting other trees or shrubs nearby that will provide a natural continuity and sequence of color. Magnolias will follow comfortably after your cherry blossoms, and the magnolia can be followed by the white flowers of a dogwood or styrax tree. What you want to avoid is having large, brightly colored rhododendrons in the background when the cherry comes into full bloom. Much better to have the still, green backdrop of a yew or cedar or privet hedge.

For your collection

Depending on the size of your garden, you could enjoy any of the trees below.

- *Prunus subhirtella* 'Autumnalis': This has white to pinkish-white flowers and blooms both in warm spells in January and February and again in fall. It has been grown very effectively in a container on a patio or rooftop garden.
- In city streets, you often find *Prunus serrulata* 'Kanzan' cherries, which also go by the names 'Kanzan', 'Sekiyama' and 'Hisakura': These are sturdy, upright, vase-shaped specimens that have very showy pink flowers in April to May and dark bronze leaves that turn green in summer. The 'Kwanzan' cherry can easily reach 30 feet (9 m). While it is not the best pick for the medium- to small-sized garden, it is still a fine ornamental tree.
- *Prunus serrulata* 'Amanogawa': A popular column-shaped cherry, this tree grows very erect and has fragrant pale pink flowers in spring. Since it is capable of going straight up at least 20 feet (6 m) without wavering and it rarely thickens out more than 3 or 4 feet (90 cm to 1.2 m), it is very useful as a screening tree that also provides striking color in spring.
- The great white cherry (*Prunus serrulata* 'Tai haku'): This grows 25 feet (7.5 m) high and just as wide, with white flowers in spring and coppery bronze leaves that green out in summer.
- *Prunus serrulata* 'Shirotae': This has pink buds that turn into lovely white flowers. It grows only 15 feet (4.5 m) high but has long horizontal branches that can reach just as far.
- The red-bark or paperbark cherry (*Prunus serrula*): This is a magnificent tree, widely appreciated for its exceptionally beautiful shiny mahogany or coppery colored bark which peels. It looks superb in winter when its bark literally glistens in the cool wet air. Its tiny white flowers in spring are less impressive, which probably rules this tree out as the ideal pick for many gardeners. It grows 30 feet (9 m) high and its leaves turn a soft yellow in autumn.
- Cheal's weeping cherry (*Prunus cerasifera* 'Kiku-shidare-sakura'): This is a very good pick for the small garden. It grows about 15 feet (4.5 m) high and 10 feet (3 m) wide and has lovely, double, bright pink flowers in April.
- The purple-leafed sand plum (*Prunus × cistena*): This is a very charming multi-branched shrub that can be trained as a single-trunk tree for the small patio or courtyard or grown close to the house. It grows 6 to 10 feet (1.8 to 3 m) high.

ℙyrus salicifolia pendula 'Silver Cascade'

Common name: Weeping willow-leafed pear, ornamental pear

Chief characteristics

This delightful tree for the medium-sized garden has silvery-gray leaves and a weeping willowlike form. It has slowly become more appreciated in recent years as more gardeners discover its virtues and versatility. It doesn't look like much in the nursery as an infant. But as it matures, it commands a special presence. With minimal care, it will grow up to form a shimmering, round-headed mass of silver leaves. The tree not only provides a striking contrast against dark green foliage in the garden, it can have a mesmerizing effect when wind catches it and breathes life into its free-flowing willowy foliage. In late spring it produces small, bright white flowers followed by small, inedible pears.

Location: Sun or light shade
Type: Deciduous tree
Size: 20 feet (6 m)
Conditions: Ordinary, well-drained soil
Flowering time: April to May

Some people don't like the tree's form. They see it as unkempt and unruly. It can look like a wild creature that has just escaped from a laboratory, but it can also make an exceptional specimen or feature tree in a lawn. It has been grown, evenly spaced in avenues, and pruned into a very disciplined but graceful umbrella shape. It is similar in appearance to the Russian olive because of the felty-gray color and texture of the leaves, but the willow-leafed pear is a smaller tree at maturity.

Where to plant it

The perfect pick for the centerpiece of an all white garden, 'Silver Cascade' was used by the celebrated English gardener Vita Sackville-West in her monochromatic white garden at the Sissinghurst garden in Kent, England.

The tree can easily be surrounded by other silver foliage and white flowering plants to complete the silver-white picture. It is best grown in a location where its foliage provides contrast, perhaps against a dark background of conifers or as an artistic counterbalance to the flat, still waters of a lily pond. It is too big for a small garden, even with attentive pruning, but for those who must have it even if space is limited, it could be grown in a planter, which would restrict its size. In a half-barrel, it would stay under 10 feet (3 m). If it got bigger than that, you could always root-prune—remove the outer growth of the rootball—which would force the tree to restrict its height.

How to care for it

Grow the ornamental pear in full sun in well-drained soil. Give it plenty of room at the sides and don't fret too much about height; its habit is to dome and droop rather than stretch and soar. It is officially classified as a small- to medium-sized tree with an ability to put up with the pollution of city smoke and grime. The rule is to thin out in the fall by pruning only dead and weak branches in the curtain of descending foliage. The aim is to achieve a healthy balance and natural symmetry. The tree's skirt, however, can be lightly trimmed each year to create a mushroom-like form that opens the underneath to creative planting of spring-flowering bulbs and low-growing perennials.

Good companions

White campanula and white summer phlox make excellent complementary companions, but for a more stimulating contrast in light shade you could try using bronze-leafed heuchera, black mondo grass or blue ajugas as groundcovers with vivid foliage. The weeping pear has been used most effectively to provide a dramatic contrast to the formal shapes of large boxwood balls and ivy-covered arbors and walls. Clematis could also be grown into sections of the tree, especially where gaps have occurred, to create a burst of color. One effective planting puts Korean goatsbeard (*Aruncus aethusifolius*) under the weeping pear's silver foliage to create rich contrast.

For your collection

- There are two other weeping trees you should consider for your garden: *Salix caprea* 'Kilmarnock', which is a small, slow-growing, umbrella-shaped tree with silvery catkins that turn yellow; and the double weeping cherry (*Prunus subhirtella* 'Pendula Plena Rosea') also known as the weeping rosebud cherry, which has a very graceful, cascading form and rose-pink blossoms. Both these trees grow less than 15 feet (4.5 m).
- For a special, feature tree you might also consider the silk tree (*Albizia julibrissin rosea*), which has exceptional fernlike foliage and pink flowers. It will thrive if planted in a sunny, sheltered, fast-draining site where the soil is not too acidic.

*R*hododendron 'Temple Belle'

Common name: Temple Belle rhododendron

Chief characteristics

It is hard to imagine a garden in the
Pacific Northwest without any
rhododendrons. You don't have to have
dozens of them, but it would be a
mistake not to have one or two. There are
reasons why rhododendrons are
considered indispensable. For starters,

Location: Light shade to shade
Type: Evergreen shrub
Size: 5 to 8 feet (1.5 to 2.4 m)
Conditions: Acidic, well-
    drained soil
Flowering time: May

they flower magnificently from early spring to mid-summer. But their
main contribution in the garden is to provide year-round structural
integrity. Their thick, green leaves clothe a sturdy framework of branches
that supply the essential botanical architecture for a garden, especially in
winter when all the perennials have vanished and deciduous trees and
shrubs are left standing leafless.

It is possible to go overboard and fill your garden with nothing but
rhodos, of course. They come in every color imaginable from fire-engine
red to metallic blue to banana yellow, to ice-cream white. There are
dastardly colorful hybrids and hard-to-find, exotic big-leafed species (the
genetic parents of the popular hybrids). Love for rhododendrons can
very easily go beyond being a mere hobby or collecting pastime and
become a full-blown obsession, driving poor souls mad with desire for
rarer and rarer specimens. Today there are hundreds of varieties of
rhododendrons in commercial production. Nevertheless, as with all
plant families, there are a few notable stars.

There is, for example, the magnificent blue-flowering *Rhododendron
augustinii* (6 to 10 feet/1.8 to 3 m), the bright red-flowering 'Taurus' (6
feet/1.8 m), the compacted form of *R. yakushimanum* (3 feet/90 cm), the
large fragrant white blooms of 'King George' (8 feet/2.5 m), and the
exquisite deep yellow trusses of 'Hotei' (3 feet/90 cm).

New gardeners and old-hand connoisseurs alike will find a common
meeting ground in their appreciation of 'Temple Belle'. It has a well-
behaved, compact form, grows to a modest 5 or 8 feet (1.5 to 2.4 m)
high, and produces delightful clear pink, bell-shaped blooms in spring.
A hybrid of the classy species *R. williamsianum* (which many experts feel
is incapable of producing an inferior plant), 'Temple Belle' has gorgeous,
rounded dark green leaves that make it very attractive even when it is not
in bloom.

Two other top rhodos include 'Dora Amateis' (3 feet/90 cm), which has white flowers tinged with pink, and 'Unique' (4 feet/1.2 m), which has clear white flowers.

Where to plant it

Grow your rhododendrons in dappled shade under the canopy of trees. They will perform perfectly well in full sun provided they are not starved of nitrogen or allowed to die of thirst. They are natural bedfellows for hydrangeas and azaleas and other acid soil–loving plants like kalmias in the mixed border. If selected carefully for their growth habits, rhodos can be arranged to create interesting levels or layers of harmonizing green leaves. Some of the compact forms make excellent container plants for rooftops and patios.

How to care for it

Our rain-drenched west coast gardens have the perfect acidic soil for growing rhododendrons and azaleas. But don't plant rhododendrons by digging a big hole and dropping the plant straight into it the way you might ordinary shrubs. Rather, make a shallow hollow, place the plant and then mound up soil and well-rotted compost around the rootball. Mulch with well-shredded leaves in winter and feed with a balanced nitrogen-rich fertilizer in the spring.

The stick remnants can be pinched or clipped off if you have the time and patience, or left to naturally decay and disappear. Pinching them off is more to do with esthetic appearance than anything. People often ask how to prune rhododendrons. But this is rarely done by expert gardeners. You can prune down new growth after flowering and still get the plant to set buds, but there are better solutions. If a bush becomes too big for its location, move it to a more spacious spot or give it away and replace it with something more appropriate. Rhodos have compact rootballs, which allows them to be moved fairly easily, even the bigger ones. There is, however, a more practical rule of rhododendron growing that makes pruning unnecessary, and that is to make sure you don't put rhodos that will grow to be giants in poky little spaces. Since rhodos mostly fall into one of three basic size categories—small, medium and large—it is not too difficult to pick the right one for the right place.

Good companions

Rhododendrons combine very easily with one another. Large gardens have even been created solely out of rhododendrons, and surprisingly the gardeners have managed to have a sequence of bloom from early spring to mid-summer by carefully selecting the right specimens. The traditional partners for rhododendrons are the lower-growing evergreen azaleas. But rhodos will combine with any flowering shrub that likes or can tolerate the same soil conditions. Camellias are a good choice.

Underplant rhododendrons with lily-of-the-valley, primulas and groundcovers such as sweet woodruff, hardy geraniums and spring-flowering bulbs such as erythronium, muscari and scilla.

For your collection

Once you fall in love with rhodos, it won't be long before you are wanting to collect species rhodos, the natural, original plants from the wild that were used to provide the genetic pool for the myriad hybrids now in existence.

- One of the best is *Rhododendron augustinii*, which has deep blue flowers that are still visible at twilight.
- One of the most heavily scented is *R. fragrantissimum*, which has white flowers with a rose blush and green tinge. It is best grown in a container so that it can be moved into a frost-free area during the winter. The fragrance is worth the effort.
- Evergreen azaleas are members of the rhododendron family. (There is no *Azalea* genus even though they are mostly listed by that name.) Some top names to look for include 'Rosebud', 'Girard's Fuchsia', 'Hardy Gardenia', 'Hinodegiri' and 'Hino Crimson'.
- Camellias are a good evergreen shrub to include in a rhododendron border. There are basically two main kinds of camellia: *Camellia japonica* and *C. sasanqua*, which bloom in the winter, starting as early as October. One of the best *C. sasanqua* cultivars is 'Bonanza', which has red flowers in the fall. *C. japonica* has slightly bigger flowers and blooms from February to March. Look for 'Bob Hope' (deep red), 'Nuccio's Pearl' (white-lilac) or 'Debutante' (pink). You should also check out cultivars of *Camellia × williamsii*, which have an excellent reputation for being hardy shrubs that flower freely and drop their dead blooms very cleanly. Names to look for include 'J.C. Williams', 'Mary Christian' and 'Donation'.

ℛobinia pseudoacacia 'Frisia'

Common name: *False acacia, golden black locust, yellow locust*

Chief characteristics

An exceptionally beautiful and graceful medium-sized deciduous tree, *Robinia pseudoacacia* 'Frisia' is suitable for small- and medium-sized gardens. Its outstanding bright, yellow-green leaves look even more sensational when seen against the backdrop of dark brooding conifers. This is a tree to lust after if you don't have one. Some people love it so much, they have planted two.

Location: Full sun to light shade
Type: Deciduous tree
Size: 30 to 40 feet (9 to 12 m)
Conditions: Well-drained soil
Flowering time: July

You don't need a lot of room to grow it, but you do need plenty of open sky as its habit is to grow up rather than out. Slower growing than its less refined cousins, 'Frisia' takes at least 10 years to reach 25 feet (7.5 m), and another 20 years to attain its full height, usually not more than 40 feet (12 m). Not a demanding or temperamental tree, it can handle cold winters, is hardy to –20°F (–29°C) and doesn't mind hot summers since it is also reasonably drought tolerant. It manages to hang onto the fabulous color of its foliage from the moment it leafs out in spring until the very cold days of fall.

What everyone loves most about 'Frisia' is its light, frothy yellow-green leaves, which always brighten dark corners and create a cheerful picture on the gloomiest of days. Less impressive are the drooping clusters of scented white pealike flowers the tree produces.

Where to plant it

The golden black locust will grow happily in full sun or light shade in almost any type of soil although, like the majority of plants, it does not like to be in ground that is perpetually wet. Some people have used this tree very successfully to give their garden a focal point or to anchor the curve in a mixed border or to create a prominent feature in the center of a lawn. It is regarded by many landscape designers as an impact tree with a delightfully cheerful character. With sunshine streaming through its leaves, it is an awesome spectacle. Its foliage can be accented even more by placing it in direct contrast with shrubs like the purple smoke bush (*Cotinus coggygria*) or the burning bush (*Euonymus alata*).

If your garden is prone to winds, try not to plant 'Frisia' in an exposed site: its branches can be brittle and if pressured too much by wind they can snap.

How to care for it

Forget about heavy pruning. 'Frisia' rarely needs it. The only pruning you will have to do is the basic: snip out whatever is dead, diseased, damaged or dangerous in spring. This tree is unlikely to display any of those problems if planted properly in the first place. However, if you do find you need to prune heavily, you will find 'Frisia' will bounce back very quickly, producing wonderful new growth.

Suckers—shoots that sometimes pop up from the ground close to the trunk—should be snipped off whenever they appear.

Good companions

Part of the beauty and appeal of 'Frisia' is its ability to share ground with a rich variety of plants and tolerate the root presence of sizable shrubs. The airy foliage of the golden black locust allows light to reach the ground rather than casting a deep shadow and that means many other plants can flourish.

Underplant with your choice of hostas or hardy geraniums. The silver foliage of *Artemisia ludoviciana* 'Valerie Finnis' and the blue flowers of *Salvia* × *sylvestris* 'East Friesland' can be combined with the green-silvery foliage of *Ruta graveolens* 'Curly Girl' to create an attractive mixture of color and textures. For a dramatic display underplant the tree with a mixture of late-blooming yellow 'Sweet Harmony' or white 'Maureen' tulips with one or two black 'Queen of the Night' tulips in the center.

For your collection

🌿 *Acer negundo* 'Flamingo' is another outstanding tree for the small- or medium-sized garden. Its new leaves have a flamingo-pink edge to them. The color is even more pronounced in cooler areas where the tree's Zone 5 hardiness rating gets pushed to the limit. It grows about 15 to 20 feet (4.5 to 6 m).

Choosing a Rose

How do you go about choosing a rose? It is a process of elimination. First, decide on the color you want. White or cream, red or pink, yellow or an orange blend (apricot, salmon, tangerine), lilac or purple or two-tone (bicolor)? Once you've done that, your shortlist will come down to a more manageable number.

Then you can decide on the rose's function or purpose. Is it to cover a fence or arch, scramble into a tree or over an arbor or along a pergola? Do you want a well-behaved bush or a less structured shrub? Do you need your roses to flower all summer or would you be content with a one-time, month-long flush of blooms? How important is fragrance to you? Some continual bloomers have beautiful flowers but no scent.

Disease resistance is important to many people now since it means not having to spray for fungal or pest problems.

All of the roses mentioned below are excellent performers. There are dozens of others worth considering. The key is to decide what you want to achieve and to do some research on the rose before buying.

osa 'Ballerina'

Common name: Ballerina rose

Chief characteristics

A terrific shrub rose, 'Ballerina' comes with excellent credentials. It flowers profusely, producing abundant clusters of small pale-pink single blooms with white centers. It is disease resistant and has a long history of consistent and problem-free performances in a variety of gardens in more than 5 different climate zones. It is not temperamental about the quality of the soil in which it is planted, and it is not the kind of rose to sulk and refuse to flower if it gets less than 6 hours of direct sunlight. 'Ballerina' grows to a manageable size, reaching 4 feet (1.2 m) high by 2 feet (60 cm) wide at maturity. Being a musk hybrid, its flowers look rather like the color of apple blossom and have a pleasant musklike, sweet-pea scent.

Location: Full sun
Type: Modern shrub rose
Size: 4 feet (1.2 m)
Conditions: Fertile, well-drained soil
Flowering time: June to July

It is not difficult to figure out how 'Ballerina' earned its name once you see the flowers. With their white centers and pink trim, the flowers resemble a ballerina's skirt. As an added bonus, the rose has few thorns and its foliage is a soft light green which blends in well with other plants in the garden. This is the kind of rose that is so versatile you can work it into virtually any situation. Use it as a flowering shrub in a mixed border or as a general mixer in your perennial border. You can use it to form a modest hedge or train it into a small tree. You can also, of course, use it as one of the focal pieces in your rose border.

Plant more than one and you'll fool visitors to your garden into thinking it is even more prolific a performer than it already is. 'Ballerina' is considered by some rose experts to be an old garden rose even though it was introduced in only 1937. That is partly because it can hold its own against top Gallica shrub roses such as 'Complicata', 'Charles de Mills', and 'Cardinal de Richelieu'.

Where to plant it

'Ballerina' will tolerate a variety of locations but it performs best in a sunny spot where it is protected from the intense heat of the afternoon sun. Give it room, if you want it to spread unhindered to its mature size of 4 feet (1.2 m) after a couple of years.

How to care for it

Resistant to most typical rose problems, 'Ballerina' rarely needs to be sprayed for black spot and seems able to repel other pests. However, make sure it is not left to starve, especially if it is in competition with heavy feeders in a perennial or shrub border. If you decide to grow it in a pot, make sure that it is a large one and that you don't forget to water routinely.

See *Rosa* 'Elina', "How to care for it," for general pruning recommendations.

Good companions

Other shrub roses make excellent partners for 'Ballerina'. Check out the red form of 'Marjorie Fair', which has many of the same characteristics as 'Ballerina'. Another smashing companion would be 'Mary Rose', one of David Austin's new English roses, which is equally hardy and disease resistant.

For your collection

Buying shrub roses can become an addiction. Many gardeners enjoy them far more than hybrids, teas and floribundas because of the way they blend in so naturally with other plants in the garden and because of their tolerance to pests and disease. Here are a few other first-rate shrub roses to consider.

- 🌺 'Blanche Double de Coubert': A tough and hardy French-bred rugosa rose that flowers in June and grows 5 feet (1.5 m). Very fragrant.
- 🌺 'The Fairy': Popular ever since its introduction in 1932, this profusely flowering rose has light pink blooms. It grows 30 inches (75 cm).
- 🌺 'Hansa': A medium-sized bushy rose with deep mauve to red blooms. It can be used for making a hedge.
- 🌺 'Fantin-Latour': This famous centifolia rose has fragrant pinkish-white blooms and grows about 5 feet (1.5 m).

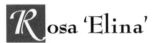osa 'Elina'

Common name: Elina or Peaudouce rose

Chief characteristics

Location: Full sun
Type: Hybrid tea rose
Size: 3 1/2 feet (1 m)
Conditions: Rich, well-drained soil
Flowering time: June to September

It is a curious thing that so many avid gardeners look down their nose at hybrid tea roses. They will talk enthusiastically about the virtues of obscure and esoteric varieties of old garden roses, but give hybrid teas short shrift. Part of the problem is that many modern roses have a reputation for being excessively prone to pests and disease. There is also a kind of disdain for the high-strung, thoroughbred nature of hybrid teas that predisposes them for a hectic, high-powered life of perpetual flower production. It all seems so unnatural to some gardeners.

Nevertheless, gardens need roses and no garden is really complete without a few hybrid teas, the celebrity flowers of summer. The challenge is to pick the best of the best. 'Elina' is certainly an unbeatable star performer. It is more disease and drought tolerant and flowers more abundantly than most hybrid teas and its exquisite, large white-primrose, lightly scented blooms make excellent cut flowers.

Bred in Ireland, 'Elina' was first introduced in 1984 and immediately began winning awards. It has been held up as a perfect example of what a hybrid tea should be: hardy, vigorous and beautiful. It was originally called 'Peaudouce' (French for "soft skin"). That turned out to be a big mistake. The breeders found the name did not help the rose make friends, so the name was changed to 'Elina'. The American Rose Society rates it 8.6 out of 10.

Where to plant it

Hybrid teas are the race horses of the rose family but they are not as temperamental or hard to care for as is sometimes suggested. They need full sun, at least 6 hours a day and nutrient-rich, well-drained soil to flower properly. They also like to be fed well and watered deeply without being drowned. 'Elina' is one of the easier hybrid teas to care for. It is less prone to black spot and probably because of its robust healthiness and vigor and subtle scent, it doesn't attract insect pests. Grow it close to the house where you can appreciate it all the time rather than at the end of the garden where you have to travel to see it.

How to care for it

Roses are killed by extremes—either neglect or overzealousness. Too much fertilizer or too little fertilizer, too much water or no water at all can all be lethal. Moderation is a good rule of thumb in caring for roses.

Pruning always seems like the biggest hassle. There is so much talk about how to prune, when to prune and what to prune, most average gardeners end up too confused and scared to do anything. The golden rule is: prune out all dead, diseased or damaged stems. Then remove thin, wiry stems that look unlikely to produce flowers. Prune out stems that rub against each other or cross one another. Keep in mind the overall shape of the bush. Finally, to promote good roots and healthy new growth in hybrid teas, prune healthy stems to about 18 inches (45 cm) from the ground. Do all this when the rose is dormant, at the end of winter or in early spring just before the buds break. If all this still makes you nervous, follow the Easy Care Method devised by Britain's Royal National Rose Society. Prune your rose bush to half its height and then take out any dead wood. The society conducted experiments and found, in most cases, this method worked as well as the more complicated methods.

Good companions

Lavender, santolina and purple alliums all go well with roses. A low boxwood hedge can provide a formal border to your rose bed and it also serves to hide the less interesting lower parts of the rose without interfering with air circulation.

For your collection

🐾 Here's a list of the top-performing hybrid teas: 'Rosemary Harkness' (a mixture of orange, yellow and salmon), 'Double Delight' (creamy white petals with raspberry rims), 'Pink Peace' (fragrant pink blooms), 'Just Joey' (scented, coppery orange) and 'Sexy Rexy' (camellia-like pink flowers).

- Other star performers include: 'Alexander' (cherry-red), 'Grandpa Dickson' (yellow), 'L'Oréal Trophy' (orange), 'Ingrid Bergman' (red), 'Pascali' (white), 'Heart Throb' (pink), 'Peace' (yellow), 'Piccadilly' (scarlet-yellow), 'Elizabeth Taylor' (pink), 'Silver Jubilee' (pink-peach), and 'Tropicana' (orange-pink).
- For outstanding fragrance choose: 'Pink Peace', 'Double Delight', 'Chrysler Imperial', 'Mister Lincoln', 'Fragrant Cloud', 'Ena Harkness', 'Granada', 'Lady Rose', 'Princesse de Monaco', 'Sterling Silver', 'Tropicana', 'Sutter's Gold' and 'Ingrid Bergman'.

osa 'Mary Rose'

Common name: *Mary rose*

Chief characteristics

Named after Henry VII's flagship, 'Mary Rose' is one of the most regal hybrids in David Austin's celebrated stable of English roses. Austin, an English rose breeder, made a name for himself internationally by

Location: Full sun
Type: English rose
Size: 4 feet (1.2 m)
Conditions: Rich, well-drained soil
Flowering time: June to September

combining the exquisite, multi-petaled beauty of famous old garden roses with the prolific flowering power of top-performing modern hybrid teas and floribundas. The result is a new class of roses called "English roses."

Everyone has his or her favorite Austin rose. 'Mary Rose' is mine. I have tried an assortment of others, but few performed as consistently or as beautifully as 'Mary Rose'. It has cheerful, fragrant, rose-pink blooms, which start to appear in early June and continue sporadically to the end of summer. Austin describes the rose's growth habit as "near to ideal—bushy, twiggy and vigorous without being unruly."

Part of my satisfaction with 'Mary Rose' is that it fits so perfectly into the perennial border, harmonizing without effort with the feathery silver foliage of artemisia and the lacy foliage of bronze fennel. 'Mary Rose' is also impressively disease resistant and it does not object to having its blooms clipped off at their peak to fill vases. The American Rose Society gave it an 8.7 rating out of 10.

There are other great roses in the Austin series you should also consider: 'Constance Spry' (soft pink) was the first to be introduced in 1961, while 'Evelyn' (apricot-yellow) is one of Austin's newer hybrids. Both are excellent. The most popular are the powerfully scented

'Gertrude Jekyll' (deep pink), 'Heritage' (light pink) and the dependable 'Graham Thomas' (yellow). One of the newest Austin roses is a fragrant pink called 'Geoff Hamilton'. It was first introduced at the Chelsea Flower Show in 1997 and is named after one of the most beloved English gardeners, who hosted a much watched television show called "Gardener's World." Certainly a rose to look out for.

Where to plant it

Like all roses, 'Mary Rose' requires full sun, but will not complain if it gets a little shade in the afternoon. It is the perfect rose for slipping into the perennial border. It will mix happily with foxgloves and campanula and give you a very relaxed, free-flowing, English cottage garden look. Consider planting more than one for a more substantial display of flowers.

How to care for it

Roses need 6 hours of sun a day. If you don't get a lot of blooms it could be because the rose is not getting enough sun. Deadhead spent blooms regularly to encourage flowering. See *Rosa* 'Elina', "How to care for it," for general pruning recommendations.

English roses and modern floribundas and hybrid teas don't seem to get along very well. If you plant an English rose, try to find a place for it outside your more formal rose bed.

Good companions

The silvery foliage of *Artemisia* 'Powis Castle' or the blue spikes of *Veronica spicata* or the bright white flowers of *Aconitum napellus* 'Albidum' all make great partners for planting around 'Mary Rose'. Pink foxgloves, blue or white campanulas and white sweet williams also make happy companions.

For your collection

If you become serious about roses, you will want to investigate more of David Austin's English roses. Austin is a fairly hard critic of his own roses, rating them with a star from 1 to 4. His own 4-star picks include those on the facing page.

Name	Color	Height
'Abraham Darby'	coppery apricot	4 feet/1.2 m
'The Alexandra Rose'	coppery pink with pale yellow centre	4 feet/1.2 m
'Brother Cadfael'	medium pink	3 feet/90 cm
'Charles Rennie Mackintosh'	dusky lilac-pink	30 inches/75 cm
'Chianti'	crimson to maroon	5 feet/1.5 m
'Constance Spry'	soft pink	6 feet/1.8 m
'Cottage Rose'	pink	30 inches/75 cm
'The Countryman'	clear pink	2 feet/60 cm
'The Dark Lady'	dusky crimson	3 feet/90 cm
'Francine Austin'	white	4 feet/1.2 m
'Gertrude Jekyll'	deep pink	4 feet/1.2 m
'Glamis Castle'	white	30 inches/75 cm
'Golden Celebrations'	coppery yellow	4 feet/1.2 m
'Graham Thomas'	warm yellow	4 feet/1.2 m
'Heritage'	clear pink	4 feet/1.2 m
'Jayne Austin'	soft yellow	42 inches/1 m
'Kathryn Morley'	soft pink	3 feet/90 cm
'L.D. Braithwaite'	crimson	42 inches/1 m
'Leander'	deep apricot	5 feet/1.5 m
'Lilian Austin'	salmon-pink	4 feet/1.2 m
'Perdita'	soft pink	30 inches/75 cm
'The Pilgrim'	yellow	3 feet/90 cm
'The Prince'	crimson turning purple	3 feet/90 cm
'Redoute'	soft pink	4 feet/1.2 m
'St. Cecilia'	buff-apricot	30 inches/75 cm
'St. Swithun'	soft pink	3 feet/90 cm
'Sharifa Asma'	soft pink with gold	30 inches/75 cm
'Shropshire Lass'	blush pink to white	6 feet/1.8 m
'Winchester Cathedral'	white	4 feet/1.2 m

osa 'New Dawn'

Common name: New dawn rose, everblooming Doctor W. Van Fleet

Chief characteristics

'New Dawn' is one of the most dependable and disease-resistant climbing roses. It can be relied upon to cover fences or walls and produce an outstanding flush of slightly fragrant, shell-pink blooms in early June. It will continue to flower

Location: Full sun
Type: Climbing rose
Size: 15 to 20 feet (4.5 to 6 m)
Conditions: Well-drained soil
Flowering time: June

throughout summer, although not nearly as profusely as at its peak.

First introduced in 1930 as the offspring of the famous rambling rose, 'Doctor W. Van Fleet', 'New Dawn' is less vigorous than its parent but is still considered by many to be the yardstick by which all other climbing roses are judged. The leaves have a healthy, shiny look while the light pink flowers, measuring 3 inches (7.5 cm) wide, are small, somewhat fragile, but plentiful. You can use 'New Dawn' to cover a fence between you and your neighbor and you can rest assured that it won't cause offence by leaving a mess or becoming too thorny or rampant.

Where to plant it

'New Dawn' will tolerate poor soil and some shade and can even be used to create a hedge or grown on the cold side of the house. Use it over an arch or arbor or fan-spread it against a fence or brick wall.

How to care for it

Prune out anything that is dead, diseased, damaged or decadent (meaning weak and unproductive). The soil in which it is planted should be enriched every year with well-rotted compost or aged manure. Feed your rose with a balanced diet of granular rose fertilizer in early spring and once again in mid-summer.

Good companions

Clematis is a perfect partner for 'New Dawn'. The purple forms such as *Clematis* 'Jackmanii Superba', 'Polish Spirit', 'Etoile Violette' and 'The President' will bloom at the same time and provide a sensational contrast. When covering a fence, another climbing rose such as the thornless 'Zephirine Drouhin', which has slightly larger, carmine-pink flowers that appear about the same time as 'New Dawn', can also be interplanted for heightened color.

For your collection

There are many other fine climbing roses worth considering.

- 🌹 'Madame Gregoire Staechelin' (Spanish beauty): This produces 5-inch (12.5 cm), very fragrant pink blooms in June. It is a classy rose with an antique appearance that gives it an old-fashioned charm.
- 🌹 'Félicité Perpétue': This has creamy fragrant white flowers and will happily clamber into trees. The 'perpétue' reference does not mean it flowers perpetually—it has one burst of blooms.
- 🌹 'High Hopes': An offspring of the more famous 'Compassion' rose, this climber has fragrant pale pink flowers and is a repeat bloomer. It is very disease resistant and a good choice for covering arches.

- 'Rambling Rector': An outstanding white, fragrant rambler, capable of covering large fences, reaching up into trees, and hiding eyesores in the garden.
- 'American Pillar': This flowers profusely in July and still rates as one of the best climbers of all time. The flowers are deep pink with a white center. You do, however, need to plant it where the air circulates freely because in stagnant air this rose is prone to mildew.
- 'Albertine': Introduced in 1921, this has highly fragrant, pale coppery pink blooms. It is a fairly rampant rambler capable of covering a long fence or pergola.
- 'Altissimo': This is not a tall climber, reaching only 10 feet (3 m), but it does produce large striking red flowers in small numbers over the whole summer rather than in one main flush. It is also a clean rose, resistant to mildew and black spot, making it a good choice for fixing against walls or fences.
- 'Compassion': A lovely, highly fragrant rose with pink to salmon–colored blooms, this is one of the best from the Harkness Rose Company, of England. It is ideal for walls and fences.
- 'Francois Juranville': This has fragrant, pale pink flowers in June and will easily scramble 20 feet (6 m). It is perfect for rose pillars, arches and arbors. It is a lot more pliable than other climbers, making it a little more flexible for bending into place over structures.
- 'Zéphirine Drouhin': This thornless climber is popular with British garden designers who often use it to cover arches along paths. It has vivid crimson-pink blooms that have been described as expressive of the "warmth of some old remembered days of summer, when roses innocently quartered their centers, and were expected to breathe a gentle fragrance into the air."

*R*osa 'Souvenir de la Malmaison'

Common name: Souvenir de la Malmaison rose

Chief characteristics

A rose is a rose is a rose? Not so. Each one is different and we all have our favorites. There are, however, some roses that are definitely more disease resistant, floriferous or sweetly scented. One of the most superbly fragranced is 'Souvenir de la Malmaison'. It was named after the famous rose garden created by

Location: Full sun
Type: Bourbon rose
Size: 4 feet (1.2 m)
Conditions: Rich soil
Flowering time: June to September

Empress Josephine, the wife of Napoleon Bonaparte, at the estate at La Malmaison, near Paris. The story goes that Josephine was so in love with roses, she tried to collect every known species. It was a natural and predictable consequence that she would eventually have a rose named to commemorate her ambitious undertaking and her passion for roses.

'Souvenir de la Malmaison' does not need an interesting history to make it desirable. It has lovely creamy white-pink, lushly petaled flowers that exude the most delicious fragrance. It is one of a group of roses known as Bourbons, which were especially popular in Victorian England because of their repeat flowering characteristic. There are several excellent Bourbons, but 'Souvenir de la Malmaison' is the most beautiful of them all. The scent has been described as an intoxicating mixture of cinnamon and ripe bananas with a hint of spice. Rain is this rose's only enemy. In drizzly, damp weather, the petals ball up because they get trapped by moisture and cannot expand properly.

Where to plant it

Grow 'Souvenir de la Malmaison' in a half-barrel or in the rose bed where it gets some protection from rain. The advantage to growing it in a container is that it can be positioned close to the house where its fragance can be enjoyed more easily and where it is less exposed to downpours. Perhaps you have a front porch that faces west or south that gives you all the sun you need plus the required rain-shielding. This rose can, of course, be planted out in the open garden. Positioned below an open window would be ideal.

How to care for it

Prune in winter and don't worry if it seems to be a slow starter. See *Rosa* 'Elina', "How to care for it," for general pruning recommendations.

Flowering may not occur until later in June, but once it begins it will be profilic and continuous. Like all plants in containers, it will need a top-dressing of well-rotted compost in spring and a sprinkling of slow-release rose food.

Good companions

Excellent partners for 'Souvenir de la Malmaison' include other classic, old garden roses such as the fabulous centifolia 'Fantin Latour' (blush pink), the outstanding 'Maiden's Blush' (soft pink) or the marvelous old Portland rose, 'Jacques Cartier' (clear pink). David Austin's English roses such as 'Gertrude Jekyll', 'Heritage' and 'Evelyn' also have the classy, old-garden rose look of 'Souvenir de la Malmaison' as well as delicious fragrance. Other heavenly scented roses worth investing in include the hybrid tea 'Double Delight' (cream, white and red), the modern shrub roses 'Sarah van Fleet' (pink) and 'Jacqueline du Pre' (soft white).

For your collection

- There is a climbing form of 'Souvenir de la Malmaison' that will grow 6 to 8 feet (1.8 to 2.4 m) high. It flowers profusely in late June and thrives if planted on a sunny, south-facing wall in a spot where it gets protection from rain.
- Other great Bourbons include the thornless 'Zephirine Drouhin' (rose-pink climber), which has a long flowering period; 'Madame Issac Pereire' (vivid crimson-pink), which has intense perfume and is considered the most fragrant of all roses; and 'Bourbon Queen' (rose-pink), which is a vigorous rose that will thrive in any soil, earning the title "queen of the Bourbons."

Salvia × sylvestris 'May Night'

Common name: Perennial salvia, sage

Chief characteristics

'May Night' was voted Perennial Plant of the Year in 1997 by the Perennial Plant Association. It is a beautiful, compact plant that produces striking deep indigo-blue flower spikes with a slight tinge of purple in early summer. It is very similar to its cousin, 'East Friesland', which flowers a little later in May. When they are both planted together side by side, it is hard to tell them apart. Both are excellent clump-forming plants, but 'May Night' has a slight advantage because of the beauty of the vivid violet-blue flowers it produces on stiff, upright stems. Drought tolerant and easy to care for, it can be used to create impressive dense drifts of blue about 3 feet (90 cm) high at the front of the perennial border at the feet of taller perennials such as lavatera. What makes 'May Night' also very desirable is its resistance to drought; it won't sulk if left unwatered for a day or two in a dry spell.

Location: Full sun to part shade
Type: Perennial
Size: 18 to 24 inches (45 to 60 cm)
Conditions: Ordinary, well-drained soil
Flowering time: May to July

Where to plant it

Grow 'May Night' in average, well-drained soil in full sun or a semi-shaded location. It can be combined with other varieties of sage like *Salvia verticillata* 'Purple Rain' for foliage contrast and the annual *S. farinacea*, for continuous summer color.

How to care for it

An easy plant to care for, salvia only needs to be tidied up at the end of its flowering period. The key to growing it successfully is to make sure that it is planted in a sunny, well-drained site. Add some sand to the base of the planting hole when you plant, to improve drainage. Heavy, prolonged rains in winter and lack of sunlight is what kills most salvia. It is tough enough to deal with frost and snow.

Good companions

Reds and silvers are excellent colors to contrast with the dark purple-blue flowers of 'May Night'. Good companions include daylilies, canna lilies, purple verbena, pastel shades of achillea, red potentilla and blue ornamental grasses.

For your collection

- Scarlet sage (*Salvia splendens*) is used to brighten floral borders in city parks in summer. It is a powerful, attention-grabbing color that needs to be handled with care in the home garden. The hot red can appear too aggressive if allowed to stand alone without flowers of calmer hues for companions.
- The deep purple-blue annual sage (*S. farinacea* 'Victoria') is another favorite for mass planting in the public landscape. However, this Texas native is a lot easier to work with. It flowers beautifully through the hot drought-days of August and is one of the last flowers to go down to dust in fall.
- The purple-leafed sage (*S. officinalis* 'Purpurascens') is an excellent plant for foliage contrast. Its soft purple-gray leaves heighten the feathery silver foliage of artemisia or stachys.
- *Salvia officinalis* 'Tricolor' is the variegated form of the common purple-leafed sage. It has green and white leaves, some with a reddish-pink tinge.
- The silver sage (*S. argentea*) is arguably the most aristocratic of the sage family. It has large, floppy, silver-gray leaves. It looks very classy when grown in a terracotta pot as a simple decorative foliage plant for patio or porch.

🐾 Salvias are coming back into popularity. It is getting easier to find some of the rarer and more exotic forms, such as these three. *Salvia nipponica* 'Fuji Snow' has arrow-shaped leaves with variegated cream tips and butter-yellow flowers in mid-summer. *S. sclarea*, the beautiful clary sage, grows 3 feet (90 cm) tall in warm sunny places and has lilac-purple flowers. *S. patens*, also known as the gentian sage, grows 2 feet (60 cm) and has very lovely gentian-like blue hooded flowers arranged sparingly along 2-foot (60-cm) high spires.

🐾 *Nepeta* 'Dropmore Blue' is another excellent blue flowering drought-tolerant plant for the front of the sunny border. Developed by a Canadian, it gets along very well with roses, grows 12 inches (30 cm) high and flowers freely from June to September.

Scabiosa columbaria 'Butterfly Blue'

Common name: Pincushion flower

Chief characteristics

What makes 'Butterfly Blue' such a must-have plant is its astonishing flower power. Starting in spring, it will continue to produce delightful lilac-blue blooms (about 1.5 inches/4 cm wide), without pausing to catch a breath, right through to fall. Only *Geranium cinereum* 'Ballerina' and *Corydalis lutea* seem to be able to do that—flower repeatedly and consistently, producing top quality blooms for at least 3 months. Scabiosa is also known as the pincushion flower because the center of each bloom looks like dozens of tiny pins pressed into a sewing cushion.

Location: Full sun
Type: Perennial
Size: 15 inches (38 cm)
Conditions: Good, well-drained soil
Flowering time: June to September

Scabiosa makes an excellent cut flower and is available in lilac-blue, pink and white. There are dozens of kinds. *Scabiosa caucasica*, for instance, grows to almost 3 feet (90 cm) and has purple-blue flowers. There is also a white form. But the pick of the crop is *S. columbaria* 'Butterfly Blue', a shorter cultivar, growing only 15 to 18 inches high, and its sister, 'Pink Mist', an almost identical twin, except that it has pale pink rather than blue flowers.

Where to plant it

Grow 'Butterfly Blue' or 'Pink Mist' in fertile, well-drained soil in full sun. They do brilliantly in containers, too. 'Butterfly Blue' combines well with the variegated Jacob's ladder (*Polemonium caeruleum* 'Brise d'Anjou'), which has small, delicate light blue flowers. The blues play off one another very nicely. If you have a sunny driveway or front entrance where you need continual color all summer, either of these scabiosa will do the trick. In the perennial border, they should be grown at the front, but they need very good drainage if you are to keep them over the years, so make sure you add some sand to the planting hole to eliminate the possibility of waterlogging.

How to care for it

If aphids become a problem, wash them away with a strong jet of water or simply squish them off the stems. Deadhead the faded flowerheads regularly for the sake of neatness and to stimulate the plant to keep blooming. It is best to use scissors because the stems can get quite spindly and they also need to be pruned away. Fertilize every couple of weeks with a half-strength solution of 20-20-20.

Good companions

Geranium cinereum 'Ballerina' or 'Lawrence Flatman' make excellent partners. The geraniums also bloom perpetually all summer and need fast-draining soil in a full-sun location. Put 'Butterfly Blue' with either of these geraniums and throw in the short clumping blue grass (*Festuca glauca*) and the purple spikes of *Liatris spicata*, and you have a winning association.

The taller forms of scabiosa combine best in the perennial border with liatris, achillea, daylilies, phlox paniculata, butterfly gaura, shasta daisies and crocosmia. You can also bring in ornamental grasses, especially the blue and burgundy ones, to put in front of scabiosa. This allows the pincushion flowers to float high above the fountain-like foliage of the grasses.

For your collection

- *Scabiosa ochroleuca* grows to 36 inches (90 cm), has gray-green felty foliage and produces small, sulfur-yellow flowers in late summer. Unlike the species recommended above, it is not very long lived, but the flowers can add interest to the perennial border.
- There is also a dwarf pincushion flower—*Scabiosa japonica*—which grows only 6 inches (15 cm) high, has mauve-blue flowers and can be used in the sunny rockery.
- If you like the look of scabiosa, you will probably also like the stokes's aster (*Stokesia laevis*), which has similarly shaped lavender-blue flowers.

Scilla (Hyacinthoides) non-scripta

Common name: English bluebell, squill

Chief characteristics

Nature uses color with immense subtlety. Yellow, purple and white flowers appear in perfect harmony and bob about on a great sea of green foliage. We can learn from this for our own gardens. It's always safe to play with colors as long as you follow nature's example and surround bright flowers with plenty of soothing, restful shades of green. Most of the problems with clashing colors occur because we ignore nature's green rule.

Location: Sun to light shade
Type: Bulb
Size: 18 inches (45 cm)
Conditions: Ordinary, well-drained soil
Flowering time: April to May

In the natural landscape, blue flowers also play a significant role. There are few blue flowers, however, that have as much simple charm or lasting appeal as the plain old-fashioned English bluebell (*Scilla non-scripta*). You will find bluebells in small woods and lanes all over England. In fact, as a boy growing up in Nottinghamshire, I remember a local copse that was known as Bluebell Wood because in spring the ground turned into a magnificent blue carpet of the magical bell-shaped flowers. I remember, as a young boy, running through them, laughing and pulling up great bunches, without ever thinking about the destruction I was causing.

The most common of all bluebells, *Scilla non-scripta* have deep violet-blue flowers with a distinctive old English bonnet. They are suspended in lovely, loose clusters on slightly arching 10-inch (25-cm) stems in April and May. They are easy to introduce to the garden and once you have found the right spot for them, you can enjoy their punctual arrival year after year.

When you go to buy bluebells, you may find them packaged under their new botanical name, *Hyacinthoides non-scripta,* or *Endymion non-scripta,* which can be confusing.

Where to plant it

Plant your bluebells in ordinary, well-drained soil. They thrive in cool, light or dappled shade, under trees or shrubs where they can naturalize. Resist the temptation to mix colors: squills look best in monochromatic drifts.

How to care for it

When colonies become too dense, dig and divide and replant bulbs immediately back into the ground.

Cut flowerheads once they are finished. Watch to see that the flowering sequence works well with other plants. The ideal match is to have bluebells in bloom just ahead or just after their companions.

Good companions

Bluebells look good pushing up through groundcovers like epimedium or mingling with the lower branches of shrubs like rhododendrons. They also work well with other semi-shade plants like bleeding hearts, astilbes, polemonium, hardy geraniums and hostas.

For your collection

- How about a pink bluebell? Mmm? Well, there is such a thing as a white bleeding heart and a yellow red-hot poker. You can get a pink form of the Spanish bluebell called *Hyacinthoides hispanica* 'Pink'. You can also get a pure white form. The Spanish bluebell (*Hyacinthoides hispanica* or *Scilla campanulata* or *Endymion hispanicus*) is larger than the English species.
- The Cuban lily (*Scilla peruviana*) is also part of the bluebell family and is loved for its spectacular hyacinth-sized blue flowerhead. It is tender, which means it has a tough time surviving in the open garden in winter in our climate. You are starting to see more of these being marketed at Eastertime.
- For the rockery, you could try the tiny blue Persian squill (*Scilla tubergeniana*), which grows only 4 inches (10 cm) high.
- *Scilla siberica* is an excellent rockery bluebell. The Siberian or Prussian bluebell (*S. siberica* 'Spring Beauty') produces particularly lovely nodding blue flowers that are dangled from short 5-inch (12.5-cm) stems. There is also a pretty white form, 'Alba'.

Sedum × 'Autumn Joy'

Common name: *Stonecrop*

Chief characteristics

'Autumn Joy' is one of those rare plants that has value in the garden from the first moment it appears in spring to the end of fall when its sturdy broccoli-shaped flowerheads hang on defiantly in the heavy frost. Large perennial borders are often anchored at the corners with giant clumps of this plant at either end. A late summer–flowering perennial, it has salmon-pink flowers in tight clusters that appear about the same time as the yellow black-eyed susans (*Rudbeckia fulgida*) and the marvelous white and pink flowers of Japanese anemones and the stately feather-duster plumes of pampas grass.

Location: Full sun to light shade
Type: Perennial
Size: 18 to 24 inches (45 to 60 cm)
Conditions: Good, well-drained soil
Flowering time: September to October

'Autumn Joy' certainly lives up to its name. One of the first perennials to appear in spring, it develops steadily through the summer, growing thick, fleshy, succulentlike leaves on erect stems. By late July to August, it will have formed large, attractive, flat-topped flowerheads. They not only offer a pleasing texture in the border, they provide valuable fall color and impressive long-lasting structure that lasts into winter. There are other cultivars similar to 'Autumn Joy', including *Sedum spectabile* 'Brilliant' and 'Stardust'. There are also some interesting types with bronze-red or purple foliage. Look for 'Atropurpureum', 'Matrona', 'Morchen', 'Vera Jameson', 'Bertram Anderson' and 'Ruby Glow'. If in doubt, stick with 'Autumn Joy' or 'Brilliant', but it is worthwhile trying to work a few others into your planting scheme. These plants are also good for attracting bees and butterflies to the garden.

Where to plant it

Grow 'Autumn Joy' where it can quietly develop without demands for flowers or color during the summer and yet have a prominent place in the fall. This could be at the front of the perennial border, but it is probably best to locate it as a foliage plant behind shorter front-runners like *Verbena canadensis* 'Homestead Purple' (an excellent trailing perennial that produces deep purple flowers all summer), *Salvia* × *sylvestris* 'May Night', *Geranium cinereum* 'Ballerina' or *Stachys* 'Countess Helene von Stein'. Wherever you plant *Sedum* × 'Autumn Joy', don't just plant one. Plant 3 or 5 to create a substantial clump.

How to care for it

Sedums are long-lived, trouble-free plants. 'Autumn Joy' will divide easily but, like hostas, it is best left to mature into a mass of impressive foliage. Let the stems stay right into winter. They will stand up in the snow and can be part of the winter garden. By spring they will have turned soft and mushy and they will give you a good reason to get outside in February to clean up for the spring explosion.

Good companions

'Autumn Joy' can also fill ground in front of rudbeckia and asters, euphorbias and shrubs like *Viburnum plicatum* 'Summer Snowflake'. Blue grasses and silver foliage plants like *Stachys byzantina, Artemisia schmidtiana* 'Silver Mound' and *A. ludoviciana* 'Valerie Finnis' make good neighbors. Also consider *Gaura lindheimeri*, which has delicate white-pink flowers at the top of long stems. It is quite drought tolerant and can even be grown very successfully in gravel-covered areas.

For your collection

- *Sedum alboroseum* 'Mediovariegatum' is the variegated form of 'Autumn Joy'. It is mostly listed as *Sedum* 'Variegatum'. Not everyone likes foliage which is green with creamy white sploshes in the center, but it has its place. It grows 2 feet (60 cm), pulls in the bees and butterflies and has pale greenish-white flowers tinged with pink.
- The sedum family provides a few worthy low-growing specimens for the sunny rockery or fast-draining slope. *Sedum spathulifolium*, for instance, grows only 4 inches (10 cm) high and has tiny rosette-shaped silver-gray leaves and bright yellow flowers. Names to look for are 'Cape Blanco' and 'Purpureum'. *Sedum spurium*, also known as dragon's blood, grows a little taller, about 6 inches (15 cm), and has pink, red or white flowers.

Spiraea japonica 'Magic Carpet'

Common name: Spiraea

Chief characteristics

There are two main groups of spiraea—
ones that have white flowers in the spring,
and ones that have red-pink flowers in the
summer. You could have room in your
garden for one of each. The white plants
give you a spectacular show of snowy
flowers in late spring while the red-flowering ones are more valued for
their yellow-green foliage than their pinkish-red blooms.

Location: Sun or light shade
Type: Deciduous shrub
Size: 3 feet (90 cm)
Conditions: Ordinary soil
Flowering time: June to July

Most outstanding is *Spiraea japonica* 'Magic Carpet'. It has delightful
foliage of gold, lime-green and red hues and produces plenty of pinkish-
purple flowers in mid-summer. The foliage is great for contrasting with
other plants and the flowers, though not immensely significant, are an
added bonus. 'Magic Carpet' also thrives in a container and is a good
plant for adding foliage interest to a patio, deck or sunny balcony.

Where to plant it

Spiraea thrives in a variety of soils and is not unhappy in full sun or
light shade. The summer-flowering spiraeas, such as 'Magic Carpet',
which bloom in June and have beautiful golden-yellow foliage, can be
used as accent plants. They need to be sited in a more visible location
where they can use their pink flowers and gold foliage for texture and
color contrast. You can, of course, become overenthusiastic about the
summer-flowering spiraeas and use them too abundantly, which
invariably ends up giving the plant a bad name. It has spoiled some
gardens, making them look needlessly boring and unimaginative.

The spring-flowering "bridal wreath" species are especially useful for
their exuberant shower of white blooms. The challenge is to grow them
in places where they can be appreciated while in full bloom, then
allowed to quietly fade into the background and become part of the
shrubbery's general foliage screen for the rest of the year.

How to care for it

All spiraeas are ruggedly disease and pest resistant. The compact
summer-flowering forms require little more than tidying up in the
spring. If they look particularly tatty, you can chop them back more
severely. The taller, cascading garland forms need to be pruned

immediately after they have flowered to promote new growth. The larger, twiggy spring-flowering spiraeas also need to be pruned regularly to prevent dead wood from building up in the center of the bush.

Good companions

Some excellent companions for 'Magic Carpet' are blue grasses (*Festuca glauca, Helictotrichon*); the blue-purple *Hebe* 'Autumn Glory' or *Hebe speciosa*; the pink flowers and silver stems of *Lychnis coronaria*; the stiff, succulent foliage and salmon flowerheads of *Sedum* × 'Autumn Joy'; and the golden-yellow foliage of *Choisya ternata* 'Sundance'.

Mix white-flowering spiraeas in the shrubbery with *Pieris japonica* 'Forest Flame', photinia, lavatera, smoke bush, and white-flowering shrubs like philadelphus and *Viburnum plicatum* 'Summer Snowflake' for continuous foliage and flower color.

For your collection

- *Spiraea japonica* 'Anthony Waterer' is called the dwarf pink spiraea, having bright green leaves and producing rosy pink flowers from July to September. It grows only 2 or 3 feet (60 to 90 cm) high.
- *Spiraea japonica* 'Little Princess' has mint-green foliage and rose-pink flowers. There is a golden form called 'Golden Princess'.
- *Spiraea japonica* 'Snowmound' is a short shrub that grows 4 or 5 feet (1.2 to 1.5 m) high and also has masses of white flowers displayed on long, graceful, arching stems in spring.
- *Spiraea japonica* 'Shirobana' is something of a novelty plant. It blooms late in the summer, producing white, pink and red flowers simultaneously from July to September. It grows only 2 or 3 feet high (60 to 90 cm) and has bright green leaves.
- Less of a novelty, but also interesting is *Spiraea japonica* 'Lime Mound', which has lemon-yellow leaves tinged with pink and produces light pink flowers in summer. This shrub grows only 3 feet (90 cm) high, but it mounds up to 6 feet (1.8 m) wide.
- The best of the white-flowering spiraeas is *Spiraea* × *vanhouttei*, which produces the dazzling cascade of snow-white flowers in May that gives spring-flowering spiraea its common name—bridal wreath. The Vanhouttei spiraea is a compact, upright deciduous shrub that grows into a fountain shape about 6 feet (1.8 m) high and has diamond-shaped, dark green leaves. It is certainly one of the best spring performers.
- *Spiraea thunbergii* has pure white clusters of flowers on long stems in April. It does, however, have a habit of becoming a dense, twiggy, spreading shrub that grows to 5 feet (1.5 m) or more.

🐾 *Nandina domestica* 'Harbour Dwarf' is an excellent spiraea-like foliage plant that fits very comfortably into a sunny terraced garden or rockery. It is a short version of the much larger *N. domestica* (heavenly bamboo), growing only 18 inches (45 cm) high and forming a very attractive shrub with yellow green leaves. It provides helpful foliage contrast against *Sedum spectabile* and support for annuals such as snapdragons, pelargoniums and nicotiana.

Stachys byzantina 'Silver Carpet'

Common name: Lamb's ears

Chief characteristics

Of all the great silver foliage plants available to gardeners, *Stachys byzantina* continues to be the most used in gardens as a groundcover or decorative edging plant or simply to provide color and textural contrast in the perennial border. It is a 5-star perennial, a top performer. The soft, silver-gray leaves are aptly named, looking and feeling rather like the ears of lambs. In mid-June, the plant sends up wonderfully solid silver spikes which by early July produce tiny lilac-purple flowers. These silver stems are not always completely rigid. At best, they all stand up in composed unison. But with rain and wind, they can flop around. Usually, the stems do not interfere too badly with other plants, but some gardeners don't care for them much or their flowers and prefer to cut out both as soon as they appear, to restore attention squarely back on the lush carpet of soft, gray foliage.

Location: Full sun
Type: Perennial
Size: 15 to 18 inches (38 to 45 cm)
Conditions: Good, free-draining soil
Flowering time: June to July

There are 3 main cultivars of *Stachys byzantina* from which to choose. 'Silver Carpet' is one of the best. It grows only 6 to 8 inches (15 to 20 cm) high, which makes it an excellent front-of-the-border edging plant. It has all the qualities we admire in lamb's ears—soft wooly gray leaves, low mat-forming growth habit—but since it rarely flowers, the foliage tends to stay more compact and dense. The taller 'Primrose Heron' (12 to 18 inches/30 to 45 cm) has pale yellow-green, felty leaves and insignificant magenta flowers, and is also useful as a groundcover in dry sunny areas. The cultivar 'Countess Helene Von Stein' (12 to 18 inches/30 to 45 cm) is gaining popularity because of its large leaves and nonflowering habit, which make it appealing to gardeners with a special interest in creating contrasts out of different foliage colors and textures.

Where to plant it

Grow *Stachys byzantina* in fertile, well-drained soil in full sun. It is very drought tolerant, using its soft gray leaves to cling on to every drop of moisture. You can use lamb's ears as a solitary specimen to add focus and textural interest, or you can plant it in a large drift to create a stream-of-silver look. It is best placed at the front of the border, even though the stems rise up almost 2 feet (60 cm). For the first 2 months in the garden it is very low to the ground. Once it does send up its spires, they can be pruned away if they start to block your view of other flowers. Lamb's ears look especially attractive next to stone walls or softening the edges of a concrete or gravel path.

How to care for it

Rain does the most damage. Being a plant that loves warm, rocky, fast-draining Mediterranean hillsides, *Stachys byzantina* is not at all happy if it has to put up with heavy rains in the growing season. The leaves become mushy and prone to disease, so good drainage is essential. Tidy up the plant in spring. Remove all dead and diseased foliage, and take out the worst-looking stems once the peak flowering period is over in July. There are no pests to worry about. Aphids, slugs and snails have no interest in lamb's ears.

Good companions

Let your imagination fly. There are always new and imaginative combinations popping up. The purple flowers on the gray spikes of lamb's ears look great against the solid purple flower spikes of liatris. Scarlet bee balm can also provide a striking contrast. Lamb's ears will sit very comfortably at the feet of *Lavatera thuringiaca* 'Barnsley' or in front of *Euphorbia characias*. Blues of salvia and scabiosa, the purple varieties of stonecrop, and the magenta and white flowers of *Lychnis coronaria* all offer interesting possibilities.

For your collection

- *Stachys macrantha* has the same first name but is nothing like any of the others mentioned here, having large green mintlike leaves, growing 2 feet high (60 cm) and producing lilac-purple flowers from June to July.
- If you like lamb's ears, you will probably also want *Ballota pseudo-dictamnus*, which has so many of the same fine characteristics—great gray foliage that is easy to care for, has no pests or disease, stays evergreen if planted in a protected spot, and offers valuable structural and textural interest to the garden. Ballota grows about

2 feet (60 cm) tall and spreads a little wider. The small, oval-shaped, gray-green leaves look like tiny bowls and are arranged in pairs up the silver stems. In a clump, they have a highly patterned, very decorative look. Ballota will tolerate lousy soil but don't make it suffer too much.

🐾 The artemisias, of course, are regarded as the true aristocrats of gray foliage. Look for 'Powis Castle', 'Silver Mound' and 'Valerie Finnis'.

🐾 Another gray-foliage plant, *Verbascum bombyciferum* has a wooly stem and yellow flowers in June and July. It is a real show-stopper that will have all your visitors oohing and aahing over its theatrical impact. It can reach 6 feet (1.8 meters) with very little effort.

🐾 Jerusalem sage (*Pholmis fruticosa*) has wooly gray-green foliage and yellow bananalike flowers.

*S*tyrax japonicum

Common name: Japanese snowbell or snowdrop tree

Chief characteristics

One of the worst gardening errors is to plant a big tree like a poplar or weeping willow or deodar cedar in a small front yard. Unfortunately, it is a mistake many have made and lived to regret. They don't, of course, start out as big trees. Deodar cedar (*Cedrus deodara*), for instance, looks

Location: Full sun to part shade
Type: Deciduous tree
Size: 25 feet (7.5 m) at maturity
Conditions: Moist, well-drained soil
Flowering time: Mid-June

like a perfectly charming, inoffensive creature as an infant in the nursery. But 10 years on and it will have outgrown its allotted space and become a headache with lanky branches full of razor-sharp needles.

If you're looking for a moderate-growing, small tree for your garden you cannot do much better than to pick the graceful snowbell tree, *Styrax japonicum*. This charming deciduous tree is a good pick for a small- or medium-sized garden. It is relatively slow growing, reaching only 25 to 30 feet (7.5 to 9 m) with a loosely rounded top at maturity. It takes about 10 years to reach 15 feet (4.5 m). An exceptionally handsome deciduous tree, it has masses of fragrant white snowdrop-like flowers in mid-June. They don't last very long, sometimes only a couple of weeks if rain comes along and knocks them about. When the tree is covered with the dainty, drooping, bell-shaped white flowers with yellow centers, it is a glorious picture. The flowers are best viewed from underneath, looking up into the tree. When it has finished flowering, the tree returns to normal with soft leaves covering its elegant framework of arching branches. In late summer, clusters of tiny green nutlike seeds can be seen dangling from the branches. They eventually turn brown in fall and drop to the ground before winter.

Where to plant it

The snowbell tree grows best in moist, free-draining, fertile soil in full sun or light shade. Plant in early spring in a sheltered location. Since the white flowers hang down, it is best to locate the tree where it is easy to look up into the branches. My snowbell tree is positioned at the top of a set of steps. This allows visitors, as they come to the house, to see the blooms from the best angle. *Styrax japonicum* is also well sited on a slope above a path or grown in a raised planter on a patio. The tree needs room either side to expand as it tends to grow out rather than up, although this habit can be managed with judicious pruning.

How to care for it

Water your tree well during the first year after planting. Mulch well to keep soil moist but not sodden. The snowbell tree is grown not only for its foliage and flowers but for its graceful form. It is important to maintain the integrity of the tree's shape when it comes time to prune. Wonder, ponder and prune wisely. The tree does not require heavy pruning. In fact, it rather dislikes it, but if you have to prune do it with intelligence and a sensitivity to the tree's natural form. No topping, please.

Good companions

Underplant with spring-flowering bulbs such as snowdrops, bluebells, crocus, grape hyacinths or daffodils. You can even use this tree in shrub form in the mixed border.

For your collection

- The fragrant snowbell tree (*Styrax obassia*) produces similar flowers to *S. japonicum*, only it blooms a little earlier and has larger, oval leaves.
- The Carolina silverbell tree (*Halesia carolina*) is also a member of the styrax family. It has attractive white bell-shaped flowers in May and could be more widely grown in the Pacific Northwest. It is more loosely structured than *Styrax japonicum* but still an excellent tree for the small garden. It grows to 20 to 30 feet (6 to 9 m).

$\mathcal{T}$ axus × media 'Hicksii'

Common name: Hick's yew

Chief characteristics

Location: Full sun to light shade
Type: Evergreen shrub
Size: 10 feet (3 m)
Conditions: Ordinary soil

Privacy is an important element in a garden. Without privacy, it can be impossible to enjoy the benefit of your hard labor in having created a garden paradise. If walls or fences won't do the job of defining borders and providing privacy, the task usually falls to a hedge of some sort. Yew makes a very classy hedge. It is slow growing and you need to have patience, but in the long run it ends up being far more attractive than other types of hedging. The yew's dark foliage will provide a dramatic backdrop for the beautiful flowers and shrubs in your garden.

The common English yew is *Taxus baccata*. Left undisturbed, this would eventually grow to 40 feet (12 m) or more. However, the best kind of yew for hedging in coastal gardens is *Taxus × media* 'Hicksii', which is a cross between English and Japanese species. Hick's yew produces a narrow, upright bush with lovely dark green foliage that holds its color and requires minimal maintenance. It is slow growing and it can take 10 years or more for it to reach 8 or 10 feet (2.4 to 3 m).

The golden yew (*Taxus baccata* 'Fastigiata Aurea') is another fine hedging plant. The new foliage in spring is golden-yellow and then turns green, retaining touches of gold on the edges of the needles. It will grow to 5 feet (1.5 m) after 10 years, ultimately reaching 15 feet (4.5 m).

Where to plant it

Grow yew in reasonably well-drained soil. It thrives in deep shade or full sun and prefers soil that is not excessively acidic or alkaline. Plant yew as an accent plant or as a formal hedge to provide screening. The dark form of the more column-shaped yews can provide a very effective, dramatic contrast in a cottage garden full of old-fashioned roses and flowering shrubs and perennials.

How to care for it

The beauty of yew is that once it is established it is very easy to maintain and does not mind being pruned into shape or cut back into place. It can handle heavy rains, cool winds and hot dry spells. It is also reasonably indifferent to air pollution.

Good companions

The best companion for a yew hedge is a perennial border. The dark foliage of a yew hedge is the perfect backdrop for the diversity of color you find in a richly planted herbaceous border. Yew contrasts well with the complex, twisted form of Harry Lauder's walking stick (*Corylus avellana* 'Contorta'), which produces pale yellow catkins in winter. You could also position a red- or yellow-flowering witch hazel—*Hamamelis* × *intermedia* 'Jelena' or 'Diane'—in front of or beside the dark shape of your yew.

For your collection

You are not likely to want to collect different forms of yew, even though there are many, including yews that make useful groundcovers such as *Taxus baccata* 'Repandens Aurea', which has dark green leaves with yellow margins. If you need a hedge and don't have time for a slow-growing yew, here are some of your other options.

- The most popular type of hedging in coastal gardens is western red cedar (*Thuja plicata*). It is fast growing, doesn't mind being sheared, bounces back from a cold winter and stays green all year. A better choice is *Thuja occidentalis* 'Smaragd', which is more compact and grows only to 8 to 10 feet (2.4 to 3 m), which means less work trimming.
- English cherry laurel (*Prunus laurocerasus*) has glossy, 5-inch (12.5-cm) leaves and is capable of reaching 15 feet (4.5 m) in 10 years.
- Boxwood (*Buxus sempervirens*) is the right pick for a low hedge for defining a rose bed or herb garden or for simply dividing one part of the garden from another. Lavender and santolina are two other possible alternatives. Boxwood, however, lasts longer and needs less maintenance.
- The foliage of hemlock (*Tsuga canadensis*) has a loose, feathery but reasonably formal look, which makes it a good candidate for a screen or windbreak.
- *Ilex crenata* is a member of the holly family and has tiny black berries in winter, but it has all the appearance of a box-type hedge and can be clipped into a formal looking waist-high barrier.
- English holly (*Ilex aquifolium*) can provide a prickly barrier to thwart burglars. It will bring birds into the garden and the red berries offer some color in the dark of winter.
- A most popular and attractive hedge used in many parts of England is plain privet (*Ligustrum amurense*), which has soft, glossy leaves. It can be sheared into a very tidy shape.

🦋 *Photinia fraseri*, like privet, is rather disdained as too common, but it has the ability to be a first-rate hedge, evergreen and colorful in spring with cheerful red leaves. It can be as low as 3 feet (90 cm) or allowed to rise well over 10 feet (3 m).

🦋 Hawthorn (*Crataegeus monogyna*) certainly has a long track record as tough, no-nonsense country hedging, making it another ideal barrier for growing under windows to deter potential burglars. Both privet and hawthorn are deciduous, of course, which means you don't get the same solid green coverage in winter that you get with evergreens like cedar and laurel, but the internal branching is usually very dense and often these do end up being partly evergreen in mild winters.

🦋 *Forsythia intermedia*, a popular deciduous shrub, is one of the heralds of spring. It can be used to create a striking hedge of bright yellow flowers in March.

🦋 Two other great deciduous hedging plants are the common European beech (*Fagus sylvatica*) and the hornbeam (*Carpinus betulus*). The hornbeam has such magnificent foliage it is surprising it is not used more for hedging, as well as for pleaching, a way of weaving the branches of a row of trees to form a hedge or a screen 5 or 6 feet (1.5 to 1.8 m) above the ground. Part of the problem with hornbeams perhaps is their tendency to hold on to their decaying leaves in winter. The European beech has a similar habit.

🦋 In gardens where space is not limited, shrub roses can be used to form relaxed barriers in areas where neat and compact formality is not required.

🦋 Other possibilities to consider are pyracantha, escallonia, spiraea, rosemary, berberis, elaeagnus, *Hebe buxifolia* and *Viburnum plicatum* 'Summer Snowflake'.

𝒯hymus × citriodorus 'Doone Valley'

Common name: Creeping lemon-scented thyme

Chief characteristics

Thyme is a low-growing, sweet-scented perennial that is very useful as a colorful, compact groundcover, ideal for growing in sunny rockeries and for filling the crevices between paving stones. It can also be grown in pots with spring-flowering bulbs like yellow crocuses and short blue irises.

Location: Full sun
Type: Rockery perennial
Size: 4 inches (10 cm)
Conditions: Ordinary, well-drained soil
Flowering time: June to July

Thymus × *citriodorus* 'Doone Valley' gives off a powerful lemon scent when the leaves are brushed. It grows 4 to 6 inches (10 to 15 cm) high and has dark green aromatic leaves tipped with gold. Other top names include 'Gold Edge', 'E. B. Anderson' and 'Argenteus'.

The common thyme (*Thymus vulgaris*) has aromatic gray-green leaves and tiny, pale lilac flowers in June. Creeping mother of thyme or wild thyme (*Thymus praecox*) grows 3 or 4 inches (7.5 to 10 cm) high, has purple, red or white flowers, and spreads to form an attractive matlike covering. You will sometimes find it in garden centers under the label *Thymus serpyllum*. Good cultivars include 'Purple Carpet' (light purple), 'Coccineus' (red), 'Elfin' (pink) and 'Albus' (white). Wooly thyme (*Thymus pseudolanuginosus*) has soft silvery foliage and bright pink flowers.

Where to plant it

Thyme is mostly useful as a groundcover in sunny rock or herb gardens. It can also be used to make an aromatic lawn as long as it does not get walked on all the time. Thyme does attract bees when in full flower, so you will want to watch where you put your bare feet! The perfect plant for filling in gaps, thyme may be used between slabs of slate to make a sitting area in a sunny corner of the garden. It can also be used to fill crevices between stepping stones or to grow over the sides of raised beds.

How to care for it

Grow thyme in slightly alkaline soil. It must have well-drained soil if it is to survive a wet winter. All thymes require sun to flower properly. If it gets straggly, gently shear it back immediately after flowering. Divide clumps in spring or fall to make more plants.

Good companions

Mixed with Corsican mint (*Mentha requienii*), thyme can make a groundcovering tapestry of soft green and purple, white or red flowers. Blue *Iris reticulata*, scillas or yellow crocuses all look great flowering above the dense, compact green leaves of lemon-scented thyme.

For your collection

🐾 Two excellent forms of variegated thyme are *Thymus caespititius* 'Aureus' (gold-green) and *Thymus* × *citriodorus* 'Silver Queen'.

🐾 Other great low-growing plants that can gently mound to cover ground with a soft, cushionlike carpet include *Phlox subulata*, *Dianthus gratianopolitanus* and *Armeria maritima*.

Viburnum plicatum 'Summer Snowflake'

Common name: Summer snowflake

Chief characteristics

Location: Sun to semi-shade
Type: Deciduous shrub
Size: 8 feet (2.4 m)
Conditions: Good, moist soil
Flowering time: April to May

Most moderate-sized gardens have room for at least 2 or 3 different kinds of viburnum. It is an extremely versatile family of shrubs, especially useful for providing groundcover or winter color or fragrant white blooms in spring.
'Summer Snowflake', a plant introduced by the University of B.C. Botanical Garden, is ideal for a low-maintenance garden. It covers itself in April to May with a full flush of white, clover-shaped flowers. The rate of flowering slows in June and continues at a more modest tempo all summer. 'Summer Snowflake' has a compact form and slow-growing habit, making it very manageable and a good shrub for small- or medium-sized city garden.

Where to plant it

All viburnums thrive in full sun in good soil that stays moist but not soggy. Where you plant them depends on the variety and the function you want it to fulfil. 'Summer Snowflake' can be planted in groups to create a low hedge or screen, or individually in the mixed border.

How to care for it

Viburnums are fuss-free plants, rarely requiring attention to deal with pests or diseases. The only pruning they need is to clear out dead and damaged branches in spring after flowering and routine pruning to keep them within their boundaries.

Good companions

'Summer Snowflake' and most of the other spring-flowering viburnums blend well with Mexican orange (*Choisya ternata*), magnolias, mock orange (*Philadelphus*), rhododendrons and small trees. They can be underplanted with spring-flowering bulbs like scilla and muscari or various spring- and summer-blooming perennials.

For your collection

🌺 *Viburnum* × *bodnantense* 'Pink Dawn' gives color in winter, producing very fragrant pink flowers on bare branches in January and February. Grows 8 to 10 feet (2.4 to 3 m) high.

- *Viburnum tinus* also flowers in late winter and early spring, and ultimately grows into a 10-foot (3-m) evergreen bush with clusters of tiny white flowers followed by blue-black berries.
- Korean spice viburnum (*Viburnum carlesii*) is an outstanding spring-flowering shrub. It grows into a small rounded, 4- by 4-foot (1.2- by 1.2-m) bush with heavily scented white clusters of flowers in March and April.
- *Viburnum opulus* 'Roseum' (also known as 'Sterile') is commonly called the snowball bush. It is possibly the best known viburnum because of its spectacular display in June of dazzling creamy white globular flowerheads that look like snowballs.
- *Viburnum davidii* is a first-rate groundcover, growing 2 feet (60 cm) high. It has long, pointed, glossy, evergreen leaves and produces tiny metallic-blue berries. Its value has unfortunately been somewhat diminished by its excessive use in the urban landscape, particularly in flower beds around shopping malls and gas stations. Nevertheless, it remains a great plant which can still serve a purpose in the home garden.
- *Viburnum plicatum tomentosum* 'Mariesii' is a spectacular shrub if you have space. It grows to 8 feet (2.4 m) and has pure white, flat lacecap flowers in spring which are elegantly displayed along the entire length of the bush's long horizontal, tiered branches. It has been planted to dramatic effect as the feature at the end of a large lawn, or as one of the stars of the shrub border.

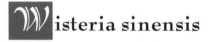isteria sinensis

Common name: *Chinese wisteria*

Chief characteristics

It can be a heavenly experience to sit beneath an arbor or walk through a pergola smothered with the fragrant flowers of wisteria in May. Gardeners lucky enough to have a well-trained wisteria doubtless have had many fond memories of warm evenings spent in late spring relaxing with friends beneath a canopy of the magnificent violet-blue blooms.

Location: Full sun
Type: Deciduous vine
Size: 20 feet (6 m) plus
Conditions: Average, well-drained soil
Flowering time: May to June

There are 2 popular types. *Wisteria sinensis,* the Chinese wisteria, is particularly vigorous and produces soft purple clusters that can measure up to 8 inches (20 cm) long. *W. floribunda*, the Japanese wisteria, is less vigorous and less bothered by extreme cold in winter. The main difference between them is their flowering habit: the blooms on the Japanese wisteria openly slowly along a cluster while the flowers on a Chinese wisteria open all at once and give a showier display. This is why the Chinese species tends to be more popular, although the Japanese wisteria has a slightly longer flowering period. Both kinds flower about the same time, from April to June.

Top cultivars of Chinese wisteria include 'Caroline' (soft lavender-mauve), 'Amethyst' (light rosy purple) and 'Blue Sapphire' (blue-mauve). Top cultivars of Japanese wisteria are 'Show Showers' (dainty white-tinged lilac), 'Longissima' (purple) and 'Rosea' (purple-pink).

Grown from seed, wisteria is notorious for taking its time to flower. You will hear people warn that new plants can take as long as 7, even 10 years, to bloom. But today most vines are grown from cuttings or grafting or layering. They are often in flower when you buy them in the pot at the nursery.

Where to plant it

You will see spectacular photographs of wisteria in full bloom covering the brick facade of old Victorian houses. In reality, wisteria is not the best choice for a climber to grow against a house. It can easily get out of hand, and the stems eventually become very woody and weighty. They can twist themselves powerfully around supporting structures and easily become a problem. Wisteria is much more suitable for growing along a sturdy pergola or over a sizable arbor. Think twice before growing one against the front of the house or over a porch entrance.

One good idea is to grow it on a standard to form a small, weeping tree. This requires diligent pruning for at least 4 consecutive years to get it trained properly.

How to care for it

Plant wisteria in a protected site where it will not be hit by severe frosts. It will thrive in average, moist, well-drained soil in full sun. Enrich the soil with well-rotted compost or manure at planting time and mulch well in spring. Prune to espalier and shape the plant in the early years. Once the plant is established, pruning usually comes down to cutting back stems in early spring to within a few inches of the previous season's growth in order to keep the vine in check. If it is still too vigorous, it can be pruned back in July, snipping back new growth to almost where it began.

Good companions

Wisteria does not leave much room for a partner but if it is trained along one side of a pergola or arch or arbor, a rose could complement it on the other side. *Rosa* 'Felicite Perpetue', which has sensational white blooms, would be a good choice.

Other top picks would be any of the following clematis cultivars: 'Madame Julia Correvon', 'Jackmanii Superba', 'Etoile Violette' and 'The President'.

For your collection

- The silky wisteria (*Wisteria venusta*) has fragrant white or purple flowers with silklike hairs.
- Other climbers for growing along a pergola or over an arbor include the purple-leafed grape (*Vitis vinifera* 'Purpurea'), vigorous roses like 'Rambling Rector' (beautiful white flowers), and the fragrant evergreen clematis (*Clematis armandii*).

*1*00 Best Plants by Type

Annuals

Brugmansia (Datura) × candida (angel's trumpet)
Heliotropium arborescens (cherry-pie plant)
Nicotiana alata (flowering tobacco plant)
Pelargonium (zonal geranium)

Perennials

Adiantum aleuticum (western or five-fingered maidenhair fern)
Ajuga reptans 'Bronze Beauty' (bugleweed)
Alchemilla mollis (lady's mantle)
Aquilegia (columbine)
Artemisia 'Powis Castle' (wormwood)
Aster × frikartii 'Monch' (Michaelmas daisy)
Astilbe × arendsii 'Elizabeth Bloom' (false spiraea)
Astrantia major (masterwort)
Aubrieta deltoidea 'Dr. Mules' (rock cress)
Campanula persicifolia (bellflower)
Coreopsis verticillata 'Moonbeam' (tickseed)
Corydalis lutea (yellow corydalis)
Delphinium Pacific hybrids (larkspur)
Dicentra spectabilis 'Alba' (bleeding heart)
Digitalis purpurea (foxglove)
Echinacea purpurea (purple coneflower)
Euphorbia characias wulfenii (spurge)
Foeniculum vulgare 'Purpureum' (bronze fennel)
Geranium cinereum 'Ballerina' (cranesbill, hardy geranium)
Helleborus orientalis (Lenten rose)
Hemerocallis 'Stella de Oro' (daylily)
Heuchera micrantha 'Bressingham Bronze' (coral bells, purple-leafed heuchera)
Hosta 'Frances Williams' (Frances Williams hosta)
Iris sibirica (Siberian iris)
Kniphofia (red-hot poker)
Lavatera thuringiaca 'Barnsley' (tree mallow)
Liatris spicata (gay feather, blazing star)
Ligularia stenocephala 'The Rocket' (ligularia)
Lupinus Russell hybrids (Russell lupins)
Lychnis coronaria (rose campion)
Lysimachia clethroides (gooseneck loosestrife, Chinese loosestrife)

Perennials cont.

Monarda 'Gardenview Scarlet' (bee balm, bergamot)
Nymphaea pygmaea 'Helvola' (water lily)
Paeonia lactiflora 'Karl Rosenfeld' (peony)
Papaver orientale 'Mrs. Perry' (oriental poppy)
Peltiphyllum peltatum (umbrella plant)
Phlox paniculata 'Mount Fujiama' (phlox)
Polemonium caeruleum 'Brise d'Anjou' (variegated Jacob's ladder)
Polygonum bistorta 'Superbum' (fleece flower, knotweed)
Primula japonica 'Miller's Crimson' (candelabra primula)
Salvia × *sylvestris* 'May Night' (perennial salvia, sage)
Scabiosa columbaria 'Butterfly Blue' (pincushion flower)
Sedum × 'Autumn Joy' (stonecrop)
Stachys byzantina 'Silver Carpet' (lamb's ears)
Thymus × *citriodorus* 'Doone Valley' (creeping lemon-scented thyme)

Bulbs

Allium aflatunense (ornamental onion)
Camassia (quamash)
Lilium 'Casa Blanca' (Casa Blanca lily)
Muscari armeniacum (grape hyacinth)
Scilla non-scripta (English bluebell)

Ornamental Grasses

Helictotrichon sempervirens (blue oat grass)
Miscanthus sinensis 'Gracillimus' (maiden grass)
Ophiopogon planiscapus 'Nigrescens' (black mondo grass)
Pennisetum alopecuroides (fountain grass)

Vines and Climbers

Actinidia kolomikta (Kolomikta vine)
Akebia quinata (chocolate vine)
Campsis radicans (trumpet vine)
Clematis × *jackmanii* (clematis)
Hydrangea petiolaris (climbing hydrangea)
Lonicera japonica 'Halliana' (Hall's honeysuckle)
Passiflora caerulea (blue passion vine)
Rosa 'New Dawn' (New Dawn rose, everblooming Dr. W. Van Fleet)
Wisteria sinensis (Chinese wisteria)

Roses

Rosa 'Ballerina' (Ballerina rose)
Rosa 'Elina' (Elina or Peaudouce rose)
Rosa 'Mary Rose' (Mary rose)
Rosa 'Souvenir de la Malmaison' (Souvenir de la Malmaison rose)

Shrubs

Buddleia davidii (butterfly bush)
Buxus sempervirens (boxwood)
Ceanothus impressus 'Victoria' (California lilac)
Choisya ternata 'Aztec Pearl' (Mexican orange, Mexican orange blossom)
Cotinus coggygria 'Royal Purple' (purple smoke bush)
Daphne odora (winter daphne)
Enkianthus campanulatus (pagoda bush)
Erica carnea 'Springwood White' (winter heather)
Fuchsia magellanica 'Riccartonii' (hardy fuchsia)
Hamamelis × *intermedia* (witch hazel)
Hebe 'Autumn Glory' (shrubby veronica)
Hydrangea serrata 'Bluebird' (lacecap hydrangea)
Lavandula angustifolia (English lavender)
Philadelphus coronarius 'Aureus' (mock orange)
Rhododendron 'Temple Belle' (Temple Belle rhododendron)
Spiraea japonica 'Magic Carpet' (spiraea)
Taxus × *media* 'Hicksii' (Hick's yew)
Viburnum plicatum 'Summer Snowflake' (summer snowflake)

Trees

Acer palmatum dissectum 'Crimson Queen' (laceleaf Japanese maple)
Acer pseudoplatanus 'Brilliantissimum' (sycamore maple)
Betula pendula 'Youngii' (Young's weeping birch)
Catalpa bignonioides 'Aurea' (golden Indian bean tree)
Cornus 'Eddie's White Wonder' (dogwood)
Magnolia × *soulangiana* (saucer magnolia)
Picea pungens 'Hoopsii' (Colorado blue spruce)
Prunus subhirtella 'Pendula Rubra' (Japanese cherry)
Pyrus salicifolia pendula 'Silver Cascade' (weeping willow-leafed pear)
Robinia pseudoacacia 'Frisia' (false acacia)
Styrax japonicum (Japanese snowbell)

Terms for New Gardeners

Acid soil: Limeless soil—perfect for rhododendrons, azaleas, heathers and hydrangeas—that has a pH of less than 6.5 and turns litmus paper red. *See also* **pH.**

Aeration: A way of getting air to grass roots by poking holes into the ground. Essential for great lawns.

Alkaline soil: The opposite of acidic soil, this chalky soil has a pH of more than 7.5 and turns litmus paper blue.

Annual: Hardy and half-hardy annuals are plants that complete their life cycle in a single season, going from seed to flower or fruit before dying.

Bare-root: A plant that has been dug up and packaged without soil around its roots. Mail orders from nurseries are mostly dispatched bare-root.

Bedding plants: Mostly annuals (although can include biennials) that are "bedded out" in spring to provide summer color.

Biennial: Plants that complete their life cycle in 2 seasons, starting from seed and establishing leaves and a stem in the first year and flowering the following year. Examples: foxgloves, wallflowers, canterbury bells.

Cambium: The green layer of living tissue just below the woody surface of a branch. A sign that your plant is still alive.

Carpet bedding: A style of planting, popular with the early Victorians, involving the tight planting of annuals to create intricate floral patterns.

Compost: Dark, blackish humus formed from the decomposition of organic matter. Can be used to enrich soil or as a mulch.

Cultivar: Short for cultivated variety, this refers to a plant cultivated by selection or hybridization, and chosen for its particular characteristics.

Deadhead: Removal of faded flowers in order 1) to maintain tidy appearance of the garden; 2) to promote flower production by preventing the plant from developing seeds; and 3) in some cases, such as with delphiniums and lupins, to induce a second flush of flowers later in the season.

Die-back: The dead part of a shoot or branch that has been incorrectly pruned.

Division: What you do to perennials every 3 or 4 years when they have grown big enough to be split into more plants. Division is usually done in spring or fall.

Dormant: Winter sleep for plants. Technically, it means there is little or no cellular activity. It's something plants do to survive winter and save energy for the new season.

Drip line: Area around a tree where the tips of roots are located, usually where water drips from the canopy of leaves.

Espalier: The art of training a tree into a variety of shapes or patterns. Perfected by French gardeners, espalier is one way of training a tree (or shrub) to lie flat against a wall or trellis in a symmetrical pattern. A popular espalier design is called the Belgian fence.

Fastigiate: A plant with a column-like shape to it.
Forcing: Getting plants to flower out of season by manipulating temperature, humidity and light.
Frost pocket: An area of the garden where cold air gets trapped during winter. Only the tougher, more hardy plants can survive in frost pockets.

Genus: The name for a group of plants related to one another. It is the first word in a plant's botanical name: *Lonicera, Fuchsia, Cotoneaster*, for example. A plant usually has 3 names: genus (first), species (second), cultivar (third), as in *Acer campestre* 'Postelense'.
Grafting: Propagating by taking the stem or bud of one plant and joining it to the root or stem of another.

Hardening off: Gradually acclimatizing a plant to being out of the warmth of the greenhouse in order to get it ready for planting in the garden.
Hardiness: Measure of a plant's ability to withstand extremes of cold and frost or other harsh conditions. *See also* **Zones.**
Heading back: Pruning back the main branches of a tree or shrub by a third to half.
Heeling-in: What you are doing when you temporarily plant a tree or shrub in a holding bed until you are ready to find a permanent home for it.
Humus: Dark brown organic material formed from the decomposition of vegetable and certain animal matter. Humus is necessary to enrich soil and give it the life needed to nourish and sustain plants.
Hybrid: A new plant produced by crossing two genetically different plants from the same or a closely related species. Not all hybrids are improvements on the parent species.

Insecticide: Chemical- or soap-based spray used to control or kill such insect pests as aphids and red spider mites.
Island bed: Novel way of growing perennials. Instead of the traditional, long, yew-backed border, perennials are displayed in a circle, with the tallest (often delphiniums) in the center.

Jardin de refuse: Polite way of describing temporary lodgings for plants you can't use, but can't bring yourself to throw away.

Juvenile foliage: New leaves that are different in their shape, size and color from the plant's more familiar adult foliage.

Knot-garden: An invention of medieval English gardeners who liked to weave low-growing herbs or boxwood hedging into elaborate, knotlike geometric patterns, sometimes with herbs or roses.

Layering: A way of propagating in which a trailing branch of a plant is bent down and anchored below ground level until roots form and the newly established plant can be safely cut away from the parent.

Leaf mold: Rotting or partly decomposed leaves that can be used as a mulch or dug into the soil to create useful organic matter.

Loam: The best kind of soil— moderately fertile, composed of clay, sand and humus with a texture that is neither too sandy nor too heavy.

Manure tea: Water in which compost has been allowed to soak to form a mild, fertilizing "tea."

Microclimate: Small area of the garden where the climate is different from the rest of the garden. When the microclimate is warmer, it means you can grow tender plants that require a climate with a higher zone rating.

Mulch: A layer of bulky organic matter usually placed around perennials to reduce moisture loss, inhibit weeds, improve soil and protect plants from frost. Good mulches include grass clippings, well-rotted compost and leaf mold.

Native plant: A species that grows naturally in a certain location and that is not created by human cultivation.

Naturalize: Informal planting that mirrors nature's own relaxed style and design to create the impression that the plants are native.

NPK: Key plant-food ingredients of fertilizer: N for nitrogen, P for phosphorous and K for potassium. The numbers in fertilizer—for example 20-20-20— represent the percentage of each element in the mix. One way to remember what each does is to memorize "Little Red Flower" (L for leaf, fed by nitrogen; R for roots, strengthened by phosphorous; F for fruit or flower, promoted by potassium).

Oxygenator: A submerged water plant that helps keep ponds clean by releasing oxygen into the water.

Perennial: A plant with the ability to survive winter and live on for several growing seasons.

pH: Measure (1 to 14) of acidity or alkalinity of soil. Lilacs won't thrive in acidic soil; rhododendrons hate alkaline soil. The lower the pH the higher the acidity.

Pinching back: A way of encouraging bushiness in a plant by using your finger and thumb to pinch off growing tips.

Pollarding: Cutting back the main branches of a tree to within inches of the trunk to create a distinct globe effect.

Pricking out: Careful removal of seedlings from the original seed tray into a roomier pot or growing space.

Reversion: What happens when a plant goes back to the color or growing habit of its parent. Roses have been known to completely change color—a red becoming a yellow—when harsh pruning forces a reversion.

Rhizome: A horizontally creeping root system from which shoots and roots develop. A good example is a bearded iris.

Rootbound: What happens when a plant has been left in a container too long, allowing roots to become tangled and choked.

Species: A division of a genus, sometimes describing some feature of the genus. *See also* **Genus.**

Standard: A tree or shrub that is trained to grow a straight stem clear of branches.

Stock plants: The parent plants from which cuttings are taken for propagation purposes to ensure new plants are an exact clone.

Stress: A cry for help. Wilting or discolored foliage are 2 signs of stress, signals that a plant is suffering from a lack of water, food or too much sun, water or fertilizer.

Tanglefoot: "Tree paste" used around the trunk of a tree to make a sticky barrier against such insects as ants (which reduces damage done by aphids, mealy bugs and some scale insects), caterpillars and cutworms.

Tissue-culture: A high-tech way of propagating by "cloning" a plant, in which tiny pieces of tissue are grown in test tubes.

Top-dressing: Putting a thin layer of new soil or compost around plants or on lawns to add nutrients to the soil.

Topiary: The shaping of shrubs and trees into decorative forms.

Trace elements: The same thing as micronutrients—various minerals that plants need in small doses in order to grow.

Tuber: A fleshy root or stem that stores nutrients for later use.

Tufa: Porous limestone rock ideal for growing alpine plants.

Umbel: A rounded, often flattened head of flowers produced at the top of a long stem. A good example is the seed/flowerhead of an angelica plant.

Underplanting: Plants that have been placed beneath taller shrubs or trees, sometimes to provide leafy groundcover or seasonal color.

Variegated: Leaves that are spotted or edged with a different color from the main one.

Variety: A subdivision of a species, which grows true to its characteristics from natural propagation. Also called wild variety.

Vermicomposting: Composting using worms to do the job normally done by micro-organisms.

Weed: 1) a plant growing in the wrong place; 2) a plant for which a useful purpose has not yet been found.

Wild garden: Informal planting style that attempts to imitate nature. Popular with avant-garde landscape architects, not with most homeowners.

×: The symbol that denotes that a plant is a hybrid species.

Xeriscaping: Method of landscaping with drought-tolerant plant material to dramatically reduce the use of water.

Zones: North America is divided into 10 climatic zones that are graded according to the average annual minimum temperatures. Zone 1 is the coldest (below $-50\,°F/-46\,°C$) and Zone 10 is the warmest ($30°$ to $40\,°F/-1°$ to $5\,°C$). Most of the Pacific Northwest falls into either Zone 7 ($0°$ to $10\,°F/-18°$ to $-12\,°C$). There are, however, colder inland areas where winter temperatures dip to $-10°$ to $-30\,°F$ ($-23°$ to $-35\,°C$), and there are hot spots where temperatures rarely fall below freezing. Zone numbers are a useful guide when buying plants that can survive in the outdoors in the garden over winter.

𝓑ibliography

It is difficult to compile a bibliography for a book such as this. So much has been taken in over the years of researching and writing gardening stories for *The Vancouver Sun*. The works listed here are constant sources of reference and have been particularly helpful in the compilation of *100 Best Plants*.

Aden, Paul. *The Hosta Book.* Portland, Oregon: Timber Press, 1988.

Austin, David. *English Roses.* London: Conran Octopus, 1993.

Brickell, Christopher. *Cavendish Encyclopedia of Pruning and Training.* Vancouver, B.C.: Cavendish Books, 1996.

Flowers by Color. Vancouver, B. C.: Raincoast Books, 1993.

Callaway, Dorothy J. *The World of Magnolias.* Portland, Oregon: Timber Press, 1994.

Hessayon, Dr. D. G. *The Bulb Expert.* London: Transworld Publishers, 1995.

Hessayon, Dr. D. G. *The NEW Rose Expert.* London: Transworld Publishers, 1996.

Hiller's Trees and Shrubs. Holland: Hiller Nurseries, 1981.

Lacey, Stephen. *The Startling Jungle.* Middlesex, England: Penguin Books, 1987.

Lancaster, Roy. *What Plant Where.* Vancouver, B.C.: Cavendish Books, 1995.

Lawson, Andrew. *The Gardener's Book of Colour.* London: Francis Lincoln, 1996.

Noble, Phoebe. *My Experience Growing Hardy Geraniums.* Sidney, B.C.: Tri Investments, 1994.

Phillips, Roger and Martyn Rix. *Perfect Plants.* New York: Random House, 1996.

Phillips, Roger and Martyn Rix. *The Random House Book of Perennials.* New York: Random House, 1991.

Reader's Digest Encyclopedia of Garden Plants and Flowers. London: Reader's Digest, 1985.

Rees, Yvonne and Neil Sutherland. *The Water Garden.* Vancouver, B.C.: Whitecap Books, 1995.

Straley, Gerald B. *Trees of Vancouver.* Vancouver, B.C.: UBC Press, 1992.

Encyclopedia of Roses, The. Portland, Oregon: Timber Press, 1992.

Gardener's Encyclopedia of Plants and Flowers, The. London: Dorling Kindersley, 1989.

Taylor, Patrick. *The 500 Best Garden Plants.* Portland, Oregon: Timber Press, 1993.

Van Pelt Wilson, Helen and Leonie Bell. *The Fragrant Year.* Toronto: George McLeod, 1967.

Western Garden Book. Menlo Park, California: Sunset Publishing, 1992.

Woods, Christopher. *Encyclopedia of Perennials.* New York: Facts on File, 1992.

*I*ndex

About the Author

Steve Whysall was born in 1950 in Nottingham, England. From 1968 to 1974, he worked as a reporter and editor for various newspapers in England, including the *Leicester Mercury, Nottingham Evening Post, Bristol Evening Post* and *London Evening News.*

He married and moved to Canada in 1975. For the last seven years he has written gardening columns for *The Vancouver Sun.* He lives in Burnaby, British Columbia with his wife, Loraine, their daughter, and two sons. Their English-style garden contains most of the plants mentioned in this book.

Courtesy *The Vancouver Sun*